Software Project
Management Essentials

Trademark Acknowledgements

All products are registered trademarks of their respective organizations.
All software is used for educational purposes only.

TABLE OF CONTENTS

Chapter 3 – Software Process Models

Chapter 4 – Software Project Scope and Resources Allocation

Chapter 5 – Software Requirements Gathering and Resource Allocation

Chapter 6 – Risk Management and Mitigation

Chapter 7 – Software Project Estimation: Tools and Techniques

Chapter 8 – Project Scheduling: Planning and Monitoring

Chapter 9 – Using a Project Management Tool: Microsoft Project 2000

Chapter 10 – Software Project Management Metrics

Chapter 11 – Managing a Project: Quality Assurance and Configuration Management

Chapter 12 – Software Implementation and Maintenance

Appendix

ABOUT NIIT

NIIT is a Global IT Solutions Corporation with a presence in 38 countries. With its unique business model and technology creation capabilities, NIIT delivers Software and Learning Solutions to more than 1000 clients across the world.

The success of NIIT's training solutions lies in its unique approach to education. NIIT's Knowledge Solutions Business conceives, researches, and develops all the course material. A rigorous instructional design methodology is followed to create engaging and compelling course content. NIIT has one of the largest learning material development facilities in the world with more than 5000 person years of experience.

NIIT trains over 200,000 executives and learners each year in different Information Technology areas using stand-up training, video-aided instruction, computer-based training (CBT) and Internet-based training (IBT). NIIT has featured in the Guinness Book of World Records for the largest number of learners trained in one year.

NIIT has developed over 10,000 hours of instructor-led training (ILT) and over 8,500 hours of Internet-based training and computer-based training. IDC ranked NIIT among the Top 15 IT Training providers globally for the year 2000. Through the innovative use of training methods and its commitment to research and development, NIIT has been in the forefront of computer education and training for the past 20 years.

Quality has been the prime focus at NIIT. Most of the processes are ISO-9001 certified. It was the 12th company in the world to be assessed at Level 5 of SEI-CMM. NIIT's Content (Learning Material) Development facility is the first in the world to be assessed at this highest maturity level. NIIT has strategic partnerships with companies such as Computer Associates, IBM, Microsoft, Oracle, and Sun Microsystems.

ABOUT THE BOOK

Almost everyday we are exposed to new software, be it application, products, solution, or systems. While a lot of research and development go into software development and software projects, software project management as an independent subject is mostly relegated to on the job learning.

The purpose of introducing the students of ISS curriculum to software project management is to emphasize the importance of project management and treat it as a formal area of study. The book Software Project Management Essentials, which is the third book in the ISS curriculum, will serve as the necessary link between technical and nontechnical roles in an organization. It will provide you with both the theoretical and practical knowledge required for managing a software project.

This book is organized to provide the best possible learning path for readers at all levels of experience. Each chapter of the book follows the simple to complex and generic to specific structure of instruction. This strategy will be of immense help to fresh aspirants in the field of project management while providing in-depth knowledge and practical tips to practicing project managers.

The book covers all the important aspects of project management. From the evolution of software project management to software maintenance management, the book covers all. It begins with discussions about the roles and responsibilities of a software project manager. It goes on to discuss the various life cycle models followed in software projects. Besides discussing software project models, the book also discusses the application of the concepts, models, tools and techniques associated with software project management.

In the chapters of this book, you will look at software project execution. The chapter on scope determination defines the framework within which the software project is managed. You will also learn about identifying and recording client requirements accurately, which is the key to a successful product. Equally important are resource allocation and effort estimation. This book covers project planning, resource allocation, and scheduling by using tools such as PERT, CPM, and Gantt charts manually and with the help of software.

The book also sensitizes you about software project risks and the risk management tricks and techniques. In addition, the book covers software quality concepts, quality assurance activities, metrics, and configuration management activities. Finally, the book discusses the implementation and maintenance activities in software projects and how to manage them.

The book includes interactive lab exercises at the end of each chapter to provide you with hands-on practice. Select chapters include homework exercises to allow you to familiarize yourself with the key concepts learned in the classroom sessions. The book makes extensive use of case studies, diagrams, and tables that are commonly used in project management activities. In addition, the chapter on using Microsoft Project 2000 includes demonstrations that guide you to use Microsoft Project 2000 to plan and control a project schedule effectively.

CONVENTIONS USED IN THE BOOK

Convention	Denotes
	A note.
	A tip.
	Just a minute
	Warning
	Reference
	Case study
Italicized text	Terms that are newly introduced
`Text in the Courier New font`	Code and file names
Text in the Arial font	Syntax for commands

Chapter 1

Introduction to Software Project Management

Objectives

- ☐ Describe the need for software project management.

- ☐ Distinguish between the management of a nonsoftware project and a software project.

- ☐ Chart the evolution of software project management as a separate discipline.

OVERVIEW OF SOFTWARE PROJECT MANAGEMENT

Today, most of the products and services that you interact with use software. Software is used so commonly that sometimes you hardly notice its presence. For example, can you imagine banks without automated teller machines (ATM) or communication without e-mail? Although some of these products may awe you, others are taken for granted. However, it is important to remember that a lot of hard work goes into the development of these software products. In this book, you will look at the range of activities involved in managing the development of a software project.

Software project management is distinct from managing any other project due to the complexity involved in the development process. The complexity stems mainly from the nature of the software product itself. A software product is composed of many programs, functions, routines, and subroutines that integrate and perform the intended functions. It has no shape or size that you can measure. Therefore, a traditional measure of performance cannot be applied to software. In addition, as software applications are growing mission critical, the margin for error is severely limited. Moreover, techniques to streamline and measure software development are comparatively new, and as yet, not calibrated for error-free use.

In this chapter, you will learn about the evolution of software project management. You will learn about the crisis that emerged as a result of the ad hoc approach to software development in the early phases of software evolution. You will also learn how software engineering and project management emerged as the answer to the software crisis.

The Product: Software

The American Heritage Dictionary defines *software* as the programs, routines, and symbolic languages that control the functioning of the hardware and direct its operation. However, software has come to symbolize much more than programs and symbolic languages. For millions of computer users, software is the magic language that enables computers to work.

Software is a key driver of the information revolution. A single software product may encompass thousands of subroutines that run on computers of varying capabilities, data that represents both figures and text, and audio and video files. However, software is still evolving. Each day you find a new milestone is achieved in the speed with which software executes on a computer.

Evolution of Software

The understanding about software and software development has come a long way from the days of punch cards and Ada. In the first stage of computing, hardware mattered the most. Computers themselves were the domains of the government, and most software was developed in defense-funded labs, dedicated to the advancement of science and technology in the national interest.

By the 1950s, large corporations realized the benefits of using computers. They increasingly started using computers to process and analyze financial and production data. These computers were huge in size. There was inadequate software available for them. Even the software that existed was designed essentially to function on a specific hardware product. The software was developed and maintained by the company that manufactured the hardware. Software design and documentation existed only in the developer's head. If the developer left the company, you would find maintenance to be a nightmare.

In the second phase of software evolution, the corporate and academic sectors increasingly started using computers, and the perspective about both software and software development began to change. By the late 1960s and early 1970s, concepts such as multisessions, multiuser systems, multiprogramming gained a foothold. Soon computers were developed to collect, process, transform, and analyze data in seconds. The focus of software development shifted from custom software to product software. Now, multiple users on multiple computers could use the same software. This phase of software evolution also saw the emergence of software maintenance activities. These activities comprised fixing bugs, and modifying the software based on changes in user requirements.

The third phase in software evolution was driven by the widespread use of silicon-based microprocessors, which further led to the development of high-speed computers, networked computers, and digital communication. Although, all the advancement in software and hardware was still largely restricted to enterprise applications manufacturers had begun to see the application of the microprocessor in something as mundane as ovens to the robots used in car plants.

The fourth, and current, phase of software evolution began in the early 1990s. This phase saw the growth of client-server environment, parallel computing, distributed computing, network computing, and object-oriented programming. This phase also witnessed the growing popularity of personal computer (PC). During this phase, the Internet facilitated easy accessibility of information. In addition to complex software to support the advanced hardware, the scope of software development widened to include software products for the common man.

Figure 1.1 sketches the path of software from the 1950s onwards.

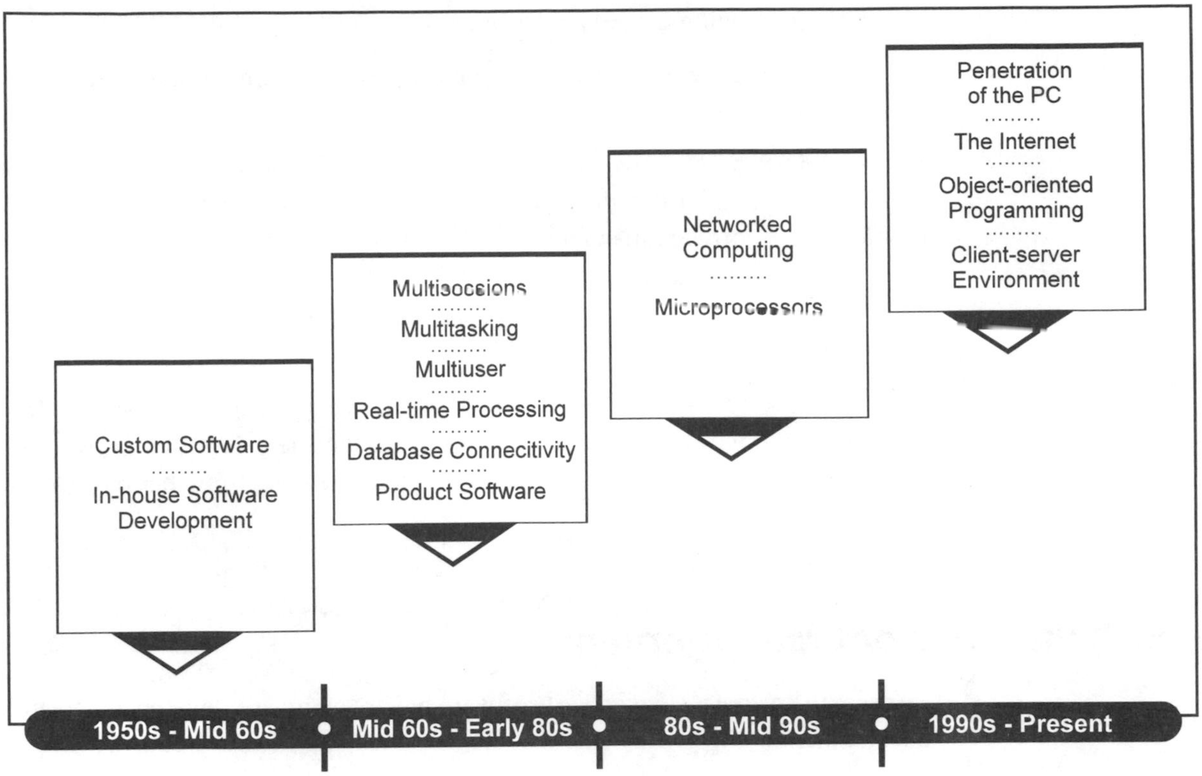

Figure 1.1: Software Evolution

The Software Crisis

The rapid evolution of software design concepts and software development methodology resulted in an ad hoc approach to software development. In the early days of computing, stress was laid more on computer hardware than on software. This happened mainly because hardware consumed the largest portion of the project budget. Project managers closely followed the process of hardware funding, budgeting, analysis and design, production, and implementation. Software development, on the other hand, was left to the developers. There was no training conducted, documentation maintained, or methodology followed for software development. You will find that this attitude persisted until the 1970s, when finally processes and methodologies for software design and development began to be created. However, the ad hoc approach to software development that was prevalent in the early stages of software evolution hampered the application of systematic processes. This conflict is referred to as the software crisis. Some of the reasons to which you can attribute the software crisis include:

- Software developers used multiple programming languages.

- Software developers used multiple variations of standard programming languages.

- Most of the requirements were complex with regard to the existing capabilities.

- Users, who had little or no experience of developing or even using software, formulated requirements.

- Software developers poorly mapped requirements to the actual product.

- Software developed had low interoperability.
- Software maintenance was costly.
- Hardware developed at a faster rate than software (better hardware requires better software to operate it).

During the period of software crisis, you will find that software that was produced was generally over budgeted, under scheduled, and of poor quality. The immediate knee-jerk response to these problems was software maintenance, which began to consume huge resources. During this period, maintaining software was adopted as a short-term solution due to the costs involved in fixing software regularly. This often resulted in the original software design approach getting lost due to the lack of documentation.

In contrast, the situation in the present times has changed to a large extent. Software costs have risen, although hardware is purchased easily off the shelf. Now, the primary concerns regarding software projects are project delays, high costs, and a large number of errors in the finished product.

Software Project Management

To meet the primary concerns of software buyers, software developers streamlined software development by:

- Applying formal engineering methodologies to software development.
- Breaking software into various components, such as modules and functions, instead of continuous lines of code to enable fast and easy software construction, upgrade, and maintenance.

Evolution of Software Project Management

As you have seen, initially, the focus of software development was just to generate a set of instructions to enable the computer hardware to work. Most of the work was mathematical, and the users themselves generally created the software they required. However, as software development projects grew in importance within organizations, organizations felt the need to assign a manager to plan, manage, and control software projects. The responsibility of a project manager ranged from planning for resources and sequencing the project activities to ensuring that all work was completed and delivered on time.

Slowly the scope of a software project manager's work enlarged. This was because, in addition to allocating resources and scheduling activities, the project manager also helped the clients who requested the software to interact with the software development team and coordinate activities between them. A project manager as a result, had to understand the requirements of the client and, based on the requirements, determine the scope of the project.

With the growth in the use of computers in the corporate and academic sectors, the role of a 'programmer' or software developer also came into being. The programmer was a person whom one could ask to create a computer program. This meant that there was now a gap between the user and computer. The user communicated the requirements for the software to a software developer, who then developed the software.

Initially, software developers created software to cater to a limited number of users because the use of software was fairly restricted. The real problems arose in the late 1960s, when the commercial viability of software projects began to be considered. Perhaps the most notable is the OS 360 project, the operating system that was developed for the IBM 360 series mainframe computers. The difficulties that such a large software project generated were clear. The techniques used by software developers and project managers for smaller software projects could not be scaled to meet the requirements of a large project. The OS 360 project started to go out of control with missed deadlines and escalating costs. Moreover, the large project team spent a lot of time understanding areas that they didn't know about. Back and forth communication between the team about design issues, standards, and overlapping objectives consumed maximum time, putting the actual development activities on the back burner.

The OS 360 project actually made both project managers and software developers aware that the development team spent a lot of precious time communicating with each other. Around the same time, the software industry felt the need to streamline the software development cycle. As a result, industry experts arrived at the conclusion that software developers must:

- Implement better management techniques.

- Use standardized programming languages and tools.

- Adopt specific standards and conventions for programming.

This conclusion meant that applying traditional engineering theories, techniques, and tools to software development would solve the software crisis.

Software Project Management in a Nutshell

Managing a software project requires a different approach from managing traditional engineering projects. You can differentiate a software project from traditional engineering projects, such as vehicle engineering or a bridge laying. The difference is caused because the product that you create in a software project is very different from a tractor or a bridge. By definition, software is invisible to the human eye. It is intangible and cannot be weighed or measured as a bridge can be. Moreover, techniques that you can use to streamline the production of software are not yet well calibrated. As a result, software project management has evolved as a separate area of expertise.

Software project management is all about effectively implementing software engineering practices. However, what exactly does software project management encompass? Software project management activities that you perform as a project manager may be summed up as follows:

- Ascertaining client requirements

- Identifying the lifecycle model for software development

- Selecting a team with appropriate skills

- Identifying appropriate metrics

- Determining the scope

- Identifying and allocating appropriate resources

- Estimating the cost and effort required

- Managing risks

- Creating and tracking a project schedule

- Managing the quality and configuration

- Maintaining the software product

- Evaluating the project and deriving lessons for future projects

As a project manager you are responsible for the overall success or failure of a software project. You can coordinate the technical and non-technical areas of the project, including software development, quality assurance, and documentation. You are also responsible for managing the relationship with the client and have the final say in all project-related decisions.

SUMMARY

✓ Software development passed through four phases during its evolution:

- In the first phase, the focus was on hardware rather than on software.

- In the second phase, software development spread from custom software to product software production.

- In the third phase, software development was still restricted to enterprise level applications with a minor focus on consumer applications.

- In the fourth phase, the scope of software development spread to include applications for the consumer market.

✓ The crisis in software development occurred because of unsound approaches to software design, development, and management of software projects.

✓ In the early phases of software development, the design, development, and management of software projects was arbitrary and not based on a systematic approach.

✓ Software engineering evolved when engineering principles, methodologies, and techniques were applied to software development.

✓ Managing software projects is different from traditional project management because traditional methodologies and measurements cannot be applied directly to a software project.

LAB EXERCISES

1. Identify the four phases in the evolution of the software development process. List the primary characteristics of each phase.

2. How is the current approach to software development different from the early phases of software development?

3. What were the different problems that affected software development activities in the early stages of software evolution? What measures were taken to address these problems?

Chapter 2

Fundamentals of Software Project Management

Objectives:

- ☐ Define the framework within which a software project is managed.
- ☐ Identify the impact of organizational factors on a software project.
- ☐ Describe the role of a software project manager.
- ☐ Sequence the phases within the SDLC.
- ☐ Identify the activities performed in each phase of the SDLC.
- ☐ Identify the problems faced by software projects.
- ☐ Clarify common software project management myths.

SOFTWARE PROJECT MANAGEMENT FRAMEWORK

You all know that a project is much more than a collection of methodologies, tasks, resources, and reviews. A project is a synchronized event where there is perfect harmony and understanding between the participants. The participants are equipped with the essential skills of planning, cooperating, helping, and communicating. However, the most important activity here is to orchestrate the movement of the participants. The onus lies with the project manager to synchronize the activities of the project to result in a perfect presentation. Although each project manager has a unique style of functioning, there are some fundamental approaches that guide a project manager. These approaches are, traditional project management concepts and software engineering concepts. To understand software projects and their dynamics, you must be aware of the environment in which a software project is executed. This further requires an understanding of the larger framework of software project management.

In this chapter, you will learn to build a connection between traditional project management concepts and software engineering concepts. Both traditional and software projects share the same methodologies, techniques, and processes. However, managing software projects requires a distinct approach. In this chapter, you will learn to apply traditional project management principles to software projects. Further, you will learn about the responsibilities of a software project manager. You will also learn about the phases in a software project and the activities within each phase. Finally, the chapter will provide you an overview of the problems that affect a software project and the myths prevalent about software project management.

Software Development Life Cycle (SDLC)

The development of a software project consists of many activities spread across multiple phases. Dividing a software project into phases helps you in managing the complexities and uncertainties involved in the software project.

Phases of a Software Project

Each phase represents the development of either a part of the software product or something associated with the software project, such as user manual or testing. Each phase is composed of various activities. You can consider a phase complete when all activities are complete.

A phase is named according to the primary deliverable set that is achieved at the end of that phase. For example, if the requirements document is required as the output, the phase is called the requirements phase. Similarly, most software projects have phases for analysis, design, construction, implementation, and testing.

A typical software project includes the following phases:

- Software requirement analysis phase
- Software design phase
- Software planning phase
- Software construction phase
- Software testing phase
- Software acceptance and maintenance phase

SDLC Models

Different organizations have different ways of assessing and arranging the phases in a project. These are called *process models*. Process models define how a software life cycle actually works. They provide you with a framework to plan and execute the various phases in the project. Typically, project life cycles display the following characteristics:

- The level of cost and effort required in a software project life cycle is small to begin with but grows larger towards the end of the project. This happens because the phases such as software construction and implementation, which come at later stages in a software project, require more resources than the initial phases of the project.

- At the start of the SDLC, external entities, such as the customer and the organization, play an important role with regard to their effect on the requirements. However, towards the end of the software project as the cost and effort required to implement changes rise, the requests for change in requirements decreases.

- The uncertainty faced by the software project is highest at the beginning of the SDLC. Their level decreases as the project progresses.

There are a few standard software process models that you can use, with some customization. Some standard process models are given below:

- The *Waterfall* model: This is the traditional life cycle model. It assumes that all phases in a software project are carried out sequentially and that each phase is completed before the next is taken up.

- The *Prototyping* model: A model that works on an iterative cycle of gathering customer requirements, producing a prototype based on the requirement specifications, and getting the prototype validated by the customer. Each iteration of the life cycle builds on the prototype produced in the previous iteration.

- The *Incremental* model: The Incremental model is an example of an evolutionary life cycle model. It combines the linear nature of the Waterfall model and the iterative nature of the Prototyping model. The Incremental model divides the development life cycle into multiple linear sequences, each of which produces an increment of the final software product. In this model, the software product is developed in builds. A build is defined as a self-contained unit of the development activity. The entire development cycle is planned for a specific number of logical builds, each having a specific set of features.

- The *Spiral* model: Another evolutionary life cycle model that combines the linear nature of the Waterfall model and the iterative nature of the Prototyping model. The project life cycle is divided into phases, and each phase is executed in all of the iterations of the Spiral model.

Note

You will learn more about different software development life cycle models in a later chapter, Software Engineering Models.

Organizational Issues and Project Management

Organizational issues have a deep influence on a software project, its progress, and the role of the project manager. The policies of an organization can affect the way the organization handles the customer, different types of technologies, and different software projects. The organizational issues that can influence a software project include:

- Reaction to external influences
- Interest in adherence to standards
- Definition of core competency area
- Existence of knowledge management system
- Interest in human resources

One organizational issue that can influence a software project is the reaction of the organization to external influences. As a project manager, it is important for you to assess how the organization reacts to changes in the external environment. For example, in the current technology environment that changes rapidly, an organization should be proactive in strengthening its capability baseline by adopting new technology and retraining its employees as per market requirements.

Interest in adherence to standards is another organizational issue that can influence a software project. The current technology environment is highly dynamic. Various nonprofit and independent organizations have developed protocols and standards for the standardization of software development and measurement. For example, the Software Engineering Institute at the Carnegie Mellon University has developed the Capability Maturity Model (SEI-CMM). The CMM rates the processes of a software development organization and classifies it into five maturity levels. Software development organizations can also get the quality-related certifications issued by the International Standards Organization (ISO). Implementing the guidelines for such certifications smoothen your project management tasks by standardizing the internal processes and optimizing performance.

Definition of core competency area also influences a software project. An organization that creates software must understand how they are created and establish processes accordingly For example, if the core competency of the organization lies in manufacturing chemicals, it should preferably not attempt software development. For such an organization, it is better to purchase an off-the-shelf software product.

An organizational issue that positively influences the tasks of software project managers is the presence of a good knowledge management system within the organization. Knowledge management is the collection of processes that control the creation and utilization of knowledge within the organization. A good knowledge management system allows you to access relevant information and make informed decisions.

Another organizational issue that can influence a software project is the interest of management in human resources. The human resources of an organization are its primary resource. You need to ensure that the people in the development team enjoy a comfortable work environment, which is conducive for smooth and trouble-free work. This includes providing suitable compensations, a friendly work environment, and smooth processes. The absence of these factors negatively affects employee morale, and therefore, productivity.

MANAGING PROCESSES

As a software project manager, you become the key player in a software project. You not only manage the day-to-day activities of the project but also ensure that the software product is delivered on time. What makes your role challenging is the performance of project related activities within a specified budget and time constraint. At the same time, you need to keep the requirements and specifications of the customer in mind.

To deliver expected results, you carry out three successive processes: studying the feasibility of the project, planning to meet the requirements, and executing the plan. These processes can be further broken down into activities, such as planning, staffing, and monitoring.

You plan and organize the software development team to complete development within the stipulated time and budget. To do this, you form a team of people who have the required technical skills. Then, you ensure that all activities are carried out as planned by the relevant people.

Your responsibilities include analyzing customer requirements, determining the scope of the software project, allocating resources to the project, scheduling the project, and executing the project. These responsibilities can be considered in terms of the areas where management skills are required. The primary software project management areas that you need to concentrate on include:

- Managing resources
- Managing cost
- Managing risk
- Managing schedules
- Managing the project plan
- Managing quality

Managing Resources

The primary input required to create software are resources. Resources for a software project may be of three kinds: human, hardware, and software. Human resource management is about effectively identifying the people with the appropriate skills, assigning roles and responsibilities to these people, and establishing reporting relationships. On the other hand, hardware and software resource management relates to identifying and ensuring resources such as workstations, disk space on servers, software tools, and software licenses. You need to ensure that human resource identification and allocation is carried out simultaneously with hardware and software resource management.

To manage resources effectively, there are two areas that require your attention. These include:

- Management of human resource
- Identification of the critical hardware and software resources

Management of human resources calls for a number of actions. First, you define reporting relationships for the software project. Reporting relationships can exist within and across organizational units, technical areas, and hierarchical levels. Next, determine the skills required for the software project, and identify the appropriate people who possess the required skills. You can review the resource pool and identify resources on the basis of their experience and availability. In case the resources are unavailable, you request for their release from another project or outsource the required resources. Depending upon the organizational practices and experiences from past projects, you can assign roles and responsibilities to the development team. Finally, create a staff management plan and an organizational chart to show the hierarchical structure of the development team.

Management of human resources also requires efficient team development. This is a complex activity because it combines managing people and organizing the reporting structure within the team. You can build cohesion and commitment within the team through team building activities. These activities include conducting team meetings to involve people from areas other than management into decision-making.

To manage human resources, you also need to implement a reward and recognition system. This helps in promoting and reinforcing positive performance. It is important that you make the link between the performance and reward explicit and achievable. You should also ensure that the training needs of the development team are met.

A second resource management area that requires attention is identification of the hardware and software resources that are critical for the project. As a software project manager, you must identify all the critical hardware and software resources and document them in the project plan. After the required resources are identified, you define control limits for each resource. Control limits for a resource are the upper and lower limit beyond which the resource is above or below the required level. For example, if a software project requires disk space on the central server, the control limits for the disk space are the required maximum and minimum disk space. Note that not all hardware and software resources are critical to the success of a software project. In some software projects, you may not find any critical resource at the beginning. However, as the project progresses, some resources might become critical. For efficient resource management, you should periodically assess hardware and software resource requirements for the software project. Just as a resource may become critical as a project progresses, a resource might also become less critical over a period of time. Therefore, plan, assess, and take corrective action for all resources through the duration of the software project.

Managing Cost

The cost factor has a considerable influence on the execution of a software project. The budget of a software project is affected by factors, such as the current orientation of the organization toward software development, number of skilled personnel available, infrastructure, and computer hardware and software. The budget can also be influenced by timely availability of resources. If a particular resource is allocated to the project later than required, the costs involved could go up drastically.

Quite often, when a software project starts to become too expensive, many project managers also tend to start cutting costs. This can have a direct impact on employee morale. When employee morale drops, so does the quality of work and the productivity. Therefore, as a project manager you must prepare for all circumstances through proper estimation and allocation. To manage costs for software projects, you need an accurate estimation of costs. To do that, there is a sequence of steps that you need to perform.

- Identify the resources required for the project
- Estimate the cost of each resource
- Set cost baselines for each activity
- Implement a control system for cost changes

To estimate costs, you first identify and describe all the resources required in the software project. You also estimate the duration for which the resources are used.

Next, estimate the cost of each resource. To estimate the cost, you can use mathematical tools. However, in the case where limited information is available about resources, you can also use expert judgment to estimate costs.

After the costs of the required resources are estimated, you set cost baselines for each activity. Cost baselines measure the performance of an activity with regard to the cost and duration defined for the completion of the activity.

Finally, as the project manager you implement a control system for cost changes. The cost control system defines cost baselines, identifies cost changes, and modifies cost baselines to adjust cost changes.

Managing Risk

Risk management is an integral part of project management. In software projects, where uncertainties are very high, risk management and mitigation is even more critical. Taking risks for high payoffs might bring in high profits but not without the danger of losses. Risk on a small scale is acceptable to most project managers as the element of loss is minimum. However, large risks pose a danger to the progress of a software project and you need to manage them. Risk management activities involve identifying potential risks, assessing them, and planning for contingent actions if a risk materializes.

As a project manager, you perform two primary activities to manage risks for a software project:

- Risk analysis
  - Risk identification
  - Risk quantification
- Risk management

The first activity in risk analysis is risk identification. Risk identification helps you point out the potential risks for a software project across all phases of the project. Risks might evolve through the duration of a software project, and therefore, risk identification is an ongoing activity. To identify potential risks for a software project, you can analyze the activities in the software project, the software product description, and risks faced by the development team in similar past projects. This exercise allows you to identify the potential sources of risks to the current software project, Assessing the factor influencing the different inputs also allows you to identify the phases in the SDLC when risk might materialize.

After potential risks have been identified, you can quantify them. This is done to ascertain their priority. If multiple risks materialize at the same time, then you must assign a priority to each risk based on the degree of impact on the project and handle the highest-risk events first. For example, the risk of change in client requirements during the software construction phase is a higher risk than a deadline for a deliverable being missed. Therefore, you first manage the risk that has a higher priority. To quantify project risks, you can use various mathematical and statistical tools. You can also use expert judgment to assess and quantify risks.

After you have identified and quantified the potential risks for a software project, you create a risk mitigation plan. The purpose of the risk mitigation plan is to help you identify procedures to choose the path of least damage and highest returns in a case a risk materializes. To mitigate risks for a software project, you first need to be aware of the opportunities and threats that can be pursued or ignored. This enables you to focus on the risks that might have a negative impact on the software project and develop contingent plans to deal with these risks. You can also mitigate risks by evolving alternative strategies to altogether prevent potential risks from materializing.

In case an unplanned risk materializes, you must be aware of the dependencies of the project activities so that ad hoc solutions can be evolved. However, as the project manager you can avoid unplanned risks from materializing by engaging in an intensive risk identification and mitigation exercise before the software project commences.

Managing Schedules

Time is a major constraint for a software project. With most software projects, the delivery dates for the software product are already committed to the customer at the time the project commences. As a software project manager you must perform various tasks to balance time and deadlines. These are:

- Identify the different deliverables that constitute the software product
- Define the activities that are required to produce the deliverables
- Identify the interdependencies between activities
- Define the duration of each activity
- Assess the project network diagram
- Create a schedule management and control plan

The first task is to identify the different deliverables that constitute the software product. These deliverables also mark the completion of the different phases within a software project.

Next, define the activities that are required to produce the deliverables. To do this, you can break down the SDLC into phases, identify the deliverables at the end of each phase, and the activities required for creating the deliverables.

After the activities are defined, you identify the interdependencies between them. The purpose of this exercise is to organize the activities and sequence them in the form of a project schedule.

Next, you define the duration of each activity. The inputs that you need for scheduling are the resources required to complete each activity. Then, assesses the availability of these resources and the duration of each similar activity in similar past projects.

After estimating the time required for each activity to complete, you assess the project network diagram. This includes an assessment of the duration estimates, resource requirements, resource pool description, and assumptions and constraints for the software. You can use mathematical tools to determine a schedule for the project. The project schedule defines the activities within each phase, the team members assigned to complete each activity, the duration of each activity, and the start and end dates for all of the activities

Finally, create a schedule management and control plan. The purpose of this plan is to identify when changes occur, implement the changes to the project schedule, and ensure that the changes are beneficial to the software project. After the changes are implemented, you might need to modify the sections of the project plan to ensure that the project is completed on time.

Managing the Project Plan

Preparing a project plan for a software project helps you ensure that the specified requirements and objectives are met successfully. It is a collation of all planning activities that have happened for a software project. This includes activities such as design and analysis, activity definition, risk planning, and cost estimation. To create the plan, you assess all planning activities, organizational policies regarding the creation of the project plan and assumptions and constraints for the project. To implement the software project plan, you require management skills, such as leadership, communication, and problem solving, along with the basic knowledge about the software. You also need to ensure that the senior management of the company has authorized work on the software project. Knowledge management techniques help you to make informed decisions regarding the project plan.

After the project plan is executed, you manage the changes to it in such a way that the performance measurement baselines are not impacted. To manage the project plan effectively, you monitor the project plan, periodic performance status reports, and requests for change. The primary tool that you can use to control the changes in the project plan is the change control mechanism. This is a set of formal procedures for changing the project plan.

Managing Quality

The quality of software depends largely on the understanding of 'quality' and quality management within the software development team. In software projects where each member has a different understanding of quality and his or her role in implementing it, the software product is usually not of the required quality.

Implementing software quality is often associated with the software developer. However, the role of the project manager is crucial in implementing quality awareness and a quality-producing work environment. When a software project starts missing deadlines and is in danger of exceeding the budget, project managers often lose the focus on quality and lay stress on meeting deadlines. However, the focus should be the other way round. A focus on delivering a quality product, even at the cost of missing a deadline or two ensures that your customer comes back for repeat orders.

On the other hand, the price of non-conformance (PONC) on quality standards simply translates into the loss of goodwill and loss of business.

Modern quality management techniques compliment project management and the role of the project manager. Quality management techniques ensure that a software product conforms to the customer requirements. Quality management further ensures that errors are prevented in the first round itself. Checks for errors and effort for removing the errors consume much more time, effort, and cost than it takes to prevent the errors in the first place. Therefore, maintaining quality in a software project is the domain of all team members.

However, as the project manager you have a critical role in maintaining quality. You provide the resources required to complete the activities of the software project and ensure that quality levels are constantly monitored.

You first identify the areas that must be monitored for ensuring quality and the quality measures to implement. Then, consider the quality policy of the organization, the scope of the project, the applicable standards, and the software product description. Next, use tools, such as a cost-benefit analysis and a flowchart, to identify the areas where you need to monitor quality and the subsequent actions for control. The output of this exercise is the quality plan for the software project. In addition, this exercise allows you to create checklists to help monitor quality.

As a software project manager, you also need to use a quality control mechanism so that the quality of the software product does not suffer. The aim of the quality control mechanism is to ensure compliance with quality standards.

PROJECT EXECUTION

You already learned in the beginning of the chapter that a software project is divided into different phases. This division is done on the basis of the activities performed in each phase. Similarly, project management activities are also arranged in phases. As a project manager, you perform the activities that map to each of these phases. The project management phases can be broadly categorized as follows:

- Project initiation
- Project planning, control, and tracking
- Product implementation
- Project closedown

Project Initiation

The tasks performed for project initiation are mentioned below:

- Requirements gathering: The first task is to gather the customer requirements. Customer requirements may be spoken or unspoken. Therefore, the challenge for the project manager is to elicit the requirements in such a way that both the spoken and unspoken customer needs and wants are gathered. After collecting the required information, you need to translate the customer requirements into technical specifications for the software project.

- Scope determination: The scope of a software project can be defined as the combination of the software product and services to be delivered to the customer. You carry out the scope determination exercise to define the scope of the software project. The scope determination exercise enables you to refine and understand the customer requirements. You can refine the scope definition further by breaking down each deliverable into smaller and more manageable activities. The scope determination exercise also helps you identify the technology for creating the software product.

- Resource allocation: During project initiation, you identify the resources required and allocate them to the software project. The resources identified may be people, reusable software components, and hardware or software tools. You allocate the resource to the software project on the basis of the activities defined in the scope determination exercise. While allocating appropriate resources for a software project, you also need to calculate the cost of each resource. The cost of a resource is calculated according to the duration of the resource in the software project. Estimating the cost of resources also helps you prepare a budget for the software project.

Note

Scope determination and resource allocation are discussed in more detail in later chapters.

- Initial project plan: Another exercise that you carry out during project initiation is the creation of a rough project plan. This plan is a draft version and carries only the primitive project plan features. This project plan carries the initial risk analysis of the software project, the initial start and end dates, the duration of the activities in the project, and the sequencing of these activities.

Project Planning, Controlling, and Tracking

This activity of the project manager involves detailed tasks. These tasks are mentioned below:

- Detailed project plan: After the scope for the software project is determined and the product design is ready, you prepare a detailed project plan. To create a detailed project plan, you define a detailed list of all the elements that make up the project deliverables. Next, the deliverables are further broken up to help in the calculation of durations, start dates, and end dates for each activity mentioned in the plan. Roles and responsibilities are assigned to people with the appropriate skills to complete each activity within the specified time.

- Control mechanism: These are set up to control the impact of changes on the software project. The control mechanism includes a detailed risk management and mitigation plan, a detailed quality plan, and quality assurance activities. You also implement a review and audit system for periodic assessment and measurement of the software project activities. The review and audit system enables you to evaluate the progress of the software project. It ensures that all necessary data is collected, deviation from the planned baselines is checked, and corrective action is taken at all checkpoints. In this way, the review and audit system ensures compliance with the organizational processes for software development.

Product Implementation

Product implementation activities involve defining processes related to the implementation of the software product at the customer site. Some of the tasks that you perform for product implementation are mentioned below:

- Implementation plan creation: An implementation plan defines the duration of implementation and the hardware and software prerequisites for implementing the software product.

- Support plan creation: The project manager also needs to create a support plan for the customer. The support plan includes considerations such as the post-implementation support activities provided to the customer. Post-implementation considerations include the number of support staff available to the customer, their names, contact numbers, and the duration of their availability.

- Training plan creation: During product implementation, you create a training plan to train the customer on the software product. The training plan includes considerations such as the duration of training, the prerequisites for training people, and the number of people that can be trained simultaneously.

- User acceptance plan: You also need to prepare a user acceptance plan. The user acceptance plan provides a detailed outline on how and when the user acceptance tests are performed. The primary focus of user acceptance test is to ensure that the final software product offers all the functionality and performance that the customer wanted. Therefore, the customer tests the software product for issues such as aesthetics, user friendliness, and scalability.

Project Closedown

The final activity for a project manager is project closedown. For most software projects, the project closedown activities take place in the post-implementation phase. However, in some software projects, the customer requests support activities for a longer duration. In such cases, the software project is considered closed immediately after implementation. The tasks that you perform in project closedown are mentioned below:

- Prepare closedown report: The project closedown report contains the results of the causal analysis that you do for the project. This contains an analysis of what went wrong, what went right, and what you could have done better in the software project.

- Identify learning: You also need to assess the entire software project and the results of the causal analysis to identify the key learning points from the software project. This helps you identify areas of improvement for future projects. The learning points can also be used by the organization as considerations while planning and executing the next software project.

- Identify reusable software components: Reusing software components enables you to lower the cost, time, and effort required to complete the software project successfully. After project closedown, you identify the software components that can be reused in future projects of similar nature. The software components prepared for a software project may be complete, partially complete, or in the design stage. These components or their designs can be assessed for usability in future projects.

- Create reference material: After the project is complete, you can create white papers and reference documents. This can be a significant contribution to the organization and the application area of the software by creating an authoritative knowledge base.

PROBLEMS IN SOFTWARE PROJECTS

Software projects are similar to traditional projects in the sense that the same types of problems affect them both. However, the difference in managing these problems lies in the approach that you take to the specific issue. For example, a technology-related problem for a software project might be the low degree of reuse of the software components created. However, for a car-manufacturing firm, there is no chance of reusing a component such as a front axle.

You can classify the problems that affect software projects into the following four categories:

- People-related problems
- Process-related problems
- Product-related problems
- Technology-related problems

People-related Problems

People-related problems in a software project are:

- Low motivation: As the project manager it is your responsibility to ensure an optimal level of motivation within the team. Lengthy projects, complex activities, and scarce resources often decrease the motivation level in a software development team. However, you need to lead in such a way that the team is constantly motivated to do a good job.

- Problem employees: some members of any team always create a problem. For example, an employee may carry a 'holier-than-thou' attitude. Problem employees raise the chances of conflicts and differences of opinions within the development team. They lower the efficiency and productivity of other team members and make it difficult to meet the objectives of the software project within the specified time. You need to ensure that employees are not allowed to create a problem for the rest of the team. Even if the employee is very competent, you need to assess the indispensability of such employees for the project. Moreover, you refrain from playing favorite with certain employees and treat everyone with the same measure.

- Unproductive work environment: the work environment is a major factor that affects the productivity of the development team. For example, a noisy or cramped workspace decreases the motivation levels of the employees. Similarly, unfriendly organizational policies also lower the motivation of the team members. As the project manager, you need to ensure that the team is protected from harmful external influences and try to make the workspace friendly to work in.

- Inefficient project management style: the project manager needs to lead by example. The team members absorb the work culture, work ethic, and attitude of the project manager and implement it in their work style. If you display a lack of leadership qualities and weak ideals, the motivation levels decrease across the software team.

- Lack of stakeholder interest: for a software project to be a success, each stakeholder needs to take an active interest in the progress of the project. All stakeholders, including the customer, the management, and the software development team, need to commit to the success of the project. For example, if the software development team is not committed to the project, then their contribution may not be to the optimal level.

- Ineffective project sponsorship by management: lack of commitment of the senior management to a software project lowers the motivation level of the team members. If the management commits to the progress of a software project and takes a keen interest in the progress, the confidence of the software development team will increase.

Process-related Problems

The process-related problems in a software project are:

- Unrealistic schedules: assigning unrealistic deadlines for a software project is a primary reason why software projects are delayed. Often, the marketing or the management team commit a delivery date to the customer in the hope of getting the project contract. However, these dates are not decided in consultation with the development team. The rationale for assigning the deadlines is unfounded. You need to ensure that the deadlines match the ability of the software team to deliver the software product. As it is not always possible to shift deadlines committed to the customer, you also need to plan the resource allocation and project execution such that the deadlines are met.

- Insufficient risk identification: unidentified, partially identified, and unplanned risks pose a threat to the success of a software project. You need to intensively identify risks and evolve a risk management plan such that the project is completed successfully, on time.

- Unsuitable life cycle model selection: different software projects require different SDLC models. For example, a project to create banking software is different from software for a satellite where the concept needs to be researched. For the former example, the Waterfall model is more applicable. For the latter example, the Spiral model is more suitable. Selecting the correct life cycle model is critical to the success of a software project.

- Abandoning quality under pressure of deadlines: when a software project faces a shortage of resources, time, and funds, project managers often push away quality concerns and focus on meeting deadlines and staying within the budget. Abandoning quality has a ripple effect that actually adds even more time, effort, and costs to the software projects. The cost of doing things right the first time is lower than the cost of inspection during product delivery. Also, the cost of inspection is lower than the cost of debugging software after the customer spots errors.

- Unstructured and hurried software development: when a software project progresses with more focus on meeting deadlines and staying within a budget, the approach to the software development is unstructured and hurried. You should plan the software project such that all the activities are identified, sequenced properly, and roles and responsibilities assigned to the various people on the project. You should also maintain the focus of the development team toward a structured approach to software development.

Product-related Problems

There are many product-related problems that you can face in a software project. These are:

- Product scope changed toward the end of the project life cycle: the project time, effort, and cost estimates for a software project can go up dramatically when the customer changes the scope of the product toward the end of the project. In such situations, you should verify the criticality of the scope change. However, if the change request is not critical, you should retain the original scope with a proper explanation to the customer. If the change request is critical, you should explain the situation to the customer. Usually, a customer gives more time and funds to a software project if proper justification is provided. In some cases, the scope change may also be because of a change in government policy. It may become mandatory for you to include such change requests.

- Research-oriented software development: many software projects digress from the original scope because of the nature of the software product or technology used. When a totally new kind of software is developed or a new technology is used, the software development team can lose focus of the objectives by getting into a research-oriented approach. It becomes your responsibility as the project manager to maintain the focus on the objective.

- Ill-defined scope: you need to define the scope of the software product in the initial stages of a software project. The scope of a software product is defined in terms of the functionality requirements, the performance requirements, the assumptions, and the constraints on the product. If the product scope is ill defined, the software project does not have a proper focus on the features required in the product.

- Fuzzy users: you also need to clarify the background characteristics of the users of the final software product at the beginning of the software project. If the description of the users is fuzzy, then the software analysis, design, and development stages may reflect the ambiguity with regard to the functions and performance of the final software product.

Technology-related Problems

You may also encounter technology-related problems in a software project. These include:

- Overestimated savings from reusable components and new tools and methods: you can reuse software components in a software project to save time, effort, and cost of creating the component again. It is important that you assess the savings that the use of such a software component provides to a software project. The expectations of both the customer and the management might not be met, if you overestimate the savings from reusing software components.

- Switching tools in mid way: the current technology environment offers new tools and technologies for software development at a fast rate. All these tools and technologies offer the benefits of a shorter development cycle, lower costs, and better functionality than earlier tools. You should identify and commit to the tool and technology for the software project before the project commences. Switching the tool or technology used during the software development stage causes the developers to relearn a new tool. In addition, there is a chance that it might not be possible to integrate the software already developed with the new tool.

- Integrating different software products in cross-platform implementations: the modern software environment requires that all software should integrate with each other. However, many software projects do not plan for integration with existing software in the same or different domain. This limits the application of such software and reduces the shelf life drastically. The key to the success of a software product is interoperability. The software project manager needs to determine the scope for the software product such that it can be integrated easily with existing software.

PROJECT MANAGEMENT MYTHS

In most cases, you learn the skills required to manage a software project while on the job. As a result, most software project managers practice a lot of management techniques that are of doubtful authenticity. Many software project managers learn about the so-called management skills and concepts that are actually myths.

Clarifying the Project Management Myths

The following list aims to clarify some of the more prevalent myths in software project management.

- Combining the best resources with the worst resources available for a software project helps to complete the project successfully.
- A general statement of objectives is sufficient to begin work on the software project.
- Allocating extra resources to a late project allows it to catch up with the project schedule.
- As software by itself is flexible, you can change the requirements at any point in the software project life cycle.
- The management and the customer always impose an unrealistic deadline for the software project.
- A software project that meets all the stated objectives is a success.
- Software maintenance is an easy task and requires less effort than actual software development.
- Identifying and reporting errors during the reviews makes the software developer unhappy and spoils the work environment.
- Web-enabling an application or adopting client/server architecture helps to run software projects smoothly.

Myth: Combining the best resources with the worst resources available for a project helps to complete the project successfully.

In software projects, combining the best resources with the worst resources drags down the efficiency and productivity of good resources. This invariably decreases the speed of the software project, and the project ends much after the specified deadline.

Myth: A general statement of objectives is sufficient to begin work on the software project.

Many software project managers and customers believe that a general statement of objectives gives a reasonable idea of the requirements. However, a formal and detailed description of the customer requirements is needed before the project commences. The software project manager must ensure that all information regarding the software project, such as the functions, performance, interfaces, constraints, assumptions, and validation criteria, is gathered.

Myth: Allocating extra resources to a late project allows it to catch up with the project schedule.

A software project is not a mechanical process such as, say, digging an artificial lake. In case of creating an artificial lake, adding more people to the job can help dig a larger area in the same time. However, in a software project, adding, more people actually increases the time required to finish the project. This happens because a new person joining the project requires time to understand the requirements of the client, software design, and standards. Moreover, the existing people in the project need to devote time and effort to train the new people on the software project. Therefore, allocating additional resources to a risky situation increases the risk to the software project.

Myth: As software by itself is flexible, changes in the requirements can be made at any point in the software project life cycle.

Requests for changes are common with all projects. However, the timing of the change for requests is critical. This is because an untimely change adversely impacts the cost of the software project. For example, a change request during the requirements gathering stage has a relatively low impact on costs. On the other hand, a change request during the software construction stage can be extremely expensive to incorporate. The software project manager must decide with the customer upon a set of objectives that must be achieved at the end of the project. In addition, the project manager and the customer must decide on a specific phase, beyond which only critical change requests are accepted.

Myth: The management and the customer always impose an unrealistic deadline for the software project.

The management and customer usually believe that project managers prepare cost, effort, and time estimates inclusive of buffers. The management and customers rationalize that if they can cut the buffers by imposing a tight deadline or a low budget on a project, the project manager would still complete the project on time.

Myth: A software project that meets all the stated objectives is a success.

Customer requirements for a software project are always in two forms, spoken and unspoken. Usually, the objectives formed from the customer requirements are based on the spoken requirements. The software project manager must to be aware of the unspoken requirements and ensure that these are met.

Myth: Software maintenance is an easy task and requires less effort than actual software development.

If change requests are made toward the end of the project, then maintenance activities can contribute to large costs and effort overruns. Moreover, contrary to the popular view, implementing changes in the software product in the maintenance stage is a painstaking task.

Myth: Identifying and reporting errors during the reviews makes the software developer unhappy and spoils the work environment.

If a developer makes an error, it is important to point it out so that the error is fixed in time. A project manager must communicate assertively so that the team does not lose focus on quality. In addition, letting an error pass may have ripple effects on the quality of the software product, frustrating the entire team.

Myth: Web-enabling an application or adopting client/server architecture helps to run software projects smoothly.

No single technology platform, language, or architecture is a one-point solution for all software projects. All approaches to software development have unique merits and demerits. For example, if a marketing firm needs to make information accessible to people at remote locations, then a Web-based application is a good option. However, mainframes are still preferred for applications created for the banking industry.

Summary

✓ The phases in a software project can be organized into a project life cycle. Some standard life cycle models are the Waterfall model, the Prototyping model, the Incremental model, and the Spiral model.

✓ Organizational policies and attitudes influence the progress of a software project and the tasks of a software project manager. For smooth progress of a software project, the organization should:

- Be proactive in adopting changes in technology and market environments.
- Be focused on developing software.
- Accept software projects that match the organizational capability baseline.
- Implement employee-friendly human resource policies.
- Implement a good knowledge management system.

✓ The role of a software project manager includes managing the following:

- Resources
- Cost
- Risk
- Schedules
- Project plan
- Quality

✓ Software project management activities can be divided into phases. The main phases and the associated activities are:

- Initiating the project
  - Gathering requirements
  - Determining the scope
  - Allocating resources
  - Creating an initial project plan
- Planning, controlling, and tracking
  - Creating a detailed project plan
  - Constructing software
  - Implementing a control mechanism

- Implementing the product
  - Implementation plan
  - Support plan
  - Training plan
  - User acceptance plan
- Project closedown
  - Preparing closedown report
  - Identifying learning for future projects
  - Identifying reusable software components for future software projects

✓ Problems affecting software projects can be classified into the following categories:

- People-related
- Project-related
- Product-related
- Technology-related

✓ There are various myths regarding software project management. A few software project management myths are:

- Adding more people to a late project can help to finish the project on time.
- Combining the best resources with the worst resources results in optimal resource allocation.
- Changes to the scope of the software project and the software product can be made at any time in the SDLC.

LAB EXERCISES

1. Why is a software project divided into phases? Identify four SDLC process models that are commonly used and discuss their application for different types of software projects.

2. A software development organization should be proactive in adopting new technologies, should have a focus towards software development, should have a good knowledge management system, and implement good human resource practices. Discuss these considerations in terms of how they impact the progress of a software project.

3. Managing human resources for a software project involves the following four activities:

   o Assessing skill requirements for the project.
   o Developing the team.
   o Creating a staff management plan.
   o Assigning reporting relationships.

   Arrange these activities in the proper sequence and explain the importance of each activity in managing human resources for a software project.

4. Why is the project closedown phase important for a software project? Discuss the activities and elements of the project closedown phase. Highlight the importance of the closedown phase for future projects.

5. Setting unrealistic deadlines, accepting product scope changes towards the end of the SDLC, and research-oriented software development are common problems that affect software projects. Discuss the impact of these problems on a software project and explain how each problem can be resolved.

6. You are a software project manager at XYZ Inc. Your current software project is in danger of falling behind schedule. Your colleague suggests that you add eight software developers, who have just been released from another project, to your project team to help finish on time. How do you explain to your colleague that adding more people would further delay the project?

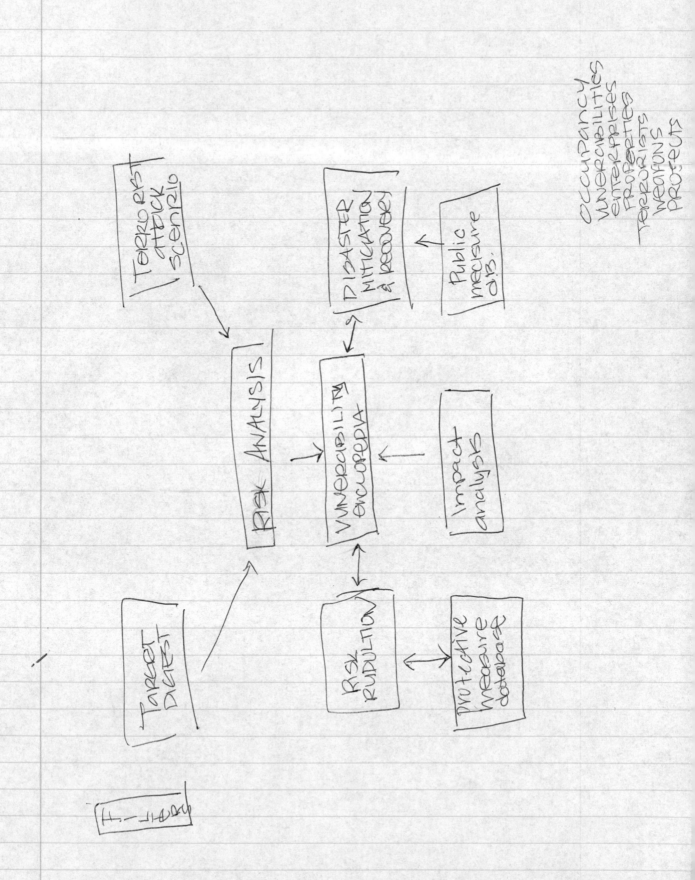

1-30-03
1ss 313

OCCUPANCY
VULNERABILITIES
ENTERPRISES
PROPERTIES
TERRORISTS
WEAPONS
PRODUCTS

Chapter 3

Software Process Models

Objectives:

- ☐ Define a process model.
- ☐ Identify the benefit of using a process model.
- ☐ Identify the primary models used for software engineering.
- ☐ Identify the evolutionary models used for software engineering.
- ☐ Select a process model based on the project requirements.

IMPORTANCE OF A PROCESS MODEL

A process is defined as a collection of related tasks with specific milestones. To ensure smooth progress of a software project, relevant processes are arranged and executed in a sequence. Every software project is discrete with respect to its complexity, size, and goals. Therefore, different process models are designed for different software projects. These process models provide approaches that decide the path of software development from the conceptualization of a project to its formal termination.

This chapter will cover the importance of processes and process models in the SDLC. You will learn about various primary and evolutionary process models. These process models help you to systematically manage and monitor a software project. This chapter will also enable you to select an appropriate process model based on the requirements of a software project.

Processes

To ensure the successful execution of a project, it is necessary to break down the project into multiple manageable tasks. Each task is performed in a series using processes. To understand what a process is, consider an example of a non software-related project. You are planning the market launch of an office management product. To create an effective plan, you need to perform certain tasks.

First, you schedule a meeting of all managers and the Finance, Marketing, Production, and Systems personnel. You can follow a process to complete this task. You may send e-mail messages or call them up personally.

Next, you decide some feasible marketing and advertising strategies. Again there are processes that help you select the strategies.

Finally, you determine the territory where the product should be launched. This is done in consultation with the Production and Marketing departments.

Just like a non software-related project plan consists multiple processes, a software development activity also consists of multiple tasks. A process or a combination of multiple processes is required to complete each task. A typical SDLC follows a consistent sequence of processes or a process model.

Process Model

A process model defines the overall processes that an organization needs to follow to manage a project efficiently. It defines a structured approach to sequence the phases and identify the requirements of each phase in the SDLC. The definition of the phases in a process model helps organize, monitor, and execute a project efficiently.

A process model is flexible and does not follow any rigid rules of implementation. An organization can deploy a totally new process model for its overall software development effort. It can also customize an existing process model to merge with its implemented process model. For example, Figure 3.1 shows two process models, A and B. Process model A was used by an organization that manufactures confidential defense applications. The management used the model to plan extensively for unexpected project risks. However, after discussing with the project managers and system analysts, the organization wants to merge its current process model with a model that has simple and consistent SDLC phases. This leads to the evolution of the process model B.

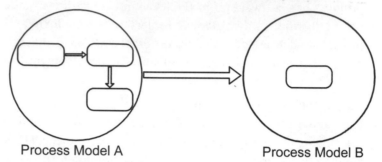

Process Model A   Process Model B

Figure 3.1: Customizing Process Models

Benefits of Using a Process Model

By following a specific process model, you can derive a number of benefits. These are:

- Repeatability in components
- Manageability of a project
- Measurability of project factors
- Clarity in work products
- Provision of a sense of completion of phases

Repeatability ensures the reusability of various supporting components, such as documentation, checklists, code analyzers, and report managers for future projects. Adhering to process models helps you reuse existing components.

Manageability is the overall capability of a project to be scheduled, tracked, and monitored against standards and specifications. In the absence of process models, the manageability of a software project becomes difficult to achieve.

Measurability is the ability of a project to be measured in terms of effort, cost, quality, and time allocation. Measuring the effort, cost, time, and quality helps plan realistically and reduce rework during the later phases of a project. Process models help you estimate and monitor a project effectively until its completion.

Another benefit of following a specific process model is that you can clearly define and justify interim work products such as documentation, plans, deliverables, and checklists. Some process models assume strict verification and completion of all work products.

Complying with a process model also ensures that developers are less likely to forget the main and supporting activities of a project. The supporting activities include documenting the deviations, scheduling team meetings, writing minutes for team meetings, and managing the software configuration. These are crucial activities that enable you to study the processes in a process model and suggest improvements.

In addition, process models provide developers a sense of direction and completion of each phase. This psychologically motivates developers to perform better than before.

Many organizations develop process technology tools to improve their software processes. These tools automate the process model of an organization, including the small tasks that comprise the SDLC. Each member of a software team can use these tools to perform tasks, create and deliver work products for the tasks, and evaluate the work products. A process technology tool can also be monitored and evaluated to analyze, control, and improve the process model from time to time. The continuous improvement of a process model is important because it helps reduce the time and cost spent on project development without compromising on the quality of the product.

PRIMARY PROCESS MODELS

Process models are of two types, primary and evolutionary. Primary models include the Linear Sequential model and the Prototyping model. The Linear Sequential model is popularly called the Waterfall model. Evolutionary models include the Incremental model and the Spiral model.

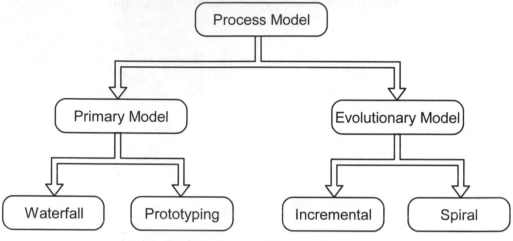

Figure 3.2: Types of Process Models

Waterfall Model

Winston Royce propounded the Waterfall model in the early 70s. It is the simplest, the oldest, and the most widely used process model in software engineering. As the name suggests, the phases in this model flow one after the other just as water flows in a waterfall from a higher to a lower level. A preceding phase is depicted at a higher level than its subsequent phase.

The Waterfall model is based on the following assumptions:

- Each phase is explicitly complete with specific baselines.

- All the preceding phases of a project life cycle are complete before moving on to the next phase.

- All the uncertainties and requirements are determined at the beginning of a project.

Phases in the Waterfall Model

Figure 3.3 displays the phases in the Waterfall model. The phases in this model are linearly sequenced. Therefore, a phase does not begin unless its preceding phase is complete. This helps track the beginning and the end of every phase. The typical phases in the Waterfall model are analysis, design, development or coding, testing, and implementation and maintenance.

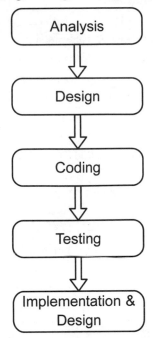

Figure 3.3: Phases of Development in the Waterfall Model

The analysis phase includes preliminary investigations that conceptualize the vision, the scope, and the basic objectives of a project. The analysis is done using a series of activities. The client requirements are documented in the *software requirements specification (SRS)* document. This document is prepared after interacting with the client in a series of meetings and discussions.

A feasibility study of the entire project is also conducted before the commencement of the project. This is performed to estimate the need for the prospective software product after its completion. The top-level plans for the project are also conveyed to the client and approved. The output work products in this stage include an SRS document and a feasibility report or a cost-and-benefit analysis report. In addition, quality review checklists and standards, a personnel skill matrix, a decomposition diagram of all the prospective phases, and a list of other deliverables in the subsequent phases are also prepared and finalized.

The second phase in the Waterfall model is the design phase. This phase is generally divided into two phases:

▨ High-level design

▨ Detailed design

In the high-level design phase, the modules, the subsystems in the project SDLC, and their relationships are determined. You can use *context analysis diagrams* (CADs) to represent the various main systems and the different modules within them. The focus of a CAD is restricted to the top-level components and the life cycle of the entire software system. The output of this phase is an *outline design document* (ODD).

Note

CADs are used to depict the main entities and the top-level processes that connect each entity. Distinct shapes are used to depict an entity, a data store, and a process. A CAD provides only superficial information about a system.

The second phase of the design phase is the detailed design phase. This phase is also called the low-level design phase. In this phase, the subsystems of the modules defined in the high-level design phase are designed. The lower-level systems exist at the unit level of a module. The output of this phase is the *detailed design document* (DDD).

Coding is the third phase in the Waterfall model SDLC. As shown in Figure 3.4, this phase begins after the analysis and design phases are complete. In this phase, you code and test the coded components for their functionality. This is the stage in which you actually begin developing the software. The coding phase is immensely supported by the outputs of the first two phases. A detailed module-wise structure provides each programmer the focus and the steps needed to develop software. Code can be generated mechanically if the design phase has been completed.

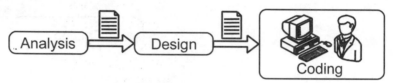

Figure 3.4: Coding Phase

The fourth phase in the SDLC of the Waterfall model is testing. As shown in Figure 3.5, testing begins as soon as software development is complete during the coding phase. During testing, the components and modules are brought together to form a complete system. The testing activity is planned for each module as well as for the entire system. Testing is done at the development site as well as at the client site. At the end of this phase, you are expected to have a fully operational system. An assessment of the quality of the system as given in SRS is also done during this phase.

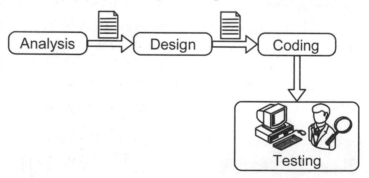

Figure 3.5: Testing Phase

Implementation and maintenance is the final phase in the SDLC of the Waterfall model. This is shown in Figure 3.6. Implementation is a one-time activity although maintenance activities are performed on an ongoing basis. The software product is implemented at the client site. The implementation can be done either in phases or at a time. Maintenance is an additional activity that is planned in this stage.

If the product is for self-use, the periodic review plan, personnel, and checklists are determined for maintaining the software. In case the product is for a client, a maintenance plan for a specific duration is drawn up for the client.

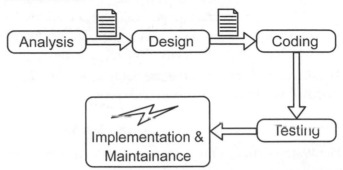

Figure 3.6: Implementation and Maintenance Phase

The phases of the Waterfall model that you have seen, display some common features. These are:

- Every phase has an input and a corresponding output. The output of one phase forms the input of the succeeding phase. This helps the closure and certification of the input documents so that they can be used as reference pointers for subsequent phases.

- The certified output of a phase that is released for the next phase is called a baseline. A baseline also marks a particular milestone in the SDLC.

- Every phase ends with verification and validation of the baselines produced in that phase.

Consider a situation. Blue Technology Inc. is an SEI-CMM level 5-certified software company that develops customized solutions. In its endeavor to create quality solutions, it adheres to the complete SDLC formally. The company has recently acquired a project on automating an accounting process and has dedicated a separate project team to complete the project. The team consists of five designers headed by the project manager, seven experienced developers, three QA professionals, two documentation professionals, and three out of the seven developers would also handle the implementation and maintenance activities. In the pre-analysis phase, the analysts with the client have assigned tentative number of days and resources that are likely to be used in each phase. The development team perceives the project to be a smooth one that can have defined processes wherein each phase has defined input and certified output.

The team is also provided defined project requirements by the client. In addition, the client has handed over all documentation of their existing accounting process with a view to assist the team in development. The team anticipates the project to be of a large size, but simple to design and develop. Therefore, the project need not be hurriedly wound up and ample quality checks need to be planned and executed according to client directions.

In such a case, you would use the Waterfall model because of the following reasons:

- The project is large yet it is clearly divided into discrete phases and each phase has defined number of days, personnel, and resources allocated. The Waterfall model requires the presence of defined phases and processes in each phase.

- The development also perceives that it can have defined set of input and certified output. This is because each phase would lead to another and the next phase would not begin until the previous phase is certified as closed. This way baselines and milestones for each phase can be identified. The Waterfall model assumes the closure of a previous phase before the successive phase begins. This ensures linear progression of a project where developers do not need to revert to an earlier phase or a process.

■ The development team is not likely to face any bumps in the development process because of clear-cut project requirements as well documentation provided to them by the client. Clarity of project vision and project requirements are the essential features of the Waterfall model, which are fulfilled in the preceding scenario.

Therefore, if the requirements are defined and a project is large enough to be divided into defined phases, you can go for the Waterfall model.

Disadvantages of the Waterfall Model

The Waterfall model faces criticism despite its popularity. This is because of the assumption that there cannot be a sudden crossover from one phase to the next. Real-time projects require sudden crossover between phases because such projects are subjected to change in every phase of the development cycle. For example, real-time projects such as embedded software development where the phases and the requirements for every phase cannot be determined at the analysis phase cannot deploy the Waterfall model.

Another reason for the unpopularity of the Waterfall model is that it requires too much effort for stringent documentation in every phase. Every phase is closed with formal documentation. Projects with predictable final product, such as banking software or an airline reservation project, usually have formal documentation. This is because the phases of these projects are defined. However, it is difficult for research and development (R&D)-related projects to complete all project documentation.

The Waterfall model does not support the development of a working model of a project first and then further development based on client feedback. Absence of a working model prevents you from detecting an issue in an early phase. As a result, you incur higher expenditure in rectifying the issue in a later phase. This in turn has an adverse effect on the effort, cost, and time spent on rework.

Finally, the Waterfall model causes, as M. Bradac [BRA94] puts it, a "*blocking state*". When a blocking state occurs, some team members wait for other team members to finish a dependent task.

For example, in Figure 3.7, the team member assigned to do the design task cannot begin work until the analysis is complete. This delays the turnaround of the software project. Many times, the blocking state wastes a lot of developers' time that could have been spent on productive project-related work.

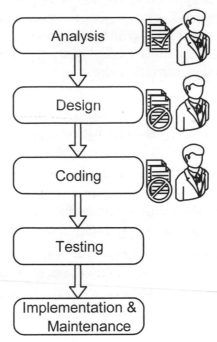

Figure 3.7 Idle Team Members in the Phases of the Waterfall Model

Conclusion

Despite its limitations, the Waterfall model still remains the most widely used model for software process engineering in many organizations, old and new. It provides a basic template into which phases such as analysis, design, coding, testing, and maintenance can be easily designed and monitored.

You apply the Waterfall model in projects that have well-defined client requirements. The projects have predictable phases that do not usually change during the project life cycle. Moreover, such projects have very few risks associated with them. The impact of these risks can be managed easily.

Table 3.1 summarizes the characteristics of the Waterfall model.

Characteristics	Applicability of Characteristics
Defined client requirements	Yes
Expected change in phases	Negligible
Risks expected	Low
Probability and impact of risks on projects	Low
Developmental environment	Familiar

Table 3.1: Characteristics of the Waterfall Model

Prototyping Model

Other software process models have emerged over the years that eliminate the limitations of the Waterfall model. The Prototyping model is another primary model. In this process model, a throwaway prototype is created based on client feedback. The prototype need not encompass all the features of the expected final product. However, the prototype includes the major features of the final product and reflects how the features are executed.

You use this model when the client is not clear about the requirements of the proposed system or when there is a conflict in client requirements. To resolve the conflict, the development team develops a working model so that the requirements of the client become defined. Defined client requirements enable the physical development of the actual product.

For example, a client feels that a list box is the best way to accept user input on an interface. However, you try to convince the client that option buttons present a more professional look to the interface. In this situation, a prototype can help convince the client.

The Prototyping model can be as simple as a drawing on a paper or as complex as the real working software. The closer your prototype is to the actual product, the more precise is your evaluation.

The development of a prototype goes through certain phases such as requirements analysis, designing, coding, and testing. However, each of these phases is promptly done and not fully completed. These phases are considered to be part of the analysis phase of the SDLC.

Figure 3.8 presents a summary of the phases in the Prototyping model.

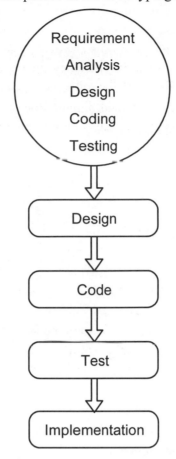

Figure 3.8: Prototyping Model

After a prototype is developed, it is delivered to the client with instructions on how to use it. After evaluating the prototype, the client provides feedback, which is then effectively used to develop the final product. Alternatively, if the client rejects the prototype, you discard the prototype and develop the product right from scratch.

There are different types of prototyping methods that an organization can implement.

- Rapid prototyping
- Reusable prototyping
- Modular prototyping

In the *rapid prototyping method*, an original prototype is evaluated and discarded. Consequently, based on the feedback, a new prototype is designed. The new prototype is evaluated again and the procedure continues until the client approves the prototype. This model is suitable when the cost and time required to create a prototype is minimal. You can also use this method if the project has a substantially long cycle and the development team wants the design to be strong.

In the *reusable prototyping method*, the previous version of the prototype design is not thrown away. Some of its components are reused and incorporated in the new prototype. This is also called Evolutionary prototyping. This model is used when the old design needs major changes but the supplementary components of the old design do not need major changes.

The third type of prototyping method is *Modular prototyping*. This implies the addition of new parts to an existing prototype as the design phase progresses. Therefore, enhancements are carried out for every design of the prototype based on client feedback. This is also called incremental prototyping. This model is used when considerable cost, time, and effort are deployed to create a prototype. It is also used if the client feedback for enhancements is not major and minor improvisations are needed to obtain client approval.

The prototyping of products can be done using two techniques:

■ High-fidelity prototyping

■ Low-fidelity prototyping

In *high-fidelity prototyping* technique, the prototype is created to resemble the actual, expected product as closely as possible. It simulates the actual product in terms of look, functionality, and timing. This is done when both the client and the development team find it difficult to conceive the final product, and the team wants client approval on most features of the prototype.

In the *low-fidelity prototyping* technique, the prototype is presented using papers and pencils. The prototype resembles, but does not look like the actual product. This technique is used when the final product is quite clear to the client and the development teams. The development team conceptualizes and highlights only some aspects of the product for approval from the client. This is a less expensive technique than high-fidelity prototyping.

Whatever be the type of prototype you choose to create, following the prototyping model is an expensive approach. This is because additional investment is first required for creating the prototype. Until the client approves the prototype, time, effort, and cost need to be divested. This may cause slippage in the estimated project time. It is only after the prototype is approved that the actual development of the project begins.

Consider a situation in which you may need to use the Prototyping model. Certified Carriers is a courier company that has decided to automate its billing, customer service, and inventory systems due to an increase in their sales volume and customer strength. The company has no experience in automation because this is for the first time that they are planning for automating their basic services. The client too has no idea about the size, cost, and the duration of the project. They have assigned the automation project to Technology Systems.

Technology Systems needs to analyze the systems of Certified Carriers and present a prospective working model of the software product. Only after the working model is approved and signed-off by Certified Carrier, will the team draw up a specific project plan and create a development team. However, an analysis team is formed to create the working model, arrange meetings with the client, accept feedback, and implement all practicable feedback to the working model. The team at Technology Systems intends to reuse the technology and the working model to further develop and complete the creation of the software product. Therefore, as of now, no resource planning, time planning, or project requirements have been drawn up by Technology Systems.

In such a case, you would use the Prototyping model because of the following reasons:

■ The project is initiated without any clear project requirements by the client. The client itself is not sure about the look and feel of the software product that it requires. Although, it is just clear about its need for automation. However, it is open to the idea of providing constant feedback for product design and development. This is the driving force of using the Prototyping model. The Prototyping model enables an analysis team to first construct a working model with their prior software experience combined with the vague needs of the client.

▪ The client is open to the idea of providing constant feedback for product improvement and shaping the prospective design of the software product. This is an important condition of using the Prototyping model.

▪ With the working model, the development team is able to estimate realistically the effort, time, cost, and resources that will be used to complete the software product. In doing so, it can also anticipate which phases or baselines in the SDLC are redundant.

Using the Prototyping model saves cost and time involved in the build-it-twice approach. The experience of developing the prototype is useful for developers while developing the final product. It reduces the risks of an unfeasible project design because the developers gain a fair idea of the resources and the probable time taken to create the final product. They also get a feel of the implementation tool to be used in the project.

Table 3.2 presents a summary of the characteristics of the Waterfall and Prototyping Models.

Characteristics	Waterfall	Prototyping
Defined client requirements	Yes	No
Expected change in phases	Negligible	Low
Risks expected	Low	Moderately high
Probability and impact of risks on projects	Low	Moderately high
Developmental environment	Familiar	New

Table 3.2: Comparison Between the Waterfall and Prototyping Models

EVOLUTIONARY PROCESS MODELS

In the light of the growing software requirements, the classical software process models could not support enhancements. With the use of an evolutionary process model, it is possible to enhance a software product. Enhancements can be in the form of additional features, such as speed, interface design, or user interaction. These enhancements are dictated by increasing client demands.

There are two popular evolutionary models, the Incremental model and the Spiral model. These models are called evolutionary because these process models help a software product evolve over a period of time. The development of a product is based on client feedback with the basic product remaining the same.

Incremental Model

The Incremental model combines the elements of the Waterfall model and the Prototyping model. In this model, the development of a software product is in builds. A *build* is defined as a self-contained unit of the development activity. The entire development cycle is planned for a specific number of logical builds. Consequently, in each build, a specific set of features is incorporated.

To facilitate consistent quality in each build, activities such as design, development, unit, and implementation testing are conducted separately. Therefore, for each build, a loop of these activities is repeated until the last build is developed for final testing.

While developing each build, it is ensured that each build is stand-alone and not dependent upon any prospective build that is yet to be developed.

Consider Figure 3.9 to understand the logic of sequencing builds.

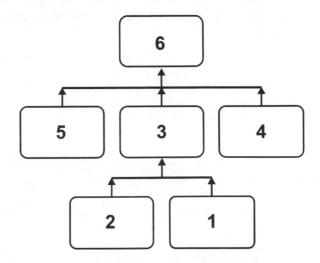

Figure 3.9: Sequential Builds

In Figure 3.9, the numbered boxes represent the builds with the arrows depicting the increasing flow of dependency. From the figure, it is clear that the lower builds labeled 2 and 1 are developed first because they are not dependent upon any other module. Next, build 3 is scheduled for development because the prerequisite builds for this build have already been developed. After build 3 is sent to the client, builds 5 and 4 are developed. These builds are prerequisites for build 6. While a particular build is tested, some time may be required to revert to an earlier build. This can disrupt the development of the subsequent builds. Finally, build 6 is developed for the client. This completes the development phase of the SDLC. In the next phase of the SDLC, all these builds are integrated, tested, and delivered to the client as a single product.

Figure 3.10 depicts the various phases of the Incremental model in which a build is developed and delivered to the client in piecemeal. The development of each deliverable is mapped to the number of days the project lasts. This way, you know when each build has been delivered as compared to its planned date.

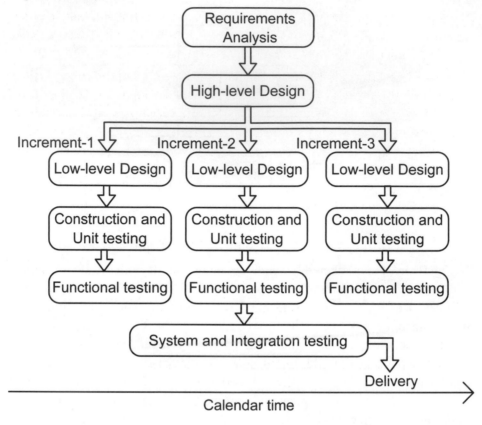

Figure 3.10: Incremental Model

You can use the Incremental model approach in software projects where human resource is scarce. In such cases, the management can decide to divide and develop a product in individual builds. When the resources are available, the subsequent builds are planned and executed. This process model is useful in real life because normally all the resources required to complete the project are not available at the same time.

Consider a situation in which you might need to use the Incremental model of SDLC. Supersoft2000 requires a software product that automates the employee and their salary details. It has assigned this project to Blue Valley Consulting (BVC) that specializes in developing Human Resources (HR)-related applications. The project requirements are defined to start the project. However, the client wants to roll out the new system for the benefit of its employees as early as possible. The analysis team in BVC has been able to divide the entire project into seven independent modules. On the basis of their prior experience, it feels each module can be executed and deployed independently by the client. After all the modules are completed, the maintenance team in BVC can assemble and implement the system at the client site. Currently, the development personnel in BVC are hired on contract and BVC faces shortage of skilled personnel.

In such a case, you use the Incremental model because of the following reasons:

Time and lack of skilled personnel are the main hindrances in this project. Therefore, by using the Incremental model, you can design, develop, and deliver independent modules. This way by using a few skilled personnel you are able to develop a system with basic features and provide it to the client immediately. The most important and the least dependent module is developed first. While the client is using the module, BVC can arrange for additional skilled personnel to complete the rest of the modules and deliver them to the client.

The Incremental model enables you to revert to an earlier phase and refine the product based on client feedback. After all the modules have been developed, the development personnel can be released. BVC can then hire or retain a few experienced personnel to create a maintenance team. This team would assemble and implement the entire employee salary details product at the client site. This flexibility of personnel can be exercised because you use the Incremental model. Using the Incremental model enables:

▓ Division of skilled labor

▓ Division of a complex project into modules

▓ Development of those modules within a short time frame

Therefore, if time and skilled personnel are constraints of a project, you can effectively use the Incremental model.

The Incremental model is compared with the Waterfall and Prototyping models in Table 3.3.

Characteristics	Waterfall	Prototyping	Incremental
Defined client requirements	Yes	No	Yes
Expected change in phases	Negligible	Low	Low
Risks expected	Low	Moderately high	Moderately high
Probability and impact of risks on projects	Low	Moderately high	Moderately high
Developmental environment	Familiar	New	Moderately familiar

Table 3.3: Comparison Between the Waterfall, Prototyping, and the Incremental Models

Spiral Model

Another evolutionary model is the Spiral model. Dr. Barry Boehm established the Spiral model theory. The theory combines the iterative nature of the Prototyping model and the organized and controlled aspects of the Waterfall model. The Spiral model focuses on identifying and eliminating high-risk problems by careful process design. The basic goal of using the Spiral model is to define ways of eliminating risks in the design phase. Consequently, minimum and manageable risks percolate into the development phase.

In the Spiral model, the entire development cycle is typically divided into four clear task areas. The task areas are:

▓ Requirements analysis

▓ Risk analysis

▓ Prototype and detailed designing

■ Construction, testing, and implementation

Requirements analysis is the first task area. It includes communicating with the client to estimate the feasibility of and the requirements for the project. The basic project objectives are established at this point. In addition, tentative plans to start the analysis and creation of a prototype are drawn up.

Risk analysis is the second task area. The uncertainties of meeting the basic project are identified in this task area. The constraints regarding resources and the cost and benefit feasibility of carrying out the project are also determined. This task area may also include deciding whether to create simulations, benchmarks, or prototypes to closely represent a project.

The third task area is the prototype and detailed designing. This task area involves the creation of a working model or a prototype. The prototype is created after deciding upon the kind of representation that has to be made based on the risks and feasibility study. The prototype maps approximately to the final product because it does not reflect all the features that an error-free software product might have.

Subsequently, when the client approves the final prototype, an overall detailed design of the prospective system is prepared in the same phase. On the basis of this detailed design, the actual software is developed. The detailed design charts out the methodologies and processes that enable effective development of software.

The last task area of the Spiral model consists of construction, testing, and implementation tasks. In the construction task area, the final product is developed after the prototype is approved following several rounds of feedback. To facilitate the development of the final software product, formal phases of development, testing, and implementation are planned and flagged off. Moreover, every phase is followed by a formal verification round to ensure that the phase is formally closed and all documentation for that phase is baselined.

In the same task area, testing and implementation are the other tasks performed. In this area, the software product is released to the client for feedback and acceptance testing.

Acceptance testing is done by the client on the basis of earlier client specifications. Finally, on the basis of the client feedback, the product is enhanced and implemented at the client site.

The four task areas of the Spiral model are represented in Figure 3.11.

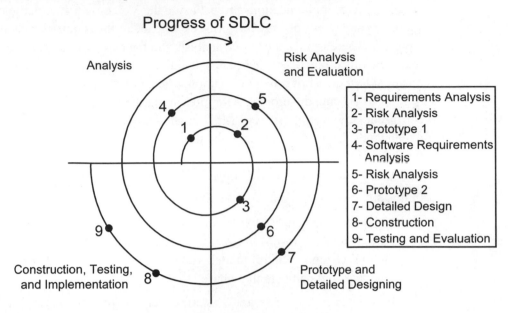

Figure 3.11: Spiral Model

In Figure 3.11, each spiral of the Spiral model represents a phase or a stage in the life cycle of the software. There are two iterations as depicted in Figure 3.11. For example, in the first iteration, the set of activities include the following:

- Requirements analysis
- Risk analysis
- Creation of a prototype

In the second iteration, based on the feedback of the client, a number of activities are performed. The second iteration begins with an analysis of software requirements. In addition, risks that are anticipated in performing the second iteration are also analyzed. Risk analysis is a discrete activity in every iteration of the Spiral model. There can be more number of iterations depending upon the seriousness of the client feedback. However, in each iteration, the set of activities continue to be:

- Software requirements analysis
- Risk analysis
- Creation of a prototype

Finally, when the client has approved the prototype, the development team can begin software development. The development phase is followed by the testing and evaluation phases.

In each iteration, all the above tasks are performed to create a quality product that conforms to the requirements and specifications proposed by the client. Therefore, for every round, there is a spiraling cumulative cost involved. The Spiral model does not require the closure of all phases. This is in contrast to the Waterfall and Prototyping models. Therefore, the development team can revert to an earlier phase if a preceding phase requires enhancements. The tasks performed for a preceding phase also affect the subsequent phases. For example, a design concern might surface in the testing phase. To address the concern, the design of the product is enhanced, which affects the coding and the testing phases.

Consider an example in which you use the Spiral model. LMN Inc. has acquired a project to develop a telecommunications project using the Voice-over Internet telephony (VoIP) technology. The company does not have any prior experience or the required level of expertise to develop such a project. There is a team of three analysts and the company does not propose to dedicate a team to complete this project. This is because it anticipates many risks and a large amount of rework that may add to the cost of project execution. The company has determined multiple models and designs to execute the project. After presenting the models to the client, the client is itself confused. However, it assures LMN Inc. of continued feedback and support. The client fully understands the ambitiousness of the project and does not consider time and budget as constraints for the project. Consequently, LMN Inc. decides to use the client feedback and risk analysis effectively until the end of the project.

In this situation, you would use the Spiral model because of the following reasons:

- LMN Inc. has no prior experience or expertise in executing such a project. Therefore, it expects a lot of rework in reverting to an earlier phase and incorporating client feedback therein. Using the Spiral model, you can to revert to an earlier phase to incorporate client feedback and compete that phase.

- It needs to perform risk analysis effectively to eliminate losses arising due to uncertain development models, resource requirements, project constraints, and time.

- It is also preferable to create a prototype for every deliverable that LMN Inc. might deem necessary to receive client feedback.

- Spiraling cumulative project costs can be covered up by the liberal budget provided by the client.

The Spiral model is typically a new model. Unlike the other models, the Spiral model incorporates some high-level management and planning activities with development activities. This model is especially suitable for high-risk projects that are uncertain in nature. Risk analysis for each phase also determines the amount of development and testing effort required in that phase. Therefore, it is applicable to large-scale projects that have adequate financial provision for evaluating risks.

Table 3.4 compares all the models with respect to their characteristics.

Characteristics	Waterfall	Prototyping	Incremental	Spiral
Defined client requirements	Yes	No	Yes	No
Expected change in phases	Negligible	High	Low	High
Risks expected	Low	Moderately high	Moderately high	Higher than all others
Probability and impact of risks on projects	Low	Moderately high	Moderately high	Higher than all others
Developmental environment	Familiar	New	Moderately familiar	New

Table 3.4: Comparison Between all the Models

Selection of a Process Model

Selecting an appropriate process model is crucial because it can provide a basic framework to initiate and carry out a project to its conclusion. It also defines the path for various project-related activities. For example, if you select a process model, you know for sure that you need to carry out certain activities, such as planning, scheduling, resource allocation, risk management, and cost and effort estimation. These activities ensure smooth progress of a project within the allocated time and ensure maintenance of quality and measurability throughout the project.

With so many process models available, a project manager is likely to face the dilemma of selecting the "right" process model for managing a software project efficiently.

To select a process model that is suitable to a project, the following criteria can be considered:

- Business goals of the organization
- Expected size of the project
- Client and project requirements
- Availability of funds and development staff
- Risks perceived in the project

Business Goals of the Organization

This criterion indicates the overall approach and mindset of an organization. If the organization has a past history of developing projects in accordance with well-defined plans and other job aids in every phase, the suitable process model can be the Waterfall model. However, if the organization is well equipped with the resources to deal with financial, technological, and personnel risks, it can choose the Spiral model. The organization can choose the Prototyping model if it is used to working in an experimental and a constant feedback mode.

Expected Size of the Project

If the size of a project is extensive and the client prefers all the features of the proposed project at the first delivery, you can select the Waterfall model. When you want the entire product to be developed and delivered in piecemeal so that the client can immediately begin the unit testing of each module, you would select the Incremental model. In contrast, if the size of the project is doubtful, you can go for the Prototyping or Spiral model. These models help to develop projects that have a vague and uncertain estimate of the project size.

Client and Project Requirements

The Waterfall model or the Incremental model is chosen if the client needs and the project requirements are defined and approved. In addition, no changes or negligible changes are expected in the future regarding design requirements. In contrast, you would choose the Spiral and Prototyping models when the client needs and system requirements are uncertain and likely to change in the future.

Availability of Funds and Development Staff

The Waterfall and Prototyping models require predetermined and adequate resources at the start of a project. However, if you expect additional funds and human resources as you progress through the different phases, you should go in for the Incremental or Spiral models. This is because the Incremental model operates on the assumption of developing a project into several builds due to lack of human resources. Similarly, the funds and staffing requirements in the Spiral model may increase or decrease depending on the changes in requirements and feasibility of the proposed project in the future.

Risks Perceived in a Project

This is yet another important criterion for the selection of a process model. You choose the Waterfall or Incremental model if the occurrence of risks and their impact perceived is minimum. However, you should go in for the Spiral model if the risks and their perceived impact are very high.

You can prepare a checklist of all these factors, similar to the one shown in Table 3.4. You can add a check mark for every factor in the checklist that meets your project description. Finally, you can select a suitable process model for your project based on the maximum number of factors checked.

SUMMARY

✓ A process model is a structured approach that defines the sequence of phases in a software development life cycle.

✓ There are two primary models, the Waterfall model and the Prototyping model.

✓ The Waterfall model is the simplest and the oldest process model.

✓ In the Waterfall model, phases follow each other in succession. A phase never begins unless its preceding phase is complete. In addition, you cannot revert to a previous phase to complete it.

✓ Using the Waterfall model ensures a steady and certain path for project development.

✓ The Prototyping model enables the developers to create a working model based on the basic features of a software project. The final product is developed based on the feedback provided by the client.

✓ Using the Prototyping model ensures that there are no risks or delays during actual project development.

✓ There are two evolutionary models, the Incremental and Spiral models.

✓ In the Incremental model, a core product is created and further enhancements are added to it.

✓ You can use the Incremental model when the staff to create a full-fledged product is scarce but additional staff can be arranged later to complete the enhancements in the core product.

✓ The Spiral model is the latest process model that is developed.

✓ In the Spiral model, analysis and risk management are the two primary activities and are implemented in every phase of the SDLC. If a previous phase is incomplete, you can revert to that phase to complete it, regardless of your current phase.

HOMEWORK EXERCISES

1. SSPT Corporation has bagged a research-oriented project in the field of biometrics. The development team is not familiar with the kind of software that needs to be developed. Therefore, project-specific requirements, milestones, and phases cannot be defined very accurately. The organization anticipates a fairly large amount of rework in the project and is in a dilemma about selecting a process model to begin development. Help the organization to select a process model by completing the following matrix with a Yes (Y) or No (N).

Considerations	Yes/No
Client requirements are well defined.	
The team is familiar with the software and the development environment.	
Serious project-related risks are anticipated.	

2. Read up some content on the fountain model and the rapid application development (RAD) model. Compare the two models and identify the situations where the two can be used.

3. The Zachman framework is a new change-oriented process model. This framework was propounded by John Zachman and is used to create an extensive enterprise system where there is enough room for rapid organizational changes. Read up some content on the Zachman framework and compare it with the Spiral model discussed in the chapter. You can limit you comparison to the following points.

	Zachman Framework	Spiral model
Defined requirements		
Anticipation of risks		
Availability of funds and development staff		
Size of the project supported		

LAB EXERCISES

1. Blue Valley Consulting has bagged a short-cycle software project that has an extremely strict deadline. As a result, the organization plans to reuse software components that were developed in the previous projects. The organization has been using a conventional process model to develop projects. To meet the deadline, the organization intends to use the existing process model. Which benefit of the process model does Blue Valley Consulting make use of by reusing existing components?

   a. Measurability
   b. Manageability
   c. Unambiguousness in work products
   d. Repeatability

2. Technology Systems has recently bagged a software project from a commercial airline to develop a Web-based application to collect client feedback. Currently, the airline collects client feedback manually. The airline has provided Technology Systems with a well-defined procedure for collecting client feedback. The airline needs the project to be completed in four months. The airline has also allocated a fixed budget for the entire project. The scope and the size of the project have already been decided in the pre-analysis phase and meetings with the client. Which process model should Technology Systems select?

   a. Waterfall model
   b. Prototyping model
   c. Incremental model
   d. Spiral model

3. Supersoft2000 is a Web-based solutions provider. The company has planned to bring out a breakthrough application in the market. There is intense competition in the market. Therefore, the company decides to bring out the application within a very short time. The company has estimated the effort and cost and defined the requirements for development. However, there is a lack of availability of skilled human resources. Which process model should the company select?

   a. Waterfall Model
   b. Prototyping Model
   c. Incremental Model
   d. Spiral Model

4.   Briefly compare the Incremental and Prototyping models.

5.   Discuss the advantages of using the Spiral model.

Chapter 4

Software Project Scope Determination

Objectives:

- ☐ Define the scope of a software project.

- ☐ Describe the phases in the scope management process.

- ☐ Identify the inputs, tools, and outputs of each phase of the scope management process.

- ☐ Obtain information for scope determination by using communication techniques and tools.

- ☐ Use communication methodologies for scope determination.

NEED TO SCOPE A SOFTWARE PROJECT

The scope of a software project is defined as the work required for creating a software product. A software project manager needs to define the scope of a software project to ensure that all processes required to complete the project are identified. The software project scope depends on the scope of the software product. After the software product scope is defined, the development team can understand the software project better in terms of requirements and constraints.

It is important for both product and project scope to be synchronized such that the completion of the product scope results in successful completion of the project scope.

Scope Determinants

The output of a successful software project is a software product. Therefore, a clear understanding of the requirements from a software product helps a development team to better understand the project requirements. The scope of a software product is the range of activities that the product can perform. It includes the functions it is expected to perform, its performance criteria, and the constraints under which the software is developed. These actually define all that needs to be done to complete the project successfully.

Function and Performance

The function and performance requirements of a software product are identified at the system engineering level as well as during project and product scope determination. The functionality of a software product includes features that enable the product to modify the user interface or process data in a specific manner. Parameters such as processing speed, data transfer speed, and request processing speed help measure the performance of a software product. An understanding of these parameters enables the software development team to understand the requirements of the software product. After the requirements of the software product are clear, the team can define the software development strategy.

Constraints

The constraints on a software product are the restrictions within which the development team will work. The constraints need to be determined while defining the scope of the project. As a project manager, you need to ensure that the required resources are identified and the constraints on these resources do not limit the execution of the software project. Identifying the constraints also help you identify the potential risks with regard to these constraints. As a result, you can ensure smoother management of the software project.

You can classify the constraints on a software product as follows:

- Technological constraints
- Resource constraints
- Time constraints
- Behavioral constraints

Technological Constraints

The technological constraints influence the technological standards used in a software project. For example, the use of a particular programming technology, platform, or environment during product development is a technological constraint.

Usually, the client defines most of the technological constraints for a software project. For example, the client may require that a particular product be created using the C programming language. However, technological constraints may arise due to the unavailability of a reliable language or platform or due to ill-defined standards and protocols.

Resource Constraints

Resource constraints arise due to a lack of facilities, equipment, funds, training, or skilled people during project development. The availability of these resources is often defined by the budget assigned to a software project.

Time Constraints

More often than not, software projects struggle to meet deadlines set by clients. However, separate phases and processes within each phase may also involve time constraints. Time constraints also arise due to deadlines set by different internal groups working on various aspects of the software. For example, the time limitation to complete an iteration of a prototyping process is a time constraint.

Behavioral Constraints

The behavioral constraints of a software project include the demographics and attitudes of the users of the final software product. For example, if an enterprise resource planning (ERP) application requires users to fill in personal details whenever they log in to any module, it could be an irritant. Similarly, if the end user is a person new to computers, the user interface needs to be simple and intuitive. It is important to take such constraints into consideration while determining the scope.

SCOPE MANAGEMENT PROCESS

The scope management process of a software project consists of different phases. You need to determine the inputs required, the tools to be used, and the output for each phase. In this section, you will learn about the phases in the scope management process.

Phases in the Scope Management Process

You can divide the scope management process into five phases. Each phase can, in turn, be viewed as a process that needs to be completed for the next phase to begin.

The different phases of the scope management process are as follows:

- Initiation — INPUT, TOOLS: BUY DECISION: CREAT/BUY
- Planning — DESCRIPTION OF SOFTWARE SOLUTION
- Definition
- Verification
- Change control

Figure 4.1 describes how these phases are arranged.

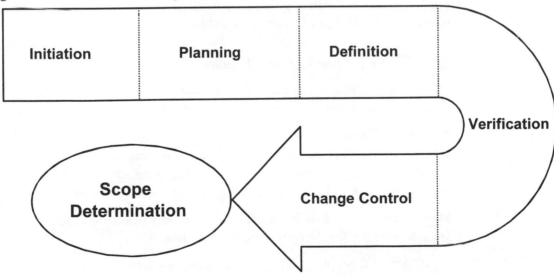

Figure 4.1: The Phases of the Scope Management Process

In the following pages, each phase is discussed in terms of the inputs required, the processes or tools used, and the output generated.

Initiation

The initiation phase marks the beginning of the scope management process. The purpose of this phase is to take stock of the software project in terms of the basic inputs required. Although preliminary feasibility surveys or some amount of software development happens to secure the project, the initiation phase of the scope determination process marks the beginning of project management activity.

If a software project is an in-house project, the initiator for the project may be either a senior manager in the software development organization or an external entity such as a consultant. If the software project is outsourced, the initiator can also be the client for the software product.

Inputs Required for the Initiation Phase

To initiate the scope management process of a software project, you first create a document describing the software product or service to be created. The description includes the required functionality and performance of the software product. The document should be detailed enough to facilitate later project planning.

Next, you create a document describing the business need of the software product or service and compare it with the planned software product. The comparison of the business need and the planned solution helps you understand the need for the software product and the requirements of the software project.

In case the client has identified the software product required, you need to identify the basis used for selecting the software solution. Understanding the selection criteria helps you evaluate the selected software solution in terms of management concerns such as market potential and financial viability.

Finally, you assess similar projects executed in the past. The historical perspective helps you reinforce the selection of a particular software solution for the business need.

Tools Used for the Initiation Phase

In the initiation phase, you use tools to decide whether or not to select a certain software project. There are two categories of tools, economic decision tools and mathematical optimization tools.

You use economic decision tools to measure the potential economic benefit derived from a software project. For example, you can use a comparative tool such as a decision tree to compare two alternative approaches to a software project. Similarly, you can use a benefit contribution tool to calculate the benefit derived from a particular software project.

Mathematical optimization tools enable you to apply constraints to the project selection process and calculate the feasibility of a software project.

In addition to the tools, you can also use experience and expert knowledge to evaluate the information given as input for the initiation phase. The expert knowledge may either exist with the development team or may be imparted through training. At times, expert consultants are sourced from outside the organization.

Outputs from the Initiation Phase

In the case of the initiation phase of an in-house software project, the senior management of the developing organization identifies a project manager for the software project. The project manager is identified and takes charge of the project as soon as possible.

Note

In the case of an outsourced software project, the client for the project determines the scope of the software product and the software project. This means that the identification of the project manager is not within the scope determination process.

The software development organization identifies a project manager after the client defines the scope and before the project activity begins.

Another important output of the initiation phase is the project brief. This document indicates the business need of the project and a description of the software solution planned to meet that need. The document should either contain this information or refer to other documents containing this information. A manager superior to the project manager authorizes the project brief, thereby authorizing the project manager to requisition and allocate resources to the project.

The initiation phase ends with the identification of a project manager, the creation of a project brief, and the definition of assumptions and constraints of the software project. For example, assumptions such as the available technology and the availability of skilled people to execute the project become clear at the end of the initiation phase. Similarly, constraints such as the budget, human resources, time, and technology are also determined during the initiation phase.

Planning

In the planning phase of scope management, the main objective is to create a scope statement. This is a formal document that contains the project scope analysis. It describes all the information required for planning the software project and measures the success of a software project.

Inputs Required for the Planning Phase

The inputs that you require for the planning phase are the project brief, the software product description, and the assumptions and constraints of the project.

Tools Used for the Planning Phase

To analyze the inputs received from the initiation phase, you use tools in the planning phase. One tool that is used commonly is a cost-benefit analysis. You can perform a cost-benefit analysis to estimate the returns on investments for a software project. It can help you in estimating the returns on both the tangible and intangible inputs.

Apart from a cost-benefit analysis, you can also use tools to analyze the currently identified software solution. For example, you can use a facilitated application specification technique

(FAST) to form a joint team of the stakeholders from both the client side and the software development organization. The joint team can then adopt an iterative approach to determine the scope of the software project.

You can also use brainstorming to identify alternatives to the currently identified software solution. This involves assessing alternatives for returns on investment.

Finally, you use experience and expert knowledge to evaluate the information given as input.

Outputs from the Planning Phase

The primary output of the planning phase is a scope statement. It provides a defined path for all the activities of a software project. In addition, it provides information on the functionality, the constraints, the interface, and the performance requirements of the software product. You can consider the scope statement as a business justification of the software project.

Along with the scope statement, the project objectives are laid down in terms of the cost, the schedule, and the quality measurements of the software project. The objectives of the software project must be quantifiable such that project execution can be measured. The objectives that cannot be quantified involve a degree of risk, because the results cannot be measured.

The scope statement acts as an agreement between the development team and the client. When the client approves a scope statement, the development team considers the document as the statement of intent from the client and initiates work based on it.

The other output of the planning phase is the scope management plan. It specifies the possible contingencies of the software project and how the scope will change to meet these contingencies. The scope management plan also identifies the change control plan. In other words, the scope management plan defines the estimated frequency of change in the scope of the project and the control measures to deal with the same.

Definition

The definition phase is the third phase in the scope management process. During this phase, you define the primary project deliverables, the elements within each deliverable, and the management and control of each element. You essentially break down each deliverable into small, more manageable chunks. The breakdown continues until you have been able to identify the smallest element that can be managed separately.

The definition phase allows you to define control criteria for each element in terms of duration, cost, and effort. The activity also helps in identifying responsibilities for each task.

Inputs Required for the Definition Phase

The inputs required for the definition phase of the scope determination process are the scope statement, a scope management plan, and the assumptions and constraints of the software project.

Tools Used for the Definition Phase

The tools required to process the inputs for the definition phase are:

- Work breakdown structure (WBS)

- Decomposition

A WBS groups all the elements of a software project according to the deliverables they are associated with. The WBS is similar to the scope statement in the sense that it helps the project team to understand the project in terms of different elements. It describes the different elements in a top-to-bottom, simple-to-complex manner. The work structure is described with the primary deliverable at the top and the lowest element within that deliverable at the bottom.

Different breakdown structures are used to organize the deliverables within a software project, such as an organizational breakdown structure (OBS). The OBS describes the allocation of different project elements to the different units within an organization. Figure 4.2 shows a sample WBS structure for a software project.

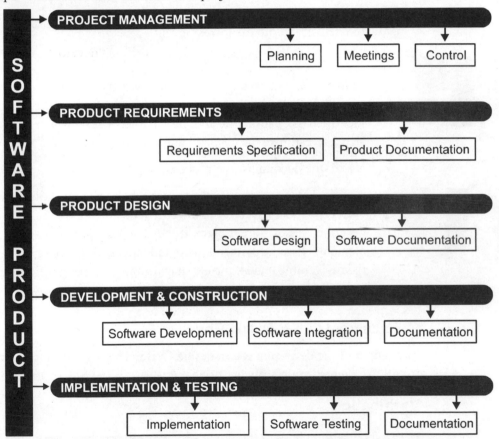

Figure 4.2: A Sample WBS Structure for a Software Project

Figure 4.2 displays the break up of a software project into multiple phases and then defines the separate activities for each phase. The product development process is divided into five phases: project planning, identification of product requirements, software design, software construction, and implementation and testing. Each phase is then divided into sub phases.

Decomposition is the second tool used to process the inputs for the definition phase. It enables you to describe the primary deliverables of a software project in terms of the subtasks or sub elements. You do this by breaking down each deliverable into smaller and more manageable chunks.

There are four steps in for performing decomposition. They are as follows:

1. Identify the primary deliverables of the software project.

    Prepare a document containing the description of all the deliverables of the software project. In the document, describe the deliverables in terms of how the software project is managed. In other words, you arrange the deliverables in the order in which they are to be processed. For example, you can decompose a project into phases and, then, into the primary deliverables in each phase.

2. Estimate the cost and duration required to process each deliverable.

    The purpose of this step is to get an idea of how much and how long it takes to process each identified deliverable. However, the deliverables that occur later in a project may not always be quantifiable. This indicates that you have not been able to decompose all the deliverables to the lowest level.

3. Decompose each deliverable.

    In this step, you decompose those deliverables that cannot be estimated, into smaller elements. Carry out the decomposition until the elements within each deliverable are identified as quantifiable and measurable. After this activity is complete, you return to step 2 to estimate the cost and duration of each deliverable.

4. Verify the decomposition process.

    The final step is to verify whether or not the decomposition process is carried out correctly. First, check if the lower-level elements within each deliverable are adequate to describe the software project. If they are not, either expand them or identify and add more elements. If some elements seem redundant, you may remove them. Finally, ensure that the deliverable and all the elements within it are quantifiable and measurable. If not, then you need to carry out steps 2 and 3 again.

Outputs from the Definition Phase

The output of the definition process is the WBS. The WBS defines a deliverable-oriented structure for all the elements of a software project.

Verification

In the verification phase of the scope management process, the stakeholders from the client side and the developing organization formally verify the project scope. They assess the defined deliverables and ascertain that each deliverable is executed successfully.

Inputs Required for the Verification Phase

The verification phase of the scope determination process primarily requires the product description as input. Thorough documentation is required for a complete understanding of the software product. The documentation describes the product in terms of functionality, performance, and constraints. The documentation may include information such as technical specifications, client requirements, details of technologies used, and details of standards followed. The actual product description may vary according to the nature of the software project and the software product.

In addition to the product description, the *work results* of the software project need to be considered. These results reflect the status of the project plan execution. The work results describe the different deliverables, their stage of completion, and the costs incurred on each deliverable.

Tools Used for the Verification Phase

The product documentation and the work results are assessed to obtain the output. The assessment includes measurement and testing of the work results.

Outputs from the Verification Phase

The output of the verification process is the acceptance of the scope definition by the client. In the case of a software project, the scope definition may include the scope statement, the scope management plan, the product documentation, and the work results.

Change Control

The change control phase is the fifth phase of the scope management process. In this phase, you define a change control mechanism for the software project. The change control mechanism covers the factors that influence change such that the change is advantageous to the software project. In addition, you identify when changes occur. You can use the change control mechanism to manage the change and its impact on the software project.

Inputs Required for the Change Control Phase

The change control phase of the scope determination process requires a number of inputs. One input is the WBS that you created in the definition phase. Another input is a periodic status report, which provides information on the performance of the software project as a whole. These reports provide information on the status of completion of various deliverables and the elements within each deliverable.

Actual requests for a change are another input required in the change control phase. Requests for change can happen at any time during a software project. These requests may be submitted in a formal written format or informally. These requests may or may not be accepted. You can consider requests for a change according to the relevance of the requesting entity to the software project. For example, you may implement a change if a new standard is defined for a programming language by the relevant standards body. Similarly, when a new government regulation makes the change legally binding, you implement the change. However, scope changes are usually not accepted in the software construction phase. Implementing the request due to scope changes could result in large overruns on cost, time, and effort estimates.

Another input required in the change control phase is the scope management plan created in the planning phase. The scope management plan describes how changes are identified, classified, and managed in the software project.

Tools Used in the Change Control Phase

A change control mechanism is the primary tool that you use to process the inputs for the change control phase. It helps in organizing the implementation of a change request. An efficient change control mechanism includes the procedures, paperwork, and approvals required to implement a change. It should be integrated with other control mechanisms at the product, project, or organizational level. This allows the change control mechanism to work synchronously with other control processes, such as time, cost, and quality control mechanisms.

In addition to the change control mechanism, another tool that you can use in the change control phase is an assessment of requests for a change. This allows you to measure the impact that the change will have on the software project. In case of any negative or positive variance from the existing process, the assessment helps take corrective action.

Outputs from the Change Control Phase

The change control phase identifies and defines the changes made to the project scope. These changes are defined as deviations from the scope defined in the WBS. When a scope change occurs, you inform all the relevant stakeholders and document the scope change for future reference.

Another output of the change control phase is the corrective action taken to compensate for the scope change. If a scope change results in a variance from the scope defined in the WBS, you need to take action to put the project plan back on track. For example, corrective action for a scope change may include activities such as modifying the objectives of the software project or the technical specifications of the software product.

COMMUNICATION TECHNIQUES AND TOOLS

You can use different techniques and tools to communicate with the client to elicit and validate client requirements. This section provides information about some of the communication techniques and tools that you can use.

Communication Techniques

A technique is a systematic procedure that is used to complete a complex task. Communication techniques allow the software project manager, the software developer, or the software development analysis team to communicate with the client in a structured way.

Some prominent communication techniques that you can use are:

- Interviewing
- Brainstorming
- Meeting
- Walkthrough and review
- The 5 Ws'
- Six universal questions
- Group discussion

Interviewing

An interview is an exchange of information between two or more people. Interviews are widely used as a requirements-gathering technique. In an interview, the software analyst gathers detailed information about the client software requirements. The software analyst asks a series of questions that focus on narrowing down the requirements. One or more people who have the relevant information may represent the client in the interview.

An interview may be structured or unstructured depending on the kind of information sought by the software analyst. For example, in a situation where the client is unsure about the requirements from the software project, the software analyst might need to follow an unstructured format for the interview. On the other hand, if the client is sure of the requirements, the software analyst can gather the relevant information through a structured interview.

Brainstorming

Brainstorming is a shared problem-solving technique. In a brainstorming session, the attendees attempt to break their existing thought patterns and generate original and creative ideas to solve a problem. The aim of a brainstorming session is to generate creative ideas. These ideas might not necessarily provide a practical solution, but may provide a general direction for a software project.

Meeting

A meeting is a process that allows the software analysis team and the client to come together for a discussion on a fixed agenda.

Walkthrough

A walkthrough is a step-by-step review of the requirements gathered by the software analysis team. In a walkthrough, the software analyst guides the client through all portions of the requirements document. In case a prototype is prepared using the requirements gathered, the client is taken through the steps manually. You can conduct a walkthrough for products, such as software, reference manuals, books, and procedures.

The 5 Ws

'The 5 Ws' is a collective term for the five questions that the analysis team asks the client to elicit requirements of a software project. You can use this technique when there is a lack of understanding about a specific requirement or a problem. The analysis team from the developing organizations asks 'why' five times to the client. Each 'why' narrows down the scope of the answer and provides a deeper level of understanding to the analyst. For example, the first 'why' could be, "Why do you need a solution?" The second 'why' progresses with the answer to the first question, "Why is the current solution not enough?" This line of questioning allows the analyst to put simple questions to the client and obtain the software requirements.

Six Universal Questions

The six universal questions technique is also used to obtain client requirements of a software project. These questions can be used at any stage of a software project to obtain the answers relevant to that stage. The six universal questions are Who, What, Where, When, Why, and How. Each question enables the analysis team to learn about the client requirements from a different perspective.

Group Discussion

The software analyst can also conduct a group discussion to decide between two alternative approaches to a software project. In a group discussion, the participants support one of the two options and argue in favor of the idea. This form of team-based argument over alternative approaches can provide the software analyst with justification for the approaches.

Communication Tools

A tool is a device or an aid to help perform an operation. You can use different communication tools to communicate with the client to elicit and validate requirements for a software project. Some communication tools are:

- Questionnaire
- E-mail and the Internet
- Query register
- Chat client
- Telephone

Questionnaire

You can use a questionnaire to ask the client questions in a structured form. It allows you to ask and receive answers to specific questions. However, a questionnaire may also have open-ended questions for abstract issues.

E-mail and the Internet

E-mail is used increasingly nowadays to communicate with clients. It provides a fast and cost-effective alternative to letters and facsimiles. You can use e-mail to send and receive information in the form of text or pictures. E-mail also allows you to send and receive attachments with information and data regarding the software project. You can also use the Internet as a research tool to locate information regarding the business need and requirements of the client.

Query Register

A query register is used when the software development team and the client are at different geographic locations. A query register contains fields such as the queries from the development team, the date the query was raised, the person who raised the query, the person to whom the query is addressed, the date when the response is required, the response date, the response time, and so on.

You use the query register primarily when the initial requirements gathering and analysis is complete but minor issues need to be clarified with the client. As the scope of the questions and answers is limited, using the query register is not recommended for gathering requirements.

Chat Client

You can also use a chat client to communicate with the client in real time. A chat client provides an inexpensive and faster alternative to e-mail. Modern chat clients allow communication through text, voice, video, and exchange of attachments.

Telephone

The telephone is a tried and tested tool for communication in real time. The telephone allows you to speak with the client and receive information and clarifications immediately.

COMMUNICATION METHODOLOGIES

Determining the scope of a software project is not a simple activity. The task requires collecting voluminous information about the business need, identifying different alternatives to meet the need, selecting a solution, defining the parameters for the software product, and implementing it. As you learned in the second section, the scope of a software project extends even after the implementation of the software product. Managing the software product, monitoring its use, and implementing changes are also part of the software scope definition.

The primary activity in determining the scope of a software project is communicating the requirements from the client to the software development team. These requirements define the functionality and performance required in the software product. In addition, client requirements define the constraints with which the software project needs to work.

This section covers three communication methodologies that you can use to elicit client requirements at the beginning of the scope determination process. These are:

- Asking context-free questions. This is similar to a simple interview of the client.

- Using FAST. This enables a joint team consisting of the client and the development team to navigate the scope determination process.

- Using quality function deployment (QFD). This can be used to translate client requirements into technical specifications.

Using Context-free Questions

At the beginning of a software project, the client and the development team are usually unacquainted. As a result, communication between them is both formal and vague. This hampers the proper flow of information and, in turn, the scope determination process.

Gause and Weinberg [GAU89] first suggested the methodology of using context-free questions for the preliminary meetings. "Context-free questions" mean that the questions are used to gain a better understanding of the business need, the required solution, and the level of effectiveness of the interview itself. The generic nature of these questions puts both the client and the representative of the development team in a more relaxed mode.

Gause and Weinberg proposed that the first set of questions to the client should aim to get an idea of the goal of the software project. For example, the representative of the development team may ask the client to clarify the person or group who first generated the request for the software project. The answer may lead to questions to help identify and determine the profile of the final user of the software product. Another question could relate to assessing alternatives to the defined solution and the economic benefit of each alternative.

The second set of context-free questions aims to gain a better perspective of the software project. It also elicits the benefits that the client expects from the software product. For example, the client may be asked what benefits the final user may derive from the software product and how the product will meet the business need. In addition, the client may be asked for a description of how the final user will use the software product. The client may also be asked about his or her expectations from the software project and the development team. Finally, the client may be asked about the various constraints of the software project.

The third and final set of questions pertains to assessing the effectiveness of the interview. The questions relate to evaluating the accuracy and authority of the answers given by the client. If the person being interviewed does not have the appropriate level of authority to provide the required details, more people can be contacted to verify the information collected.

Facilitated Application Specification Techniques

Context-free questions in an interview help to make the relationship between the client and the development team less formal. However, the benefit of using context-free questions is limited to the first few meetings when preliminary information about the project is collected. After that, the interview format needs to become more comprehensive. At a more advanced stage in the scope determination process, information is required for solving problems, negotiating terms, and specifying requirements. Then, more advanced communication techniques need to be implemented.

All software development organizations have multiple departments and teams working on a single software project. Interactions with the client tend to be on a team-wise basis. Each team communicates with the client through a series of formal forms, memos, and interview sessions. Queries sent by multiple teams often confuse the client and hamper the determination of the overall scope of the software project. As a result, information does not flow properly and misunderstandings occur between the client and the development team.

To prevent situations that impede scope determination, FAST evolved. It adopts a joint team-based approach to information gathering from the client. FAST involves a joint team consisting of the client and developers who identify the problem, the solution, elements of the solution, alternatives, and a preliminary set of requirements for the software product. The FAST approach involves the following steps:

1. Setting up a joint meeting of the client and the development team

2. Establishing guidelines for the scope determination process

3. Preparing an agenda for the meeting

4. Identifying a facilitator to control the meetings

5. Creating a definition mechanism

6. Determining the scope

In the initial interview sessions, the development team understands the basic business need. Later, the schedule for a FAST session is decided between the client and the development team. As part of the preparation for a FAST session, a facilitator is chosen to conduct the session. The facilitator may be a client, a developer, or a person unrelated to either.

The attendee list for the FAST sessions include the client, the software development team, the hardware engineering team (if any hardware is part of the project scope), and the marketing team. You select people from different departments for the sessions such that the broadest level of requirements and concerns may be listed. A comprehensive list of requirements and concerns helps you determine the scope of the software project effectively. All the information collected in the interviewing phase is distributed among the identified attendees.

Each attendee is then given a preparatory task for the FAST session. Each attendee needs to prepare a list of all the objects or entities to be produced by the software solution. The attendee also needs to list the objects in the environment that the solution is intended to operate in and the objects on which the software solution will operate. In other words, the attendees prepare a list of all the inputs that they think are required, the outputs that will be produced, and the parts of the environment that the software will function in.

Next, the attendees prepare a list of all the services or functions that the software product will provide to different users. In addition, each attendee prepares a list of the constraints on the software project, such as time or cost. Finally, each attendee prepares a list of performance criteria for the software project. All these lists, prepared by a number of people with different interests, ensure that the broadest possible concerns are elicited.

When the FAST session is convened, the facilitator ensures that everyone has the same understanding of the business need and the identified software solution. Next, the lists prepared by the different attendees are collected and collated. At this point, no criticism or vetting of any point submitted is allowed. The task is simply to collate the unique items on the different lists.

After the lists are collated, the facilitator conducts a joint discussion to add, modify, or delete the items on the lists. The discussion ensures that the scope of the software project is determined according to the business need of the software solution. Next, all the attendees are divided into teams and each team is assigned one item or a group of similar items. These teams then create mini specifications for the item in question.

After the different teams create the mini specifications, all the attendees jointly collate a list of mini specifications. The items on the collated list are again added to, modified, or deleted by a unanimous decision. In this manner, a set of mini specifications of the separate lists of objects, functions, constraints, and performance constraints is produced. The list is again checked to verify whether any mini specifications can be elaborated further.

After the final list is created, each attendee is asked to list the validation criteria for the software product. As with the other inputs, a final list of the validation criteria is unanimously prepared by a process of collation, addition, modification, and deletion.

At this point, the FAST session generates all the inputs required for determining the scope of the software project. All the inputs gathered are then used to create a draft scope document for the software project.

Quality Function Deployment

The QFD technique was first used in the early 1970's at the Kobe shipyard of the Mitsubishi Heavy Industries, Ltd. Its primary purpose is to translate the spoken or unspoken client requirements to technical specifications and deliver a high quality product or service.

According to the Kano model of the QFD technique, there are three types of requirements that a client has from a software project: basic, performance, and excited requirements.

The basic requirements are those that define the objectives and goals of a software project. They can be presented to the client during meetings. The client only checks if the objectives and goals are identified and assessed. Basic requirements such as performance criteria and specific functions may be presented through charts and graphs.

Performance requirements are those that the client does not state explicitly. These requirements are implicit and fundamental to the software product. However, they must be identified by the development team and stated explicitly. If performance requirements are not replicated in the software product, the client could be dissatisfied. The performance requirements include the interface designs, the ease of use of software, the ease of software installation, and reliability.

The excited requirements are the requirements beyond the basic requirements that the client has from a software product. Meeting the excited requirements would result in increasing client satisfaction. For example, a modular design for a corporate firewall system that facilitates upgrades and installation could be considered as exceeding client requirements. Translating the excited requirements into a software product also helps to differentiate it from the competition.

The QFD technique uses client interviews, observation, and surveys to gather information for scope determination. The information gathered is then presented to the client for review.

There are six steps in the QFD technique to collect client requirements and determine the software project scope. In the QFD technique, you need to:

1. Identify the client.

2. Determine the client requirements.

3. Prioritize the client requirements.

4. Benchmark the competition.

5. Translate the client requirements to measurable technical specifications.

6. Build and deliver a quality product through a focus on client satisfaction.

The first step in the QFD technique is the identification of the client. The client for a software project could be an external, paying client or a group within the organization. For example, the product of the software department of a bank could be a face recognition system and the client could be the ATM department of the bank.

After identifying the client, you determine the client requirements. The Kano paired question model is used to determine the client requirements. The model suggests that you ask the client a paired question to determine the requirement type. In a paired question, a combination of questions allows you to determine the reaction of the client to the possible outcomes of a given scenario. For example, you ask a question to determine the reaction of the client if an upgrade facility existed for a product. Next, you ask another question to determine the reaction of the client if an upgrade facility did not exist. These questions help determine if the requirement is a basic requirement, performance requirement, or excited requirement.

In the third step, you prioritize the stated requirements. As a result of the prioritization, measurement criteria are generated for the entire group of requirements. Then generate a weighted factor for each requirement to determine the cost, time, and effort needed to achieve the requirement. You can prioritize each requirement by asking the client about the end user of the requirement and the benefits the end user will get from it.

The fourth step is to benchmark the competition and how the client perceives the competition. This activity raises awareness of the currently defined requirements and what else could be done to enhance the requirements.

Tip

While benchmarking, it is a good idea to compare the top products from the competition with each client requirement. These comparisons may be subjective or objective.

In the fifth step, translate the requirements into measurable engineering specifications. These engineering specifications help you evaluate the requirements on the basis of measurable tasks.

Finally, build and deliver a quality software product. You need to carry out two activities at this stage. First, you ascertain the method used by the competition to reach their targets. Second, you use the information regarding the method used by the competition to develop measurable targets for software development. The best targets are the ones that have a specific value. Values within a range are less precise but still usable for a software project.

AN EXAMPLE OF SCOPING

AB Corp. is a leading manufacturer of synthetic yarn. It has a large plant where an X-Base system is implemented. All these systems run in a legacy X-Base environment. As the systems were developed a while ago, their performance and functionality are more or less obsolete with regard to the current performance requirements.

In addition, the old system is not very scalable. This adds to the problem of scaling up to the requirements of the proposed new manufacturing facilities. The management has decided to implement a new system that caters to the requirements of the old systems as well of the new facility.

The Business Need

The business need of AB Corp. can be articulated as: "To cater to the IT needs of the existing facilities and those of the upcoming facilities."

The IT systems team at AB Corp. has evaluated the business need and the functionality required from the proposed software solution. It has identified two possible solutions:

- An ERP system implementation to integrate all the functional areas of the facility using one enterprise-level application

- A client/server environment to allow different functional areas to connect to central databases

Scope Determination

To determine the correct software solution for AB Corp., the IT team began to collect information from the relevant stakeholders to determine the scope of the software product. First, the IT team created an analysis team to interview the group of supervisors and managers who had first expressed the need for an updated IT system. After collecting information regarding the required performance, functionality, and constraints, the analysis team prepared a scope brief document. They used a decision tree to decide whether the solution should be created within the organization or bought from outside.

Next, the analysis team created a scope statement and a scope management plan. This is done to specify the project objectives, the functionality and performance requirements, and the contingency plan for the software project. The analysis team evaluated the performance requirements and the constraints of the two different software solutions, the ERP and the client/server solution.

The analysis team found that the client/server solution was more apt for implementation at AB Corp. for the following reasons:

- A client/server environment would provide better control of the existing systems than an ERP solution. In addition, the new systems could be mapped to it.

- Unlike an ERP system, there was no need to customize or tailor the processes to fit the solution.

- The client/server solution could be made in-house, thereby avoiding the cost of purchasing proprietary ERP software.

- As the processes did not have to be changed with the client/server solution, the users could easily adapt to the new system.

Finally, the analysis team distributed the information gathered among selected stakeholders and convened a FAST session. The FAST session allowed all the stakeholders to identify the inputs, outputs, and processes required for the software solution. After much iteration, the FAST team unanimously produced a list of performance criteria, mini specifications, and valuation criteria. These lists were then used to prepare the scope document for the software project.

As a result of the scope determination process for the optimal software solution for AB Corp., the IT team was able to implement an integrated manufacturing support system based on the client/server architecture. The IT team at AB Corp. reused the production, warehousing, dispatch, and quality control modules from the existing X-Base system.

SUMMARY

✓ Before a software project commences, the scope of the project needs to be determined.

✓ The scope of a software project is linked to the scope of the software product it aims to create.

✓ The scope of a software product is defined by the functions and performance required of the product and the constraints under which it needs to be created.

✓ There are five phases in the scope management process:

- Initiation

- Planning

- Definition

- Verification

- Control

Each phase is defined by the inputs required, the tools required to process the inputs, and the output of the processing.

✓ The initiation phase requires:

- Inputs: The product description, the business need for the product, and the selection criteria used for the software product

- Tools: Economic tools, mathematical tools, and experience

- Outputs: Identification of the project manager for the software project, the project brief document, and the assumptions and constraints of the project

✓ The planning phase requires:

- Inputs: The project brief document, the product description, and the assumptions and constraints of the software product

- Tools: A cost-benefit analysis, analysis techniques such as QFD and brainstorming, and experience

- Outputs: A scope statement and the scope management plan

✓ The definition phase requires:

- Inputs: The scope statement, the scope management plan, and the assumptions and constraints of the software project

- Tools: A WBS and a decomposition activity
- Outputs: The WBS

✓ The verification phase requires:

- Inputs: The product description, product documentation, and the project work results
- Tools: Assessment of the product documentation and the work results
- Outputs: Acceptance of the scope definition by the client

✓ The change control phase requires:

- Inputs: The WBS, periodic status reports, change requests, and the scope management plan
- Tools: A change control mechanism and assessment of requests for change
- Outputs: Scope changes and corrective action taken to compensate for scope changes

✓ Different communication techniques and tools, such as interviewing, brainstorming, group meetings, and questionnaires, are used to communicate with the client and elicit the requirements of the software project and software product.

✓ Context-free questions are used for preliminary interviews between the client and the software development team.

- They are used to relax both parties and initiate the communication process.

✓ FAST techniques provide a joint team-based approach for gathering information from the client and creating a scope statement for the software project.

- FAST techniques employ an iterative process of collecting requirements, performance criteria, technical specifications, constraints, and validation criteria for the software product.

✓ The QFD technique is used to translate the spoken and unspoken client requirements into technical specifications.

LAB EXERCISES

1. AB Corp, a synthetic yarn manufacturer, uses an X-Base system for its computing needs. It decides to implement an enterprise-wide client/server computing solution to upgrade its computing environment. AB Corp's management team approaches you to develop the software. AB Corp specifies various requirements and limitations for the software product. Identify the options that are functionalities, performance criteria, and constraints from the table below.

Activity	Functionality/Performance/Constraint
Process data from the shop floor and present status reports to the floor manager.	
Monitor the level of raw materials in the inventory and automatically place a purchase order in case the reorder level is reached.	
Create the software product based on client/server architecture, while integrating the existing X-Base systems.	
Allow users to personalize the software interface.	
Generate management information system (MIS) reports within three seconds each.	

2. The initiation phase is the first phase in the scope management process. Identify the inputs required for the Initiation phase from the following list.

   a. Product description

   b. Assumptions and constraints for the product

   c. WBS

   d. Scope statement

   Briefly describe the importance of these inputs for the initiation phase.

3. List and discuss the different communication techniques used for gathering and validating client requirements. Which techniques and tools have you used in your work environment? Do you think all the techniques and tools you listed can be used in a software project?

4. What is the benefit of using context-free questions in the preliminary meetings with the client? List and describe the three sets of questions you put to the client.

5. You are a project manager at Blue Moon Computers. The preliminary meetings with your client clarified the understanding of the purpose of the software project. However, you now need detailed information to develop technical requirements. You decide to convene a FAST session to involve all concerned stakeholders in the process. Assuming that you are also the facilitator for the session, discuss how you would conduct the session.

Chapter 5

Software Requirements Gathering and Resource Allocation

Objectives:

- ☐ Use an SRS document to list client requirements for a software project.
- ☐ Identify the resources for a software project.
- ☐ Identify the requirements for resource allocation.

MANAGING SOFTWARE PROJECT REQUIREMENTS

Determining the client requirements is the starting point of a software project. In the early days of software development, understanding client requirements was easy because, in most cases, the client and the software developer were the same person. However, the current technological environment is quite different from the early days of software development. Now, the software developer is a distinct entity in a software project. The requirements of the client need to be understood, documented, and communicated to the software developer. The success of the software project depends on how well the development team understands the requirements.

Requirements Specification

Often, software projects start off with badly stated requirements. In addition, frequent changes in requirements from the client mean an increase in effort for the software developer. These cause delays in the delivery of the final software product to the client. The primary reasons for poor requirements specifications are:

■ The client is not clear about the requirements. This often makes the requirements inconsistent and conflicting. The client may be unaware of the capabilities of existing software and hardware and the process of developing the software.

■ The client and the software developer are from different backgrounds. Both the client and the software developer may be unaware each other's needs and capabilities, causing miscommunication and misunderstanding of requirements.

These reasons make the specifications phase one of the most important phases in the SDLC. As a project manager, you need to ensure that the development team gets as much information out of the client as possible.

Software Requirements Specifications

During the requirements specification phase, you create an SRS document. It contains requirements for the project and provides the development team with a clear understanding of the quality required from the final software. You may define quality in terms of the functionality of the software, its performance, ease of use, interoperability, conformance with standards, and so on. The SRS document also captures all processes and the inputs and outputs required for the processes.

Development of the SRS document is an iterative process. You must keep in kind that client requirements generally keep changing till the very end of the SDLC. In fact, many customers themselves do not realize the full scope of the requirements in the initial stages of the requirements specification process. To deal with the problem of clear requirements specification, you need to ensure that there is an open channel of communication between the client and the development team. Identifying and refining requirements for a software project is not a one-time activity but involves several iterations. An open channel of communication allows back-and-forth communication over the requirements until all doubts are clarified. You must also ensure that the client is part of all activities involved in the SRS process.

Ensure that constraints, such as a specific architecture or interface for the software, are not imposed on the software project. Such over-specification may result in constraints on the developers and may also prevent them from exploring using better options. However, this rule of thumb is broken quite frequently. Both clients and developers frequently commit themselves to certain architecture, standard, or protocol while framing the specifications for software.

Finally, while specifying requirements, you ensure that software developers are able to understand the client requirements completely and comprehensively.

Identifying the Stakeholders

During the SRS activity, software developers identify all the entities that may be impacted by the software being developed. For example, consider developing software for the ATMs at a bank. Here, the stakeholders are the bank's clients, the clerical staff, the technical staff, and the director of the bank. Each stakeholder has a different requirement from the ATM software being developed. The bank's clients will want the ATM to enable them to make withdrawals and deposits easily. On the other hand, the clerical staff will want the ATM to be able to generate data and financial records for each client.

As the software project manager, you need to ensure that requirements of each stakeholder are clearly identified. Although individual requirements may present only a partial view of the problem and may even appear contradictory, it is important that you consider all requirements while preparing the SRS document.

Nature of an SRS Document

The SRS document is created for two purposes. First, stakeholders in the project use it to confirm that their requirements are accurately captured and understood by the development team. Second, the software development team uses the document to create a design for software based on client's requirements.

The format of the SRS document is not created on an ad-hoc basis. Most software development organizations generally maintain requirements on standardized document formats. Standards lend form and structure to the requirements, besides ensuring that each category of requirements is elicited from and validated by the client. In addition, standard formats also ensure that you are able to capture analysis methods, tools, and necessary reviews and approvals.

An SRS document must specify:

- The intended functionality of the software.
- The way in which users will interact with the software.
- The way in which the software will interact with the existing software.
- The performance criteria for the software, such as processing speed and response time.
- The attributes of the software, such as modularity and security.
- The design constraints, such as the use of a specific programming language or encryption standard.

Characteristics of a Good SRS Document

The characteristics of a good SRS document require that the document must be:

- Correct
- Unambiguous
- Complete
- Consistent
- Categorized
- Measurable
- Achievable

Correct

All requirements in an SRS document need to be correct. Both software developers and client need to verify that the document is factually and technically correct.

Unambiguous

Each requirement must be stated in a way that has only one meaning. To create a document that is not misinterpreted, you need to state the requirements in simple language.

Complete

You fill all the different sections of the SRS document based on requirement of the document format, such as the functionality, performance, external interfacing, attributes, and design constraints. In addition, you should also ensure that there are no decisions left for later phases of the SDLC.

Consistent

Make the SRS document consistent by making consistent references to input, output, processes, tools, and names across the document.

Categorized

Categorize the requirements of the SRS document in terms of their importance and priority. This helps you in focusing on requirements that have higher priority. Typically, you can categorize requirements as 'Essential', 'Conditional', and 'Optional', in terms of their decreasing importance in the project.

Measurable

Ensure that the requirements in the SRS document are quantified. This will help you in measuring the quality of the output of each phase of development in the SDLC against the stated requirements. For example, if you quantify that the response time of the software must be in minutes, you can measure the actual response time against the requirement stated by the client.

Achievable

Articulate the requirements in such a way that they are achievable. For the requirements to be achievable you can define them as tasks for developers that can be performed and their output measured.

Structure of an SRS Document

While creating an SRS document, list the requirements in their order of priority. This helps software developers to use a modular approach to different types of requirements, prevent redundancies, and easily modify any part of the document.

An ideal SRS document comprises the following three sections:

- An introduction
- A description of the entire project and requirements
- Specific requirements

Introduction

The first section of an SRS document is an introduction. It provides an overview of the entire document. The introduction has the following categories:

- Purpose: states the purpose and the audience profile for the document.
- Scope: defines the scope of the document in terms of the software project.
- Definitions and conventions used: contains all the definitions, acronyms, and abbreviations used in the document.
- Overview: describes the structure of the document and how to approach it.

Description

The second section describes the software and the issues that impact its development. This portion has the following categories:

- Product behavior: describes the various elements of software, such as the user interface and interoperability.
- Functions: are the primary functions that the software performs in a specific environment under specific conditions.
- User profile: describes the user profiles to which the product is targeted. This section describes the technical background, tasks, and responsibilities of the users.
- Design constraints: are the technical and non-technical considerations that the software adheres to, such as encryption, architecture, safety issues, and so on.

Specific Requirements

Software developers use this information to design, create, test, implement, and deliver a software product. This section provides the details about the required inputs, intermediate work products, and output of the entire software project. The specific requirements of a software project may be described in a number of ways, depending on the type of software.

Figure 5.1 provides a sample template for an SRS document. This is a generic template for an SRS document. You can modify it according to your requirements.

1.Introduction
    1.1 Purpose
    1.2 Scope
    1.3 Definitions and conventions
    1.4 Overview

2.Description
    2.1 Product behavlor
    2.2 Functions
    2.3 User Profile
    2.4 Design constraints

3.Specific Requirements
    3.1 Functional requirements
        3.1.1 Introduction
        3.1.2 Data flow diagram
        3.1.3 Inputs
        3.1.4 Outputs
        3.1.5 Processing   3.1.5.1 Validations
                          3.1.5.2 Tolerance limits
                          3.1.5.3 Exception conditions
                          3.1.5.4 Security considerations
                          3.1.5.5 Error recovery
                          3.1.5.6 External interface/Dependencies on other functions
                          3.1.5.7 Response time consideration
                          3.1.5.8 Estimated volume of transactions
                          3.1.5.9 Any assumptions made

    3.2 Performance requirements
    3.3 Design constraints
        3.3.1 Standards compliance
        3.3.2 Hardware limitations
    3.4 Attributes
    3.5 External interface requirements
        3.5.1 User interface
        3.5.2 Hardware interfaces
        3.5.3 Software interfaces
        3.5.4 Communications interfaces
    3.6 Other requirement
        3.6.1 Other requirement 1
        3.6.2 Other requirement 2

4. APPENDIX A - TITLE

5. APPENDIX B - TITLE

SOFTWARE REQUIREMENTS SPECIFICATION (SRS)

Figure 5.1: Sample Template for an SRS Document

The Introduction and Description sections of the sample SRS template in Figure 5.1 remain the same for most software projects. However, the specification section changes according to the need of specific software projects. For example, Figure 5.2 describes the specific requirements of an SRS document based on Use-cases. In this template, the requirements are captured using a case-based approach. Section 3.1 in this template provides a brief description of the Use-case activity. Section 3.2.1 describes the main flow of events and section 3.2.2.1 describes the alternative activities, such as validation and pop-up messages. Similarly, section 3.3 represents the special requirements of the software project.

3 Use case name

3.1 Brief Description

3.2 Flow of events

3.2.1 Basic flow
(The normal flow of activity)

3.2.2 Alternative flows

3.2.2.1 First alternative flow
(First level branching action)

3.2.2.2 Second alternative flow
(Second level branching action)

3.3 Special requirements

3.3.1 First special requirement
(Any special activity such as generating an acknowledgement at the end)

3.4 Pre-conditions

3.4.1 Pre-condition one
(pre-check)

3.5 Post-conditions

3.5.1 Post-condition one
(Post processing activity, such as generating a report)

Figure 5.2: Template for the Specification Section of an SRS Document Based on Use-cases

RESOURCE ALLOCATION

After the requirements specification of the software project is complete, the next task is to plan for the resources required for the project. Resources include all the inputs needed to successfully complete the project.

Resource Types for a Software Project

The resources for a software project can be classified into three broad categories: people, reusable software components, and tools for development. Figure 5.3 shows the three levels of resources.

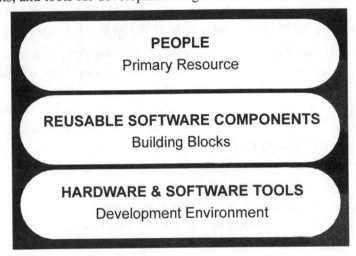

Figure 5.3: Resource for a Software Project

People

The people required for a software project make up the topmost level of resources. After the scope of the software project is determined, the people requirements also become clear. You can identify people with the appropriate skills for the software project. These skills include organizational skills, such as project management, design engineering, and senior quality engineering, and functional skills, such as database and application-level functions. The time available to finish a software project defines the number of people required for a software project.

While allocating people to a software project, you need to keep some considerations in mind. For example, there might not be people with the appropriate technical skills required for a software project. In addition, a software development team is composed of a project manager, one or more lead developers, and software developers. It is possible that the people required at a certain hierarchical level are not available.

A work-around for the unavailability of skilled people is to create a team composed of both skilled and unskilled people. For example, the project can have 80 per cent of a software development team with skilled personnel and the rest with people who need to be trained. Although the exact composition depends on the availability of people, it is recommended that skilled personnel make up at least 60 per cent of a team.

The other problems that you could face are the lack of training facilities for personnel. Moreover, the behavioral, attitudinal, and motivational issues in individuals also demand due consideration before people are allocated to a software project.

Reusable Software Components

Reusable software components speed up software development by allowing software developers to create and reuse generic software components. They allow a software project to operate at reduced costs and with shorter development cycles. You need to catalogue, standardize, and validate the reusable software components for easier reference.

Reusable software components can be classified into the following four categories for the purpose of resource allocation:

- *Off-the-shelf components*. These are existing software components developed by a third party or an internal group. They are fully standardized and validated for use in a software project. Off-the-shelf components constitute a low risk and can be used if available internally or bought from outside instead of new components being created.

- *Full-experience components*. Software components that have been developed for similar projects in the past or have validated specifications and designs are referred to as full-experience components. The developers on the current project are assumed to be experienced in these components, making their modification and implementation easy. Full-experience components can either be completed internally or the completion work can be outsourced, depending on the availability of time and people.

- *Partial-experience components*. These software components are similar to full-experience components in the sense that they too have been developed for past projects or are validated specifications and designs. However, the difference in this case is that the developers on the current project are assumed to be only partially experienced in the application area of these components. Therefore, a high degree of modification is required for these components. This associates a high degree of risk involved with partial-experience software components. It is best to use them only if no other option is available.

- *New components*. These are software components that need to be created by the software development team.

Hardware and Software Tools

Different hardware and software tools make up the development environment within which a software project is executed. Within a software development organization, there are various constraints on allocating environmental resources to a software project. In a software development organization, various software projects run concurrently. In addition, the supply of hardware and software tools is limited. Therefore, the demand from different projects for hardware and software tools overlaps and strains the limited supply.

As a project manager, you need to plan ahead for the availability of the hardware and software resources required for a software project. You also need to requisition resources and verify their availability for the required duration.

Requirements for Resource Allocation

Resource allocation for a software project primarily determines the physical resources required for a software project. In addition, it involves determining the quantity of each resource required. You need to carry out resource allocation in close association with cost and effort estimation.

The resource allocation process is similar to the scope determination process in the sense that the inputs, the tools required to process the inputs, and the outputs need to be determined.

Inputs Required for Resource Allocation

For the resource allocation process, you require different kinds of inputs. These are:

- Work breakdown structure
- Scope statement
- Organizational policies of the software development organization
- Resource pool

One input required is the work breakdown structure that is created in the scope determination period. The WBS organizes the elements of a project according to the deliverables they are associated with and identifies the elements that require inputs.

The scope statement that is generated by the scope determination process also supports the WBS as an input for the resource allocation process. In addition, data from similar past projects that reflect the kind of resources required for the current project serves as an input for the resource allocation process.

Apart from the WBS and the scope statement, you also require the organizational policies of the software development organization to determine issues, such as staffing, hierarchy, team structure, purchase, and rental of equipment.

Finally, you require a resource pool to clarify the resources available for allocation. The resource pool description may be less detailed at the start of the software project and may grow more detailed as the project progresses. There is a low level of detail at the start of a software project because finite descriptions and numbers for the resources required do not emerge until the relevant project activity is initiated.

Tools Required for Resource Allocation

This activity in the resource allocation process is concerned with identification of the tools required. For decisions such as these, you need experience and expert knowledge of the software project scope.

Outputs from Resource Allocation

The outputs from the resource allocation process are the requirements for different types of resources. In addition, you also get information about the quantity of the various resources, the time when the resources will be required, and the duration of their availability.

SUMMARY

✓ Software requirements are unclear because:

- The client is either unaware or unclear of the requirements.
- The client and the software developer are from different backgrounds and unable to understand each other's perspective.

✓ An SRS document includes the perspective of all stakeholders in the software project.

✓ An SRS document describes:

- The functionality to be delivered in the software product.
- The nature of interaction with the user and the functionality of the software product.
- The performance criteria for the software product.
- The attributes, such as modularity and security, of the software product.
- The constraints for the software product.

✓ An SRS document has three sections:

- Introduction: gives an overview of the entire SRS document.
- Description: contains information to understand the SRS document in detail.
- Specific requirements: describes the actual requirements of the software product in detail.

✓ There are three types of resources for a software project:

- People
- Reusable software components
- Hardware and software tools

✓ The inputs required for allocating resources to a software project are the WBS, the scope statement, the relevant organizational policies, and a description of the resource pool.

✓ The tools required to process the inputs in the resource allocation process are experience and expert knowledge.

✓ The outputs of the resource allocation process are the requirements for different resources, the quantities required, the time at which they will be required, and the duration for which they will be required.

LAB EXERCISES

1. List five characteristics of an SRS document. How do these characteristics contribute to an SRS document?

2. Safest Software Co. is commencing on a software project to create a reservation system for an airline. The company management asks the project manager to reuse software components from past projects to save on development costs and time. The software component repository in the company has two kinds of reusable software components, full-experience and partial-experience components. Discuss the considerations involved in choosing either category of software component.

Chapter 6

Risk Management and Mitigation

Objectives:

- ☐ Identify the potential software project risks.

- ☐ Determine the impact of risks on a software project.

- ☐ Sequence the steps in the risk management process.

- ☐ Create a risk management plan for a project.

- ☐ Mitigate risks in a software project.

RISK MANAGEMENT CONCEPTS

Ever wondered why people insure their lives, their homes, their cars, or their valuables? Suppose your house, along with all the valuables, is burgled. You will be definitely disheartened. However, you will suffer less if all your valuables are insured. At times such as these, you realize the importance of planning in advance for the uncertain events in your life. Just as you plan for unforeseen events in your life, project managers also need to prepare for uncertainties affecting projects. All project management skills of a project manager can fall flat in the face of uncertainties and unplanned problems.

Any project can encounter uncertainties in the form of increased costs, schedule delays, and diminished qualities. Unless tackled, these uncertainties can lead to major project disasters. The uncertainties encountered during project execution are the potential project risks. Every software project has to grapple with the new risks threatening information security along with the conventional risks, such as hardware failure, time and cost escalation, defects, or resource crunch. Risk can be defined as the possibility of loss. Risk arises due to the inability to achieve objectives within defined cost, schedule, and technical constraints. Risk has two components. The possibility of not achieving a particular outcome is one, and the result of failing to achieve the outcome is the other. The former is the probability of loss, and the latter is the loss. Software project management deals with managing both these components of risk.

According to the risk management guru Barry Boehm, "Risk management focuses the project manager's attention on those portions of the project most likely to cause trouble and compromise participants' win conditions." In other words, risk management is a set of actions that helps the project manager plan to deal with uncertain occurrences. It is through risk management that project managers assess risks and manage to reduce risks to an acceptable level.

Software risk management is not about managing risks faced by a software organization. Here, the focus is on managing risks encountered during software development process. Therefore, the concern is about managing the future of a software project.

In this chapter, you will look at the unforeseen events that might affect a software project. You will also learn about the steps for managing and mitigating software project risks.

Types of Risks

To be able to manage project risks, you must first understand what constitutes a risk. All uncertain occurrences are not risks. Only those occurrences that have an adverse impact on the progress of a project are risks to the project. Risk is not a bad thing. Risk is bad only when it results in loss for an organization. Unless there is a potential for loss, there is no risk. Moreover, loss can be interpreted as either a bad outcome or a lost opportunity. The tendency of most project managers is to jump at the statement "this is a risk." However, the desired reaction is to pre-empt all possible outcome and plan for them. Project risks can be broadly categorized into development process risks and product risks.

Development Process Risks

The risks encountered during product development are categorized as development process risks. These comprise developer errors, natural disasters, disgruntled employees, and poor management objectives.

Developer errors could be attributed to poor training due to budgetary constraints and inadequate skills and software tools. Ergonomic problems, environment problems, and interruptions or distractions at office also account for developer risks. Other risks in this category include problems in personnel acquisition and retention.

Similarly, natural disasters such as flood, cyclone, fire, storm, and snowfall are also risks to a project.

Disgruntled employees can also become a risk to an organization. For example, a sacked employee can use password sniffers to gain unauthorized access. A dismissed person can flood the system with senseless messages. A disgruntled employee can also try to sabotage the project work by destroying files and programs.

A poorly defined management objective is another development process risk. If the language in the management objective is ambiguous and not stated clearly, the risk management program will not function properly. Narrowly focused and changing objectives that are not updated can also be counted as risks. Lack of contingency plans, incomplete cost estimates, and unrealistic schedules are also potential risks in a project. Similarly, unrealistic performance standards are also potential risks to the development process. Other possible risks include contractual risks, technological risks, and inadequate documentation of other concurrent projects.

Product Risks

Product risks crop up in the form of changing requirements during product development. Incomplete and unclear requirements are a risk to the product during development. Similarly, problems in meeting design specifications can also be categorized as risk to product development.

Risks could arise if the project deliverables or objectives are not clearly defined or if technical data is missing. The possibility of several alternatives at any given time during the project is also a cause of concern. If errors are not recognized during the design phase, they could turn into risks for the project. Similarly, risks could arise due to the size and complexity of the product or while achieving client acceptance of the product.

Note

The key idea in risk management is not to wait passively for a risk to materialize and become a problem. The objective of risk management is to ensure that for each perceived risk, you know well in advance how to tackle it.

RISK MANAGEMENT PROCESS

The process of risk management begins during the analysis phase of software development life cycle. However, the actual process of managing risks continues throughout the product development phase. Risk management is a dynamic process because it deals with the activities that are yet to happen. Risk management has a two-fold agenda. First, deciding actions for preventing risks from happening, and second, deciding actions for tackling risks that materialize. Therefore, risk management is all about pre-empting a risk, coming up with a plan for resolving the risk, and finally executing the plan.

Figure 6.1 displays the steps of the risk management process. Formally articulated, risk management process consists of three steps:

1. Risk identification
2. Risk analysis
3. Risk mitigation

Figure 6.1: Risk Management Process

Risk Identification

In this step, the project manager gathers information about the potential risks in the project. The project manager plans the strategies for avoiding risks or controlling them. The project team conducts brainstorming sessions and discussions among team members about the requirements document. They discuss the available technology, manpower, prevailing environment, and all project-related factors. The project manager picks up the thread from these and creates a risk log. After the risk log is prepared, the project manager calls a meeting within the team and technical experts to discuss the risk log and the mitigation plans. An effective way of identifying risks is using a questionnaire.

Table 6.1 displays a sample risk identification questionnaire.

Risk Description	Yes/No/Not Applicable (NA)
A. Product Engineering	
1) Are requirements changing continuously during product development?	
2) Do the changing requirements affect each of the following:	
Quality	
Functionality	
Schedule	
Integration	
Design	
Testing	
3) Are the external interfaces changing?	
4) Are the requirements missing or incompletely specified?	
5) Are there any missing requirements?	
6) Can these requirements be incorporated into the system?	
7) Does the client have unwritten requirements or expectations?	
8) Is there a way to capture these requirements?	
9) Are requirements unclear or in need of interpretation?	
10) Are you able to understand the requirements as written?	
11) Will the requirements lead to the product the client wants?	
12) Are there any requirements that may not specify what the client really wants?	
B. Product Design	
1) Do you encounter problems in meeting functionality requirements?	
2) Are there any specified algorithms that may not satisfy the requirements?	
3) Will the design and/or implementation be difficult to achieve?	
4) Are there any requirements or functions that are difficult to design?	
C. Reusability	
1) Are you reusing the program?	
2) Do you foresee any problems in documentation?	
3) Do you foresee any problems in performance?	
4) Do you foresee any problems in functionality?	

Table 6.1: Sample Risk Identification Questionnaire

The sample questionnaire in Table 6.1 includes an exhaustive list of risks that might be encountered during the progress of a project. The answers to the questions in the risk identification questionnaire enable the project manager to estimate the impact of risks. In the sample questionnaire Table 6.1, the risks are categorized under product engineering, product design, and reusability. From this table, you obtain a list of risks that are relevant to each category. You compare the information obtained from this table with past results and estimate the criticality of risk. In short, during risk identification, you obtain answers to the following queries:

- **Why** is the risk important?
- **What** information is needed to track the status of the risk?
- **Who** is responsible for the risk management activity?
- **What** resources are needed to perform the activity?
- What is the **detailed plan** to prevent the risk and/or mitigate it?

Risk Analysis

After identifying the risks, the project manager needs to analyze the risks. Uncertainty and loss are the two characteristics of risk. The uncertainty factor in risk means that the unknown event may or may not happen. While analyzing risks, the project manager needs to quantify the level of uncertainty and the degree of loss. Based on this, the project manager plans schedules and costs. During analysis, information on risk is converted into information on decision-making. Analysis provides the basis for the project manager to work on the "right" risks.

Risk Description	Probability of Occurrence (0-1)	Impact on Project (1-10)	Risk Factor (Probability x Impact)

Table 6.2: Risk Analysis Table

Table 6.2 displays a risk analysis format. There are various tasks involved in risk analysis. First, the WBS elements are identified. One of the tasks in the risk analysis phase is to describe the risk. The risk can be product-related, process-related, organization-related, client-related, or infrastructure-related.

Second, the WBS elements are evaluated to determine the risk events. Then the project manager quantifies the probability of occurrence of risk. The project manager can assign probability values between 0 and 1. For example, a risk with a low probability of occurrence is marked 0.2 while that with a high probability of occurrence is marked 0.8. The reason why a particular risk has a high or low probability depends on the actual circumstance of the project.

Third, the risks are rated depending on their probability of occurrence. Based on the probability of risk, the project manager identifies the impact of the risk. The impact of risk on cost, schedule, and quantity needs to be calculated and graded. The impact of risk can be graded on a scale of 1 to 10, 1 being the lowest, and 10 being the highest.

Then the risk factor is calculated by multiplying the probability of risk and the impact of risk. Finally, each risk is prioritized relative to other risks. The risk factor is used to prioritize the identified risks. For example, the risk with a probability value 0.1 and an impact value 2 will have minimal impact. While risks close to probability value 0.8 and with an impact value 9 will have greater impact. Therefore, the project manager can prioritize risks based on the probability and impact of risks. A risk that has a high impact and low probability will not absorb a significant amount of the project manager's time. However, high-impact risks with moderate to high probability will catch the attention of the project manager.

Risk Mitigation

Risk mitigation is the best possible approach adopted by the project manager to avoid risks from occurring. The probability of the risk occurring and the potential impact of the risk can be mitigated by dealing with the problem early in the project. Essentially, risk mitigation involves three possibilities and the project manager needs to adopt a risk mitigation strategy aimed at them. The three possibilities include:

- Risk avoidance
- Risk monitoring
- Contingency planning

Risk Avoidance

To avoid risks from occurring, the project team prepares the risk plan before the commencement of the project. The project team identifies the potential risks and prioritizes them based on their probability of occurrence and impact. Then, the team prepares a plan for managing risks. In most software projects, this plan is popularly called the risk management plan. Table 6.3 displays the format of a risk management plan.

Risk Description	Probability of Occurrence (0-1)	Impact on Project (1-10)	Risk Factor (Probability x Impact)	Mitigation Steps	Responsi-bility	Start Date	End Date

Table 6.3: Risk Management Plan

To prepare the risk management plan, the project team first identifies and assesses the risks associated with the project. Then, the probability of occurrence of each risk is estimated and the possible impact is calculated. In the plan, the probable cost and damage is also quantified. The project team also identifies the contingency plans for all the identified risks. The contingency plan for each risk is based on the project's defined operational software process. The plan is modified throughout the software development life cycle of the project based on the changes taking place. The contingency plan also includes the cost, in terms of effort, in carrying out the plan. The software risks identified are tracked, reassessed, and re-planned at the end of each phase. The project manager revisits the plan if significant changes are introduced in the software project.

Risk Monitoring

As the project proceeds, risk-monitoring activities commence. It is not possible to monitor closely all the risks that are identified for the project. For example, if 100 risks are identified for a project, only top 20 risks are monitored. There are re-planning checkpoints where the information obtained from monitoring the risks is used to refine the risk assessments and management plan. The project manager monitors the top 20 percent of the factors that may indicate the status of the risks in the project. In the case of large teams, the project manager also needs to monitor the attitude of the team members and their problems. This helps the project manager monitor any possible team-related risks.

Besides monitoring the top 20 percent of the risks, the project manager needs to monitor the mitigation steps also. Consider an example. To ensure that particular software is browser-independent, the software is created on the lowest compatible browser. Such software will work on any browser thus making it browser-independent. Therefore, mitigating a project risk involves working hard at reducing the possibility that the risk will ever occur. Mitigation includes nearly all actions that a project team takes to overcome risks. For example, choosing a more expensive but proven technology over a newer, less expensive technology is a step toward mitigating project risks.

Contingency Planning

The possibility of contingency planning arises when mitigation efforts fail and risk becomes a reality. Contingency planning is used to monitor risks and invoke a predetermined response. According to the plan, a trigger is set up. If the trigger is reached, the contingency plan is put into effect. Contingency planning involves maintaining an alternative plan if the original plan fails. A simple example could be the savings people make for a rainy day. Contingency plans are a must for the top 20 percent of the risks identified. These plans are put to use after the risks become a reality. The importance of contingency planning can be realized from this example. Despite the massive attack on WTC, the stock markets in the US resumed functioning within a few days. This was possible because the finance companies had backed up their data and information on computers elsewhere. The contingency planning of finance companies prevented the risk of huge data loss for the stock market.

MANAGING RISKS: CASE STUDY

Consider a scenario. Your organization is a vendor of software solutions. A bus transport company in the US wants you to develop a Schedule Adherence system. The team that will develop this software is new and the platform selected for development is also new to your organization. The project team needs to be trained intensively for this.

During this project, the team is expected to manage a large volume of data. The team has never had any experience in managing such a large volume of data. The system also needs to use this data to generate various MIS reports related to delays or adherence of bus services.

The performance requirement is less than fifteen seconds for all popular browsers. Your organization is anticipating numerous requirement changes during the development process. The system needs to be implemented across several states in the country. The data related to the system is highly confidential because it can provide an edge to the competitors.

Now, as a project manager, you need to prepare a risk management plan for this project. The project starts on May 15 and should be completed on November 15.

First, you need to identify the potential risks involved in the project. The potential risks to the project are described in Table 6.4.

Risk Description
Inexperienced staff
Performance risk due to high volume of data to be processed
Cross-browser compatibility
Involvement of new technology
Design changes during development

Table 6.4: Potential Risks to a Project

After identifying the risks, you need to estimate the probability of their occurrence and their impact on product development. Based on this, you calculate the risk factor and plan the mitigation steps.

Your risk management plan is displayed in Table 6.5.

Risk	Probability (0-1)	Impact (1-10)	Risk Factor (Probability x Impact)	Responsibility	Mitigation Steps	Start Date	End Date
Inexperienced staff	0.8	3	2.4	Project Manager	Conducting training sessions before the commencement of project	May 15	July 15
Performance risk due to high volume of data to be processed	0.6	7	4.2	Architect	Massive tuning of architecture during the design phase and conducting a proof of concept for the design	May 15	Till the end of the project
Cross-browser compatibility	0.6	5	3.0	Developer	Using the lowest compatible browser for development	May 15	Till the end of the project
Involvement of new technology	0.5	5	2.5	Project Manager	Ensuring all details pertaining to the technology is available and keeping in close touch with the technology vendor	May 15	Till the end of the project
Design changes during development	0.6	8	4.8	Architect	Designing a flexible architecture that can accommodate future changes and enhancements	May 15	Till the end of the project

Table 6.5: The Risk Management Plan for Building a Schedule Adherence System

In Table 6.5, the risk factors with high values are the high priority risks. Here, the high priority risks are design changes during development, performance risk due to high volume of data to be processed, and cross-browser compatibility. The high priority risks need to be monitored closely and continuously. The rest of the risks can be monitored periodically. Certain risks need contingency planning despite being low in the priority list. For example, the risk due to involvement of new technology is a low priority risk. However, the probability of occurrence of this risk is 0.5, which is fairly high. This calls for contingency planning because you may not be aware of all the details of the new technology. Suppose the system fails to respond if the number of users exceeds a certain number. In such a situation, you need to have a contingency plan ready. You need to discuss with the vendor regarding a workaround for such a situation. The workaround should be ready in the case of failure of the system.

SUMMARY

✓ Risk is defined as the possibility of loss. It is the inability to achieve program objectives within defined cost, schedule, and technical constraints.

✓ Risk management is a set of actions that helps the project manager plan an approach to deal with uncertain occurrences.

✓ A software project encounters two types of risks, development process risks and product-related risks.

- Some of the development process risks are developer errors, natural disasters, disgruntled employees, and poor management objectives.

- Some product-related risks are incomplete requirements, unclear project deliverables and objectives, and complexity of the product.

✓ The steps of risk management involve: risk identification, risk analysis, and risk mitigation.

- Risk identification involves identifying risks. Risks are identified after discussion with team members about the requirements documents, available technology, resources, and other project-related factors.

- Risk analysis involves quantifying risks based on the probability of occurrence and the impact of risk on the project.

- Risk mitigation involves risk avoidance, risk monitoring, and contingency planning. The risk management plan is prepared to manage software project risks.

✓ Contingency planning involves maintaining an alternative plan if the original plan fails. Contingency plans are put to use when risks become a reality.

LAB EXERCISES

Suppose your organization, Global Systems Inc., is a vendor of software products and solutions. ABC Transport Authority wants Global Systems Inc. to develop a driver license testing software. The testing will be conducted for users belonging to varied geographical areas. Therefore, the system should provide questions in multiple languages.

ABC Transport Authority has an existing system in multiple platforms and the license testing system must integrate to the existing system. The license testing system should also be available outside the organization for demonstration in kiosks. The system should be such as to be installed on multiple platforms.

The client has not specified its requirements very clearly. ABC Transport Authority expects your organization to provide inputs on what could be the best thing to do. The response time of the system should be less than five seconds for all user transactions.

The audio and video should also be played wherever applicable. The system should be delivered on the intranet and the Internet by using popular browsers. The system must be ready within two months. The above software is the first of its kind Global Systems Inc. has ever developed.

1.   Identify the risks in the above scenario.

2.   Prepare a risk management plan for the above scenario.

Chapter 7

Software Project Estimation: Tools and Techniques

Objectives:

- ☐ Divide project tasks by using the WBS technique.
- ☐ Use SLOC to estimate effort.
- ☐ Calculate function points to estimate effort.
- ☐ Estimate effort by using the COCOMO technique.
- ☐ Sequence the steps to use the Delphi technique.
- ☐ Select a suitable estimation technique based on the project type.

SOFTWARE PROJECT ESTIMATION

Watts Humphrey in his book, Managing the Software Process, has said, *"If you don't know where you are, a map won't help."* This saying is very relevant while dealing with software project estimation. In a software project, unless you are sure that your estimation is accurate, you cannot make much progress. Estimation of factors such as cost, effort, risks, and resources is crucial. It gives you a fair idea of the size of the project. You can use the information about size to estimate the cost, effort, and duration of the project. This further helps plan for resources and schedule the project.

In this chapter, you will learn to create project estimates by breaking down a project into multiple tasks. The chapter will also cover some of the techniques that you can use to estimate the cost and effort required for a project. You will learn about source lines of code (SLOC), Function Points (FP), and the *COnstructive COst MOdel* (COCOMO) technique. Finally, this chapter will help you select a suitable estimation technique based on the type of your project.

Work Breakdown Structure (WBS)

To correctly estimate the effort, size, or cost of completing a project, it is important to be aware of the multiple tasks that comprise a project. You can divide a project into logical units or tasks by using the WBS technique. Creating a WBS is a prerequisite for any estimation activity. It enables you to conceptualize an abstract entity, such as a project, into distinct, independent units. After dividing a project into tasks, you can categorize them as logical, broad tasks. For example, tasks, such as drawing up a marketing strategy, planning a phase-wise product release, and interacting with media agencies and the production department can be compiled under a common category, Marketing.

Benefits of Using a WBS

Using a WBS provides a number of benefits to the management and to the development teams. First, it gives the management an idea about the size and complexity of the project.

Second, it helps in planning, scheduling, and monitoring a project realistically. This is possible because all the tasks in the project can be performed with measurable targets for each task. To aid planning, scheduling, and monitoring a project, you can use tools such as Program Evaluation and Review Techniques (PERT), Critical Path Method (CPM), timeline charts, and Gantt charts. These tools use WBS as the fundamental basis for assigning resources to tasks, computing the number of days needed, and the cost required to complete the tasks. These tools will be covered in detail later in this book.

Steps to Create a WBS

A project can be compared to a large system. A large system consists of multiple, independent subsystems that achieve a common goal. Similarly, a project consists of small, independent tasks. Each task can be subdivided into subtasks. For example, in a general software project, a task is to perform project analysis. To complete this task, there are multiple subtasks, such as interviewing client and system analysts. You may also consider studying the organizational objectives and preparing a project proposal to present to the client. Therefore, in a project analysis task, there are three subtasks. A subtask is also known as a work package. A work package is a unit-level entity in a project system.

You can create a WBS by following the three steps listed below. These are general steps, and they can vary in relation to an individual or an organization.

1. Brainstorm to arrive at broad tasks for a project.
2. Refine the broad tasks.
3. Categorize tasks into logical task headers.

Brainstorming to Arrive at Broad Tasks

The first step in creating a WBS is to organize a meeting of all senior managers, system analysts, and prospective developers. The objective of the meeting is to brainstorm and come up with a set of broad tasks that need to be performed in a project. During the brainstorming session, you can make a note of all possible tasks.

Subsequently, the feasibility of each task is assessed. In addition, any conflict of common tasks can be eliminated. To enable you to perform this activity better, you can arrange tasks as and when they are brainstormed. For example, XYZ Inc. conducts a brainstorming session to divide the tasks into multiple subtasks that are performed during the analysis phase of a project. During the session the project managers and the analysts come up with tasks on the basis of prior project experience. These include tasks such as determining the scope of a project, drafting the software specifications, and securing resources for the project. Some additional tasks are also determined based on client requirements. Preparing the initial project budget and estimating the approximate project timeline are examples of such tasks. In addition, personnel responsible to complete each task are also determined. The subtasks are subsequently arranged in the order in which they are executed.

Figure 7.1 depicts the subtasks in the analysis phase. Note that after a questionnaire is prepared, you can either arrange to meet the client or document the feedback collected by the questionnaire. It is clear from the figure that preparation of the SRS document can begin only after the preceding three tasks are complete.

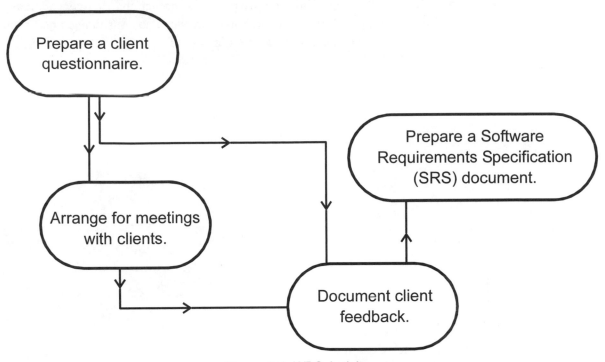

Figure 7.1: WBS Activity

Dividing a main task into multiple subtasks also enables you to estimate the duration and the effort required for individual tasks. Subsequently, at the end of the phase, you can evaluate the actual effort and duration. This helps you compare the estimated values with the actual values and prepare a schedule for the subsequent phases. The duration of each task affects the total duration of a phase. This, in turn, affects the schedule of the subsequent phases. You can make similar deductions while comparing the estimated costs with the actual costs of a task.

Refining Broad Tasks

In the second step of creating a WBS, you refine the list of tasks that was compiled during brainstorming. Refining the tasks may include adding more tasks or combining the existing ones. During this step, you may also change the arrangement of tasks. A change in the arrangement of tasks can occur on the basis of two theories of WBS.

- Deliverable-based theory
- Project life-cycle-based theory

You use the deliverable-based theory when the deliverables of a project are more important than its phases. This normally happens when the deliverables are decided before the project begins. However, if the phases of a project are completely defined, you use the project life-cycle-based theory. You can use the project life-cycle-based theory to arrange the tasks in a project.

Categorizing Tasks into Logical Headers

Finally, after defining tasks and arranging them, you categorize each task into a logical task header. For example, preparing test plans and test cases and drawing up the test plans can be categorized as "Testing." This activity provides another chance to ensure that you have not missed any task during brainstorming. In addition, you can also consult an expert such as a senior manager to review and validate the tasks identified.

MEASURING EFFORT FOR A PROJECT

Measuring the effort for a project is a specialized activity. It enables you to derive cost estimates that are critical for project management. An incorrect measurement of effort at the beginning of a project can result in inaccurate project plans and frequent slippages. It can also lead to inaccurate cost estimates, which can cause steep cost deviations between estimated and actual cost values. There are many techniques, such as SLOC, FP, and COCOMO that you can use to accurately estimate effort. These are quantitative estimation techniques because they rely on the use of formulae to calculate effort. In addition to quantitative estimation techniques, there is a human-based technique known as the Delphi technique. This technique is based on soft skills and relies more on human factors, such as collecting information during group discussions.

SLOC Technique

At the beginning of a software project, it is important to determine the size of the project. The project size helps determine the resources, effort, and duration of the project. There are many techniques to calculate the size of a software project. You can calculate the size by using a directly measurable technique, the SLOC technique. It is defined as the source lines of code that are delivered as part of the product. The effort spent on creating the source lines of code is expressed in relation to thousand lines of code (KLOC). The SLOC technique is an objective method of estimating the size because there are no multiple ways of calculating the lines of code. Therefore, the effort estimate is close to being accurate.

This technique includes the calculation of lines of code, documentation of pages, inputs, outputs, and components of a software program. Components are again of multiple types, such as reports, screens, and files. The SLOC technique is also used to directly calculate the effort to be spent on a project.

Figure 7.2 is a simple example of counting source lines of code. The code displayed here contains four lines of code.

```
If (emp_code<=1200)
     Print ("Welcome to the Inventory
database.");
Else
    Print ("Access denied to the Inventory
database.");
```

Figure 7.2: Code Snippet

Counting SLOC

You can use the SLOC technique to estimate the effort required for a project when the programming language and the technology to be used are predefined. In addition to the programming language and technology, the complexity and effort required to write a program should be easily predictable. The use of the SLOC technique requires that the technology or language remain unchanged throughout the project. Generally, you can use the SLOC technique when you are using third-generation languages, such as FORTRAN or COBOL.

While counting the source lines of code, there are some general considerations that you need to keep in mind. However, these can vary in every organization. The general considerations include the following:

■ Only the delivered lines of code are included in SLOC calculation. For example, test drivers and other support software are not part of the number of lines developed for a project.

■ Only the source lines of code written only by the development team are counted. This excludes the code created by applications generators.

■ Only declaration statements are counted as source lines of code. This excludes comments inserted to improve the readability of programs.

Disadvantages of Using SLOC

Despite being accurate in providing figures to calculate the effort required for a project, the SLOC technique has a drawback. The SLOC technique is language-dependent. The effort required to calculate source lines of code may not be the same for all languages. For example, to conceive and write 8 lines of code that accomplish a task in the assembly language may require 15 minutes. However, you may need only five minutes to complete the same lines of code if it is written in Visual Basic.

FP Technique

The FP technique is a direct indicator of the functionality of a software application from the user's perspective. This is the most popular technique used to estimate the size of a software project. This fact is further supported by a quote of Capers Jones, chairman of Software Productivity Research, Inc. in Burlington, Massachusetts, on page 1 of Computer Finance brought out in November 1997. He quotes "*80% of the Fortune 500 are using function points, at least somewhere in their application development organizations*".

You use the FP technique to estimate the total size of a project. The total size of a project is estimated as a single FP value. After calculating the total size of a project in FP, you divide the total FP into the different phases of the SDLC. This way, you can determine how much effort per FP is required in that particular phase. For example, the testing phase is planned for 20 FP of work. The project managers, based on their past project experience, determine the amount of effort in man/person months required in the testing phase.

Similarly, you can express the cost required to complete FP of work for a particular phase. At the end of a project, you can also express the number of defects reported in terms of per FP for a phase.

History

Function points were developed as an alternative to lines of codes to measure the size of software. Allan.J.Albrecht invented function point estimates in 1979 at IBM. Thereafter, he introduced General System Characteristics (GSCs) in 1984. From 1990 onwards, International Function Point Users Group (IFPUG) made periodic revisions to the function points theory.

Features of Function Points

The total size of a software project is expressed in total function points. It is independent of the computer language, development methodology, technology, or capability of the project team developing the software project.

The specific user functionality of the application is evaluated in terms of relation to what is delivered by the application and, not how it is delivered. Only user-requested and user-defined components are counted. To calculate FP for a project, some major components are required. The major components and their relationships are represented in Figure 7.3.

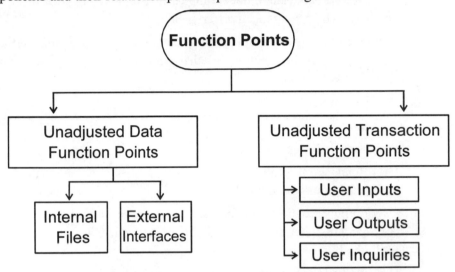

Figure 7.3: Function Points Components and their Relationships

You can calculate the function point estimates for a project or a particular phase by following four steps:

1. Identify the unadjusted function points.
2. Calculate total GSCs.
3. Calculate Value Adjustment Factor (VAF).
4. Apply a formula to calculate Adjusted FP (AFP).

Identifying the Unadjusted Function Points (UFP)

The first step in the calculation of FP is the identification of unadjusted function points. This involves assigning a value to the information domains that exist in a software application. An information domain is a collection of data objects, such as text, numeric, audio, static graphics, video, and files. These comprise a single information domain for a project.

The information domain of a software application also includes the structure, flow of data objects, and the control objects that make up a system. Control objects manage the movement and behavior of data objects in the information domain. For example, a control object, Add function, requires data objects. The type of data object for the emp-name field is text type and that for the emp-code field is numeric. Multiple such combinations of data and control objects comprise the information domain of a software application.

Unadjusted function points are of two types:

- Unadjusted data function points
- Unadjusted transaction function points

Unadjusted data function points (UDFP) is the functionality provided to a user to meet the internal and external data requirements of a software program. UDFPs include internal files and external interface files. An internal file could be a separate master file that contains data about an entity. For example, to update the Customer file, the data from a master file named Orders is required. Therefore, Customer and Orders are two different logical master files.

An external interface is defined as a medium that is used to either collect data or communicate with an external system. For example, the Employee payroll form needs data from the Employees database, which exists on a different server.

The second category of unadjusted function points is unadjusted transaction function points (UTFP). This is the functionality that provides a user with the components to process data. UTFP require you to count:

- User inputs
- User outputs
- User inquiries

User inputs are the values entered by a user and saved on a database. The number of such individual inputs is counted. An example of a user input is entering a customer name.

User outputs are the results in response to a user input. For example, you may provide the command to create reports in a software program. The number of user outputs is also counted individually.

User inquiries are inputs related to queries by a user. Each query generates an output from an existing database. An example of a user inquiry is retrieving the hire date of an employee on entering the employee identification number. User inquiries are different from user inputs because inputs are saved into a database whereas user inquiries are not. Moreover, you count the number of user inquiries individually.

For each information domain value for the UDFP or UTFP, you multiply the total number of unadjusted function points with a suitable weight. This weight can be low, medium, or high. The standard values for weights followed globally are displayed in Table 7.1. This table is provided by IFPUG.

Table 7.1 represent a value that is assigned to each domain parameter depending on the complexity of coding that parameter. For example, if a user input is simple to code, it is assigned a weight of 3.

Information domain	Low	Medium	High	Total
User inputs	*3=	*4=	*6=	
User outputs	*4=	*5=	*7=	
User inquiries	*3=	*4=	*6=	
Internal files	*7=	*10=	*15=	
External interfaces	*5=	*7=	*10=	
TUFP				

Table 7.1: Information Domain Weights Table

These values enable you to determine the size of a software project in relation to unadjusted function points of the code being developed. Assume that the code you are developing has 10 simple screens. The unadjusted function point value for that code is 30 (10*3). Similarly, you can determine the unadjusted function point values for other domain parameters, such as user outputs, user inquiries, internal files, and external interfaces. These values are then added to arrive at a figure for Total of Unadjusted Function Points (TUFP). This value is used later to calculate FP.

Calculating the Total GSCs

Calculating GSCs is the second step in the process of calculating FP. GSCs are factors such as data communication, which determine the complexity of the software being developed. There are 14 GSCs in every application that is developed.

The 14 GSCs are listed in Table 7.2.

General System Characteristics Table		
S. No.	Characteristics	Brief description
1	Data Communications	The degree to which an application communicates with the other applications
2	Distributed Functions	The degree to which an application transfers or shares data among the components of applications
3	Performance	The degree of the response time and throughput performance of an application
4	Heavily Used Configuration	The degree to which the computer resources, where the application runs, are used
5	Transaction Rate	The frequency of transactions that are executed, on a daily, weekly, or monthly basis
6	On-line Data Entry	The percentage of data that is entered by using interactive transactions
7	End-user Efficiency	The degree to which human factors and user friendliness are to be considered
8	On-Line Update	The degree to which the number of internal logical files is updated online
9	Complex Processing	The degree to which the complexity of logic influences the processing logic Processing logic, in turn, influences the development of the application
10	Reusability	The degree to which the application and code in the application are specifically designed, developed, and supported to be reused in other applications
11	Installation Ease	The degree to which conversion from a previous environment influences the development of the application
12	Operational Ease	The degree to which the application attends to operational aspects, such as backup, start-up, and recovery processes
13	Multiple Sites	The degree to which the application is developed for multiple locations and user organizations
14	Facilitates Change	The degree to which the application is developed for easy modification of processing logic or data structure

Table 7.2: GSCs

In the second step to calculate FP, the unadjusted FP value is further refined. This is done by assigning a value to each GSC factor depending on its complexity. This is known as the *degree of influence* (DI) of each factor. The DI ranges on a scale of 0 to 5. A degree of 0 represents no influence although 5 represents a very strong influence. For example, an application should be able to respond to a user within a time frame of five seconds. Then, the DI value for the performance factor will be 5.

In this way, the values from 0 through 5 are assigned to all the GSCs in the second step. These values are finally added to arrive at a consolidated value, F_i, where i represents each GSC from 1 through 14.

It is important to note that DI is a subjective decision of an organization. The same factor may be assigned different DI values by different organizations. Table 7.3 displays the DI values.

Degree of Influence in values	Description of the degree of influence
0	No influence
1	Incidental influence
2	Moderate influence
3	Average influence
4	Significant influence
5	Very critical

Table 7.3: DI Values

Calculating Value Adjustment Factor (VAF).

The third step in FP calculation is to apply a formula to calculate VAF for a software application. VAF consists of the GSCs with suitable DIs applied on each one of them. In addition to the GSCs, VAF contains the constant values, 0.65 and 0.01, that are multiplied to the total of the weighted GSCs. These constant figures have been determined based on the experience compiled from multiple projects and incorporated in the function points theory. To calculate VAF, you use the following formula.

```
VAF = (0.65 + [0.01 * sum of Fi])
```

The last step is to calculate AFP. This provides the actual function points value. This value is a combination of the total number of information domain elements counted and the GSCs that are weighed according to suitable criticality ratings. Multiplying TUFP with VAF, adjusts the final function points value to reflect a realistic value. Therefore, the formula to calculate AFP is:

```
AFP = TUFP * VAF or
AFP = TUFP * (0.65 + [0.01 * sum of Fi])
```

To understand the calculations involved in the four steps which you learned, consider an example. Table 7.4 displays information domains for an antivirus application being developed. Weights are assigned to each information domain.

Information domain	Count	Low	Medium	High	Total
User inputs	19	3 * 5 = 15	4 * 8 = 32	6 * 6 = 36	83
User outputs	15	4 * 5 = 20	5 * 6 = 30	7 * 4 = 28	78
User inquiries	5	3 * 2 = 6	4 * 2 = 8	6 * 1 = 6	20
Internal files	6	7 * 1 = 7	10 * 2 = 20	15 * 3 = 45	72
External interfaces	3	5 * 0 = 0	7 * 2 = 14	10 * 1 = 10	24
TUFP					277

Table 7.4: Weighted Information Domains for an Antivirus Application

In Table 7.4, there are 19 user inputs. Of these, five are of low importance. Therefore, according to the table of information domain values provided by IFPUG, you multiply the five user inputs by three. Similarly, eight user inputs are of medium importance. These are multiplied by four. Finally, the six user inputs of high importance are multiplied by six. After multiplying the user inputs by specific weights, you add the multiplied weighted user inputs. In this case, the total of weighted user inputs is 83.

In this way, you calculate the total weighted values of the other information domain values, such as user output, user inquiries, internal files, and external interfaces. The TUFP value for the antivirus application is 277.

Next, DI values are assigned to all the 14 GSC factors. For example, Data Communications is assigned a DI value of 5. This is because the software system that is to be developed exercises very high influence on data communications in software.

Table 7.5 displays the DI values for the antivirus application.

General System Characteristic	DI Value
Data Communications	5
Distributed Functions	4
Performance	5
Heavily Used Configuration	2
Transaction Rate	3
On-line Data Entry	4
End-user Efficiency	3
On-Line Update	2
Complex Processing	4
Reusability	5
Installation Ease	2
Operational Ease	2
Multiple Sites	3
Facilitates Change	4
Total complexity adjustment value	48

Table 7.5: DI Values for an Antivirus Application

The DI values are added to arrive at a figure for F_i. For the antivirus application, the value of F_i is 48.

Next, you substitute the derived TUFP and VAF values in the following formula to calculate FP.

FP = TUFP * VAF

FP = 277 * (0.65 + [0.01 * 48])

FP = 313

You can assign this total FP to the entire project. Thereafter, to express the effort, cost, defects, and productivity of the different phases in the SDLC, you can appropriately divide this total FP into phase-wise FP.

Using FP for Initial Estimation

Consider an example to understand the use of FP in the process of estimation. It is estimated that to complete one FP of work, the project requires 10 hours. In a project, the total FP estimated is 200 FP. Therefore, to complete a project of 200 FP, you require 200 FP * 10hrs = 2000hrs. In relation to 8 hours on a working day, the value of working hours is 250 person days. Assuming 20 working days in a month, to complete a project of 200 FP, you require 12.5 person months. This implies that to complete 200 FP of work, a person requires 12.5 months. If you deploy two persons on the project, they would require six months to complete the work.

Using FP for Post-Project Analysis

FP is generally used to create software metrics, such as productivity, cost, testing, and effort. In addition to calculating FP to estimate the probable project size, you can use FP to express factors such as productivity, effort, defects, and cost used in a completed project. Expressing these factors in FP helps analyze a project effectively. Analysis of a project enables to apply the learning derived from a particular project to future projects.

Note

You will learn more about software metrics and their uses in the chapter, Software Project Management Metrics. The chapter will detail how you can use FP to create software metrics.

Consider an example to understand how you can use FP to express the number of defects reported per FP of effort. You need to compare the project quality of three projects on the basis of their respective project size in FP. Table 7.6 summarizes the defects-related data collected for the projects. The total project size is calculated the same way you calculate FP, by multiplying total unadjusted function points with value adjustment factor. To reiterate, the formula to calculate FP is:

`AFP= TUFP*VAF`

	Total number of defects reported	Total project size in FP
Project 1		
	10	150
Defect density	10/150=0.067 defects/FP	
Project 2		
	20	200
Defect density	20/200=0.10 defects/FP	
Project 3		
	40	1000
Defect density	40/1000=0.04 defects/FP	

Table 7.6: Defects/FP for Different Projects

Table 7.6 depicts the defect density calculated for each project. Defect density is defined as the occurrence of a software defect per FP of development effort. The formula to calculate the defect density of a project is:

`Defect density=Total number of defects/total project size in FP.`

From Table 7.6, you can conclude that Project 3 is of superior quality as compared to projects 1 and 2. Project 3 is of superior quality because it reported least number of defects per FP of development effort. In contrast, Project 2 is of inferior quality because it reported the highest number of defects per FP of development effort.

Advantages of Using Function Points

Function points are language-and technology-independent. Therefore, you can use them to estimate any kind of project. They can also be used to estimate the effort, cost, and schedules of projects that use the Prototyping and Spiral models because such projects have uncertain user and project requirements.

In addition, you can use function points as a project estimation technique when you anticipate changes in the middle of a project. These changes may disturb the estimates if you had used SLOC to estimate the effort, cost, or size of a project. The FP estimation uses a subjective and holistic approach for project estimation. Consequently, the estimates calculated by using the FP are unlikely to be incorrect.

Disadvantages of Using Function Points

Estimation by using FP generally uses data from past projects for assigning weights to GSCs and the information domain values. To be able to do this realistically, it is important for the organization to have developed similar projects in the past. The organization should also be prepared with adequate data and tools for FP estimation of the new project. In addition, FP provides a vague estimation. This characteristic of FP does not usually provide precise or approximate estimates of the effort, cost and size of a project. Consequently, at the end of a project, deviations from the estimated to the actual values of each of the factors may be quite extreme.

COCOMO Technique

The COCOMO technique is another popular estimation technique. Dr. Barry Boehm propounded this technique in 1981. COCOMO uses cost driver attributes to calculate the effort and duration of a project. The COCOMO technique has three levels of implementation. With each level, the complexity of the model increases. The levels of the COCOMO technique are:

- Basic
- Intermediate
- Advanced

Basic COCOMO

The basic COCOMO technique estimates the effort and cost of a software project by using only the lines of code. You use basic COCOMO when you need a rough estimate of effort, such as during maintenance projects. This is because in such projects, a majority of the work is already completed. Estimating the effort in the basic COCOMO technique involves three steps.

1. Estimating the total delivered lines of code
2. Determining the effort constants based on the type of the project
3. Substituting values for lines of code and effort constants in a formula

You have already seen how the total delivered lines of code are estimated. The next step in the COCOMO model is to determine the type of the project being developed. The basic COCOMO technique considers three types of projects to calculate effort.

- Organic
- Embedded
- Semidetached

Organic projects have sufficient and defined objectives. The organizations that undertake organic projects have ample experience in development and use small development teams. These are simple business and financial applications, such as a banking system and inventory system.

Embedded projects have stringent and specialized hardware, software, and human resources requirements. Organizations usually have less experience in developing such projects. Examples of such projects include real-time operating systems (RTOS), industrial automation systems, and sophisticated space and aviation systems.

Semidetached projects are a combination of the preceding two types of software projects. A new operating system and a database management system (DBMS) are examples of such projects.

The last step in calculating effort by using the COCOMO technique is to substitute the values of lines of code and effort constants in the following formula.

$$E_i = a1 * (KLOC)^{a2}$$

In the formula, E_i is the effort for a project. The effort constants, a1 and a2, depend on the type of project being developed. The values for a1 and a2 are displayed in Table 7.7.

Project Types	a1	a2
Organic	3.2	1.05
Embedded	2.8	1.20
Semidetached	3.0	1.12

Table 7.7: Effort Constants

For example, you estimate that the total number of delivered lines of code in 1,000 lines of code for an application is 4 KLOC. The application is of an organic type. Therefore, the value for a1 will be 3.2 and a2 will be 1.05. When these values are inserted in the formula of the basic COCOMO technique, you derive that 14 person months are required to complete the application. The calculation of project effort is done as follows:

$$E_i = 3.2 * 4^{1.05}$$

$$E_i = 3.2 * 4.28$$

$$E_i = \sim 14$$

Intermediate COCOMO

Calculation of effort by using the intermediate COCOMO technique involves an additional step of calculating the effort adjustment factor (EAF). The effort adjustment factor is calculated by assigning ratings to 15 cost driver attributes. These cost driver attributes relate to the various aspects of a software project, such as project, product, personnel, and computer attributes. Using the intermediate COCOMO technique, you can accurately estimate effort and cost required for a project. Accurate estimates are very helpful to start new development projects.

Calculating the effort by using the intermediate COCOMO technique is a three-step process.

1. Estimate the initial development effort by using SLOC. To do this, you use the following formula:

$$E_i = a1*(KLOC)^{a2}$$

In the formula to estimate the initial development effort, KLOC refers to 1,000 lines of code. The constant values a1 and a2 differ with every project.

2. The second step is to determine the relevant cost driver attributes that affect your project intensively. This provides you with the value for EAF.

Table 7.8 summarizes 15 commonly used project, personnel, and product-related cost driver attributes. The values for each cost driver under each rating are filled in by an organization based on past experience.

Cost Drivers	Rating					
	Negligible	Low	Average	High	Very high	Extremely critical
Analyst Capability (ACAP)						
Applications Experience (APEX)						
Programmer Capability (PCAP)						
Programming Language Experience (LEXP)						
Virtual Machine Experience (VEXP)						
Required Software Reliability (RELY)						
Database Size (DATA)						
Software Product Complexity (CPLX)						
Execution Time Constraint (TIME)						
Main Storage Constraint (STOR)						
Computer Turnaround Time (TURN)						
Virtual Machine Volatility (VIRT)						
Use of Software Tools (TOOL)						
Modern Programming Practices (MODP)						
Required Development Schedule (SCED)						

Table 7.8: Cost Driver Attributes

3. Finally, you calculate the actual effort by multiplying the weighted cost driver attributes with the initial effort estimate. Typically, the values that rate each cost driver attribute range from 0.9 through 1.4. For example, if software reliability (RELY) is of prime importance according to the requirements specifications, it is provided a rating of high or a value of 1.4. Similarly, if the time to execute a software program is of negligible importance, you assign a rating of low or a value of 0.9. For software attributes that are of mediocre importance, you can assign a value between 0.9 and 1.4.

Usually, in organizations, the average rating is assigned a static value of 1.0. To calculate the estimated effort using the intermediate COCOMO technique, you use the formula:

```
E = EAF * E_i
```

Consider an example for using the intermediate COCOMO technique to calculate the estimated total effort of a project life cycle. In a customized insurance project, there are four modules. The total effort estimate of the modules is 3.0 KLOC. The management has identified four cost driver attributes with the respective multiplying factors that might affect the project most. In this situation, the values of a1 and a2 are 3.2 and 1.05, respectively, because the insurance project is an organic project. Therefore, you apply the following formula to calculate the initial effort estimate.

$$E_i = a1 \ (KLOC)^{a2}$$

$$E_i = 3.2 * 3^{1.05}$$

$$E_i = 3.2 * 3.16$$

$$E_i = 10.11$$

The values assigned to the cost driver attributes that are applicable to a particular software application are displayed in Table 7.9. According to the table, the time to execute a software program is of high importance. Therefore, the attribute TIME is assigned a value of 1.35. In contrast, the software application does not require a very high analyst involvement. Therefore, the value assigned to ACAP is very low or 0.95. Using the same logic, the values for other cost driver attributes are assigned.

Applicable cost driver attributes	Rating	Multiplying factors
CPLX	High	1.2
TIME	Very high	1.35
ACAP	Low	.95
MODP	Average	1.00

Table 7.9: Applicable Cost Driver Attributes

Referring to Table 7.9, EAF can be calculated as,

```
EAF = 1.2 * 1.35 * 0.95 * 1.0
EAF = 1.53
```

After obtaining the values for the variables E_i and EAF, you can substitute these values in the formula to calculate the total effort.

```
E = EAF * Ei
E = 1.53 * 10.11
E = 15.5 person months
```

Advanced COCOMO

The advanced COCOMO technique uses the steps of the intermediate COCOMO technique. In addition, it uses costs driver attributes assigned to each phase of the SDLC such as analysis and design.

Applicability of COCOMO

COCOMO is flexible and capable of using SLOC, FP, and even object points. Object points are measurable code sections in an object-oriented programming language, such as C++, Ada, and Java.

You can use COCOMO when the size of a project is extensive and the requirements of the project are vague. In contrast, SLOC and FP can be used for projects where either the requirements are more or less known or developers possess the relevant experience in developing projects.

COCOMO is suitable for complex and sophisticated projects that are expected to operate within intensive hardware, software, and personnel constraints.

Generally, you can use COCOMO when the software development environment is new to an organization. In addition, you can use COCOMO when you do not have baseline data about past projects. However, you need complete data about your current project to assign weightage to each cost driver attribute. You can use FP or SLOC techniques when you have enough past project data to assign accurate weightage to the 14 GSCs and the various information domain value elements.

Delphi Technique

The Delphi technique is a human-based estimation technique. Human-based estimation techniques use human experience and analytical skills to estimate the size, productivity, and effort required for a project. This is a trusted technique and is widely used in many established organizations to facilitate practical and reasonable estimation.

The rationale of using the Delphi technique is that when many experts independently arrive at the same estimate on the basis of similar assumptions, the estimate is likely to be correct.

The Delphi technique has eight basic steps.

1. Identify the teams that need to perform the estimation activity. In an estimation activity meeting, three distinct groups of people need to be present.

   - Estimation experts: They usually consist of groups of five or six experienced project managers. The estimation values provided by the project managers are based on past project history and their knowledge. However, only those project managers should be invited for estimation whose experience of a past project matches that of the current project. Otherwise, estimation values may turn out to be far from realistic.

   - Estimation coordinator: An estimation coordinator is very similar to a moderator in a usual meeting. The coordinator facilitates the meeting and ensures that the goals of the meeting are fully achieved.

   - Author: An author is similar to a recorder of minutes in a meeting.

2. The author presents the project details including clients' needs and system requirements to the group of experts. The author also describes the expectations from the group. The author and

experts jointly identify the tasks that need to be estimated. They also identify the valid assumptions that they need to consider while estimating. For example, while estimating the effort needed to create a high-level design, they can assume that the SRS document is approved by the client.

3. The author and experts arrive at a consensus that any estimation with a specific variance value will not be accepted. For example, they may decide that any variance above 25 percent will not be accepted as an estimation value for computing the project effort or the productivity.

4. The coordinator prepares a list of tasks jointly decided by the team and distributes the list to all experts. These tasks comprise a project plan.

5. The experts independently make their estimates for each task. After recording their estimates, they hand over their estimates to the coordinator. This is a critical step. While making estimates, no discussions or consultations are permitted because a mutual discussion may influence the estimation logic of the fellow experts. The coordinator and the author jointly ensure this.

6. The coordinator prepares a summary of estimates for each task in a table as represented in Table 7.10. After calculating the percentage of variance, the coordinator marks each task as accepted or not accepted based on the agreed accepted value.

Task	Maximum Estimation (Hours)	Minimum Estimation (Hours)	Percentage of Variance	Accepted or not Accepted (A/NA)
Cost and benefit analysis	20	15	25	A
High-level design	50	30	40	NA

Table 7.10: Summary of Estimates Table

7. The coordinator hands over the summary to the group of experts and the author. The group of experts and the author discuss tasks and assumptions where the percentage of variance is more than the acceptable level. The maximum and minimum estimates of tasks are not disclosed or discussed. For example, in Table 7.10, the group and the coordinator do not accept the high-level design task because it exceeds the agreed variance value of 25%. Therefore, the team would discuss this task to estimate its maximum and minimum effort afresh. To resolve the high percentage of the variance value, some tasks may be broken down further or combined. This activity of breaking down tasks into smaller levels involves fresh estimates for those tasks at the smaller levels.

8. Revert to step 5 and repeat the steps. You do this until all tasks are assigned estimates that have an acceptable percentage of variance value. Figure 7.4 summarizes the steps of the Delphi technique in the form of a flowchart.

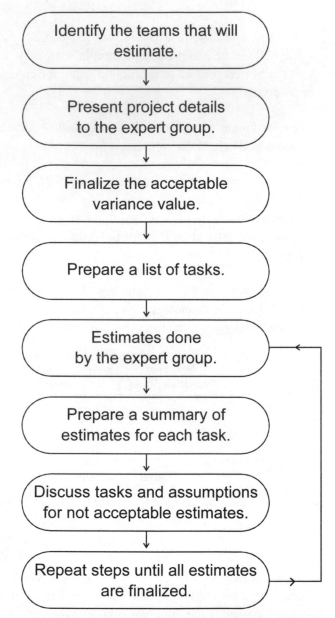

Figure 7.4: Steps of the Delphi Technique

The Delphi technique is a simple and subjective method of estimation. However, it is a very effective method because most of the estimates are tried and tested. You can use this method if the project is small or if you have the data and expertise that can enable unambiguous estimates.

Conclusion

Estimation is an important activity in the SDLC. For efficient project management, you need to estimate the effort, cost, and the defects reported. These estimates help you to plan a project realistically. In addition, comparison of data across projects can enable you to identify the loopholes in the process and improve them.

You can use scientific estimation techniques such SLOC, FP, and COCOMO. You can also use human-based estimation techniques such as the Delphi technique. All these techniques have different requirements and provide variable estimation values.

However, it is recommended that you use a mix and match model to estimate efficiently. Therefore, you could use FP and COCOMO to calculate the effort and cost of a project.

SUMMARY

✓ Estimation is an important project management activity. Estimation is required to plan a project realistically.

✓ WBS technique divides a project plan into multiple and manageable units called tasks. This is a prerequisite activity to estimate the size and effort of a project.

✓ You can create a WBS in three steps.

- Brainstorm and identify a list of possible tasks.

- Refine the list of tasks and look for gaps.

- Categorize each task into appropriate task headers.

✓ The SLOC estimation technique is used to estimate cost, effort, and defects. This is done by counting the number of source delivered lines of code.

✓ FP technique uses the general functionality of a software application from the user's perspective.

✓ You can calculate FP in the following steps:

- Calculate the total unadjusted function points value.

- Calculate the total complexity adjustment values.

- Calculate the final FP value by using the function points formula.

✓ COCOMO is a cost-driven estimation technique. You can estimate using COCOMO in three main steps:

- Calculate the initial effort estimate based on the types of projects. The value provided is represented as E_i.

- Calculate the effort adjustment factor by assigning ratings to the 15 cost driver attributes. The value represented is EAF.

- Calculate the adjusted effort estimate by multiplying E_i with EAF.

✓ Delphi is a human-based estimation technique. It is a group-based activity where a group of experts estimate the maximum and minimum effort values for a task.

HOMEWORK EXERCISES

1   IBG Inc. traditionally uses the Delphi technique to estimate the effort required in every phase of a project. It needs to estimate the average effort on a small enhancement project. Sequence the following steps of estimating effort by using the Delphi technique.

    a.   Prepare a list of tasks.

    b.   Identify the teams that would perform estimation.

    c.   Discuss tasks and assumptions for not acceptable estimates.

    d.   Finalize the acceptable variance value.

    e.   Repeat the steps until all estimates are final.

    f.   Estimate effort.

2.   Explore the various methods and perspectives that organizations use to create a WBS. List them and discuss the advantages and disadvantages of using each method.

3.   In the chapter, you learned about the intermediate COCOMO technique. The intermediate COCOMO technique was revised by Ray Kile and is known by the name of Revised Enhanced Version of Intermediate COCOMO (REVIC) technique. Read up content on the REVIC estimation technique. List down the points that are an improvement over the intermediate COCOMO technique.

LAB EXERCISES

1. Safest Software Co. has recently bagged a software project contract to develop an embedded software system. The organization has not developed such a project before. The technology and the delivery medium of the software project have not been anticipated. However, the system analysts have roughly projected the functionality of the prospective software. To arrange for resources and estimate the initial project cost, the organization needs to use an estimation technique. Which estimation technique should the organization select? Give reasons for your answer.

2. Calculate the adjusted function point value for a project. The number of information domain elements anticipated in the project is provided in the following table. Assume that all information domain elements have a rating of average. Similarly, the degree of influence for all GSCs is an average value of 3.

Number of user inputs	30
Number of user outputs	15
Number of internal files	6
Number of external interfaces	2
Number of external inquiries	25

3. XYZ Inc. develops sophisticated financial applications. They have bagged a software contract from an international banking firm. They have been asked by the client to estimate the effort required for the project. The organization feels that they would require 30 KLOC to code for a single module. The organization needs to accurately estimate effort in terms of cost spent on every aspect of the project. Compute the effort by using the intermediate COCOMO technique. Assume that all the cost driver attributes are assigned a rating of high.

4. "The FP technique of estimation is more popular than the SLOC technique of estimation". Agree or disagree with the preceding statement providing reasons.

Chapter 8

Project Scheduling: Planning and Monitoring

Objectives:

- State the need for project scheduling.
- Identify the guidelines for creating a software project schedule.
- Create a project schedule by using a Gantt chart.
- Create a project schedule by using PERT.
- Derive the critical path of a project schedule by using CPM.
- Identify the advantages of different project scheduling tools for different kinds of projects.

SCHEDULING A PROJECT

Ever wondered why you create a To Do list for yourself? Ever reflected on the importance of a calendar in your life? These lists and calendars help you plan your day-to-day activities. They serve as the indispensable road map in an unfamiliar terrain. Similarly, while managing a software project, you need a schedule to see it through smoothly. In the previous chapters, you learned that there are multiple activities involved in a software project. In this chapter, you will learn to schedule the activities. As a project manager, you need to assign durations to all activities and monitor their progress. You also need to plan the order in which the activities will be performed as well as the start and end dates for each activity. In short, you need to create a project schedule.

The project schedule reflects the start dates and end dates for each activity in the project. It also reflects the resources required to complete the activities. To create a schedule, you can use project management tools.

This chapter explains the need for scheduling a software project. In this chapter, you will learn about two tools to create and monitor a project schedule:

- Gantt charts
- Network-scheduling techniques

Need for Project Scheduling

Software projects have a tendency to get out of control because of the multiple activities that need to be monitored, tracked, and controlled. When a project goes out of control, the original deadlines, the budget, and the effort required overshoot the initial estimates. This not only impacts the product, but also the credibility of the development team.

What Delays Software Projects

There are various reasons why a software project is delayed. Some of the reasons are listed below:

- The initial estimate of the effort and resources required to complete the software project was incorrect.
- Changes in client requirements were not accounted for in the project schedule.
- Known risks were not mitigated.
- Technical difficulties surfaced during software product development.
- Human difficulties, such as interpersonal problems and team attitude, became unmanageable.
- The initial deadline set for the project was unrealistic.

How to Prevent Delays

While most of the above reasons result in project delays, unrealistic deadlines cause the maximum damage. Unrealistic deadlines are caused either by the client wanting a quick delivery or the management wanting a return business from a client. However, unrealistic deadlines are the norm for software projects. You need to resolve the conflict between an unrealistic deadline and the constraints of the software development team. As a project manager, you need to balance the limited resources and the final deliverable committed to the client. To do this, you can follow the points listed below:

1. Study similar past projects for the methods of dealing with similar situations. Use the historical information to project time and effort estimates for the current software project.

2. Use an incremental process model to create a schedule to deliver the required functional module of the software product.

3. Present the schedule created on the basis of past projects to the client. Explain the projected delays and the reasons for the same.

4. Present the incremental model as a strategy for developing the software product.

All the strategies have their advantages and disadvantages. If the schedule created using inputs from the past project does not help meet the deadline, you can use the incremental model. In the incremental model, the strategy is to deliver each module as and when it is completed. However, historical trends show that clients opt for either strategy if provided reasonable time and effort estimates.

Scheduling Basics

Only a small percentage of all the activities in a software project have a direct impact on the on-time completion of the software project. Therefore, you need to identify the activities that are critical to the completion of the project. In addition, you ensure that all inputs are available to complete the critical activities. This is where a software project schedule comes into the picture.

The goal of a software project schedule is to determine the duration of the software project and the phases within the project. A software project schedule enables you to distribute the estimated effort to be spent in performing the critical activities.

There are a few basic principles that determine how a software project schedule is created. To create a project schedule, first you group similar activities together. Then, you determine the dependencies of the different activities. Next, you allocate the estimated time and resources to each activity. Finally, you define the roles and responsibilities and the output and validation criteria.

Some of the guidelines for creating a software project schedule are discussed below:

- Classification
- Interdependence
- Time and effort allocation
- Validation criteria
- Defined responsibilities and outputs

Classification

While managing a software project, you need to group similar tasks and activities so that they are completed successfully. The primary tools used to group similar tasks are the WBS and decomposition technique. Using these tools, you can divide a software project into different phases. The phases can be further subdivided into activities. The software project schedule is prepared according to the arrangement of the phases.

Interdependence

As you have seen, a software project is composed of multiple phases and each phase is composed of multiple activities. Although each activity is treated separately, it is linked to other activities. As a project manager, you determine the interdependence and sequence of activities. For example, some activities can be completed without any inputs from other activities, whereas other activities cannot start unless a preceding activity is completed.

Time and Effort Allocation

Each activity in a software project needs a certain amount of time and effort for completion. To manage the project, you assign start and end dates to each activity. You also need to allocate appropriate effort to each activity. Most software projects operate with time and effort constraints. Therefore, managing within the available resources is very important for a software project manager.

Validation Criteria

You also determine the validation criteria for time and effort allocation in a software project. Determining the validation criteria allows you to ensure that the optimal level of resources is available for a particular activity. Suppose 5 people are assigned to an activity that requires an effort of 3.5 person days. This means resources allocated are more than the actual requirement.

Defined Responsibilities and Outputs

As a software project manager, you assign roles and responsibilities to all people assigned to a software project. This defines the hierarchy in the development team. You also define the outputs from each activity. This helps in identifying the results expected at the end of every activity. Next, you link the roles to the outputs. When each role is linked to the expected results, you can track each person's effort and the progress of each activity towards closure.

GANTT CHART

You have seen the importance of scheduling and the activities involved in scheduling. There are various tools that help you create a schedule. One of the simplest project management tools used to represent the timeline of activities is the Gantt chart. A Gantt chart has horizontal bars plotted on a chart to represent a schedule. In a Gantt chart, you plot time on the horizontal axis and activities on the vertical axis. You represent an activity by a horizontal bar on the Gantt chart. The position of a horizontal bar shows the start and end time of an activity and the length of the bar shows its duration. You can have one look at the Gantt chart and make out the progress of the project. Figure 8.1 displays a sample Gantt chart.

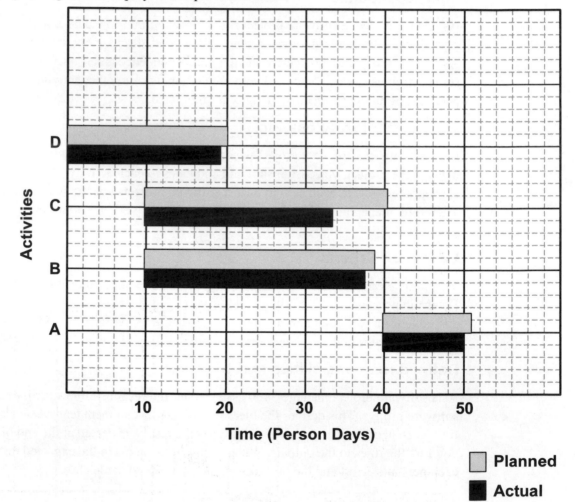

Figure 8.1: A Gantt Chart

In Figure 8.1, activity D starts on day 1 of the project. The planned duration of this activity is 20 days. The planned duration is shown in a lighter shade on the Gantt chart. This is done to differentiate planned duration from the current status of the activity. In the case of activity D, the current duration of the activity is 19 days. Therefore, activity D is still one day short of completion. This can be discerned from the length of the gray and black bars. Activity C, planned for completion on day 40, is much behind schedule. This can be observed from the smaller length of the black bar in the Gantt chart.

To understand how you can use a Gantt chart to schedule a project, consider an example. Table 8.1 displays a set of activities in a software project and the start and end time for each activity.

Tasks	Time Allocation (person days)	Planned Start	Planned End
Requirements analysis and project planning	10	01/01/2002	01/14/2002
Setting up the environment	6	01/01/2002	01/08/2002
Software construction	80	01/15/2002	05/15/2002
Unit testing	30	05/16/2002	06/28/2002
User training	5	07/22/2002	07/26/2002
System testing	15	07/01/2002	07/19/2002
User documentation	30	01/15/2002	02/28/2002
Data migration	20	01/15/2002	02/15/2002
Conducting user acceptance test	20	08/01/2002	08/31/2002

Table 8.1: Project Activities and Time Allocation Details

Using the data shown in Table 8.1, you can create a Gantt chart. The Gantt chart is displayed in Figure 8.2.

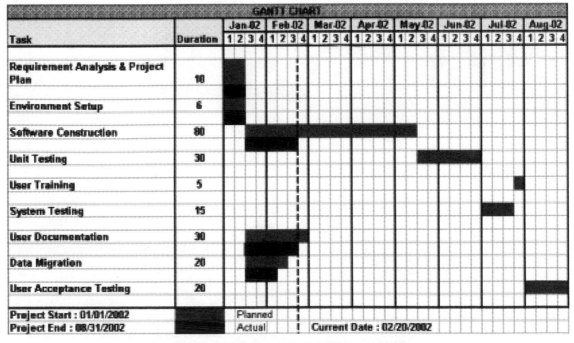

Figure 8.2: Gantt Chart for Activities of Table 8.1

In Figure 8.2, the Gantt chart displays the week-wise status of a software project. A vertical dotted line is drawn through the chart to represent the current date. This line indicates the status of the project on a specific day. The left side of the line indicates the tasks that are completed. On-going activities run across the line. The future activities lie completely to the right of the line. After drawing the Gantt chart, you can extend the bars every week to a length proportional to the work completed during the week. Therefore, the bars describe the status of the project at any point of time.

This process of creating a Gantt chart as discussed above is manual. Nowadays, automated tools are available for creating Gantt charts. For example, you can use Microsoft® Project™ 2000 developed by Microsoft to create a project schedule automatically.

NETWORK SCHEDULING TECHNIQUES

To plan the activities in a project, you can also use network-scheduling techniques. Network scheduling techniques use network schedules to trace the completion of predetermined activities. There are two basic network-scheduling techniques, PERT and CPM. You can use either of these techniques to analyze a wide variety of projects. Each technique depicts a project as a sequence of activities. This helps you perform an analysis of individual activities or the complete project.

The network-scheduling techniques also enable you to analyze the dependencies that exist between the activities. Using PERT and CPM, individually or in combination, helps you complete a project on time. By using these techniques, you can determine the latest time by when an activity should start to be completed on time.

Creating a Network Schedule

Despite the different approaches followed by PERT and CPM, both techniques have some common components. These include:

- Activities
- Nodes
- Network
- Critical path

Activities

Activities are the basic building blocks of network schedules. An activity is defined as a task that consumes time, effort, money, or any other resource. It is necessary to specify all the activities of a project by breaking down a project into several steps. You need to define the steps in such a way that they are distinct, homogeneous tasks for which you can estimate resource requirements.

Each activity is represented on a network schedule by using an arrow with its head indicating the direction in which the project will progress. Each activity is identified by a description or an alphabet. In addition, the estimated duration of each activity is placed below the activity. Figure 8.3 shows an activity with an expected duration of 15 days.

A

15 Days

Figure 8.3: An Activity

After identifying all the activities in a project, it is necessary to schedule them. This enables you to arrange the activities in the order of completion. You sequence the activities based on their types. The different activities that are possible in a project are predecessor, successor, and concurrent activities. Predecessor activities need to end before the next can begin. After a predecessor activity is completed, the successor activity becomes the predecessor for another activity. However, unlike the predecessor and successor activities, the concurrent activities can be completed simultaneously with other activities.

Some activities in a project, irrespective of whether they are predecessor, successor, or concurrent, may depict a float period. Float is the amount of time by which an activity may be delayed without affecting the completion date of the entire project. However, the complex dependencies that exist between activities result in sequencing constraints for projects. To a large extent, these constraints limit the flexibility that you may otherwise have in project planning.

Nodes

A node on a network schedule is that point in time at which an activity either begins or ends. The point where an activity begins is called a tail node and the point where it ends is called its head node. On a network schedule, a circle represents a node. A number identifies each node in a network schedule. Figure 8.4 represents the tail and head nodes for the activity of interviewing clients in a project.

Figure 8.4: An Activity Connecting Two Nodes

Network

A network is the graphic representation of the activities in a project. It depicts all the activities and nodes in the project. On a network, the arrows terminating at a node need to be completed before the following activity can begin. Figure 8.5 shows a sample network consisting of five activities in a project.

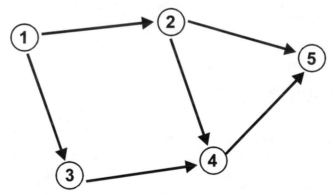

Figure 8.5: Sample Network Schedule

Critical Path

The critical path is the longest path through a network. It consists of those activities that cannot be completed concurrently. In other words, the critical path represents the maximum duration for a project. You can determine the maximum duration by adding the duration of each activity on the critical path. Typically, a double line in a network schedule represents the critical path for that project. Figure 8.6 shows the critical path for a network.

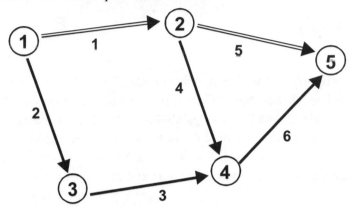

Figure 8.6: Network Schedule with Critical Path Identified

All the activities on the critical path are critical for a project. If an activity on the critical path is delayed, the entire project is delayed by the same amount of time. You need to monitor the activities on the critical path because the project depends on the successful completion of these activities. If required, additional resources can be applied to these activities to shorten the project duration. However, some of these activities may also depict a float period.

Rules for Creating a Network Schedule

There are a few basic rules that are followed while constructing a network schedule.

1. Each activity has a preceding node and a succeeding node.

2. Each node has a distinct number. As a convention, the number that is assigned to the head of the arrow is greater than the number that is assigned to the tail.

3. The network schedule has no loops. For example, in Figure 8.7, activity 1 is the predecessor of both activity 2 and activity 3. This places activities 1, 2, and 3 in a loop.

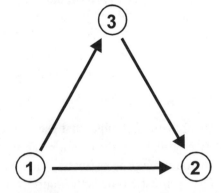

Figure 8.7: A Loop is Not Permitted

4. Each activity has a unique preceding and succeeding event associated with it. For example, in Figure 8.8, activities A and B have common preceding and succeeding events associated with them. This is not allowed in a network schedule.

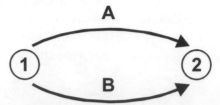

Figure 8.8: Activities with Common Preceding and Succeeding Events

At times, you need to introduce a dummy activity in a network schedule. This is an imaginary activity that enables the network schedule to display parallel activities. For example, in Figure 8.9, consider A and B as two parallel activities that can be executed simultaneously. Both A and B must end so that activity C can begin. A dummy activity is introduced as a dashed arrow to mark the start of activity C. The dummy activity is introduced to show the dependency between activities in the network schedule and does not have a description or duration.

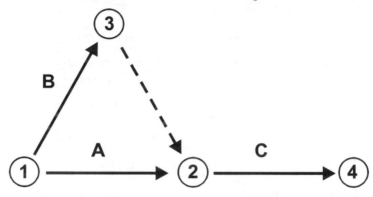

Figure 8.9: Dummy Activity

Using PERT to Schedule a Project

PERT was developed in 1957 to cater to the needs of the Polaris Fleet Ballistic Missile project of the US government. PERT uses a probabilistic approach to time estimates. You normally apply it to projects that are characterized by uncertainty. For example, in a complex software project where you require research to identify activities. PERT allows you to account for the uncertainties that are common to most software projects. PERT uses the network schedule to represent a project schedule while taking the uncertainties into account.

Time Estimates in PERT

PERT is a probabilistic technique that uses three time estimates. It assumes that activity times are represented by a probability distribution. To finish an activity, it bases the probability distribution of activity time on three time estimates: the *optimistic time*, the *pessimistic time,* and the *most likely time*. The optimistic time is the shortest time period within which an activity can end if everything goes well. The pessimistic time is the time that an activity takes to complete if everything that can go wrong goes wrong. This is the longest time that an activity can take to complete. The most likely time is the estimate of the normal time that an activity takes to complete. From these three estimates, you derive the expected time to complete an activity. The expected time is also referred to as the average time for the activity.

To calculate the expected time for each activity, you use the following equation:

$$T_e = \frac{T_o + 4T_m + T_p}{6}$$

Where T_e is the expected time, T_o is the optimistic time, T_m is the most likely time, and T_p is the pessimistic time required to complete an activity. According to this equation, you calculate the expected time for an activity as a weighted mean of the optimistic, most likely, and pessimistic times. The weights attached to these times are 1, 4, and 1, respectively.

Consider the example of the activities in a software project as given in Table 8.1. The time estimates provided in Table 8.1 are the estimated times for each activity. Table 8.2 provides the break-up of the estimated times into the optimistic, pessimistic, and most likely times for each activity.

Tasks	Optimistic Time Estimate (person days)	Most Likely Time Estimate (person days)	Pessimistic Time Estimate (person days)
Requirements analysis and project planning	7	10	13
Setting up the environment	3	6	9
Software construction	48	83	100
Unit testing	20	28	33
System testing	4	5	6
User training	10	15	20
User documentation	23	28	45
Data migration	18	18	30
Conducting user acceptance test	14	21	22

Table 8.2: Optimistic, Most Likely Time, and Pessimistic Estimates for Activities

Using the formula for calculating estimated time for an activity, the estimated time for requirements analysis and project planning is:

$$T_e = \frac{7 + 4\,(10) + 13}{6} = 60/6 = 10 \text{ person days.}$$

Similarly, you can calculate the estimated times for all the activities in Table 8.2 using the above formula.

Figure 8.10 shows the PERT network schedule created using the time estimates.

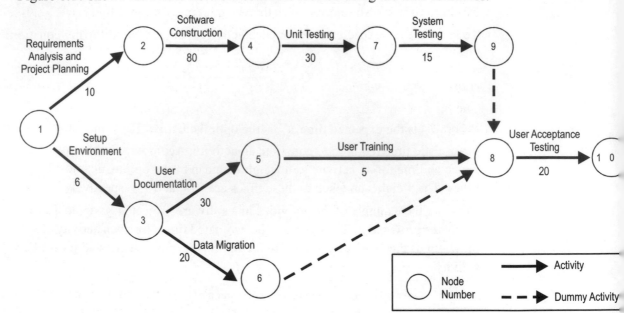

Figure 8.10: PERT Network Schedule for Activities

Using CPM to Derive a Critical Path

CPM was developed in the 1950s by DuPont to solve scheduling problems in an industrial setting. This method was used successfully by a number of projects that use a stable technology and are relatively risk-free.

CPM is also based on the concept of a network schedule. CPM uses the time estimates that are calculated using the PERT technique. CPM treats the time estimates from PERT as a known value. This means that CPM is a deterministic technique whereas PERT is a probabilistic technique that estimates the duration of activities. CPM and PERT were developed as two separate techniques. However, over time, both the techniques evolved into one scheduling and tracking tool for project managers.

CPM allows you to derive the critical path for a project schedule. The critical path is the longest path in a software project. The critical path is composed of critical activities in a project. These activities are well defined and independent. This means no activity in the critical path is dependent on another activity for successful completion. To derive the critical path for a network schedule, you need to calculate the earliest finish (EF) time and the latest finish (LF) time for each activity.

Calculation of the Earliest Finish Time

The earliest finish time for an activity is the minimum time required to complete it. The EF time of the first node is always zero. To calculate the EF time for a network schedule, you need to move along the schedule from left to right.

Starting from the first node, you add the EF time of each node to the duration required by the immediately succeeding activity. In case a node has more than one preceding activities, you use the largest EF time of the preceding activities. This rule also applies in case one of the preceding activities is a dummy activity.

For example, apply the rules for calculating the EF time to the activities listed in Table 8.2. The EF time of node 1 is 0. Therefore, the EF time for node 2 is 10 person days. The EF time for node 4 is calculated by adding the duration of the software construction activity, which is 80 person days, to the EF time of the preceding node 2, which is 10 person days. Therefore, the EF time of node 4 is 90 person days. This means that the earliest possible time within which the software construction activity can be finished from the start of the project is 90 person days.

The EF time for the rest of the activities in the network schedule is calculated in a similar manner. Figure 8.11 shows the network schedule with the EF time calculated for all activities.

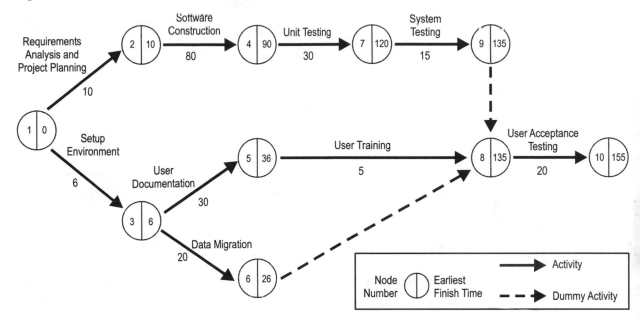

Figure 8.11: Network Schedule with EF Times Calculated

Calculation of the Latest Finish Time

The latest finish time for an activity is the maximum time required to complete it without delaying the project. To calculate the LF time for a network schedule, you move along the schedule from the right to the left.

Starting from the last node, you subtract the duration of the following activity from the LF time. If a node has more than one following activity, subtract the smallest activity duration from the LF time to obtain the LF time of the next node. This rule also applies if the following activity is a dummy activity.

For example, apply the rules for calculating the LF time to the activities listed in Table 8.2. The LF time for node 8 is calculated by subtracting the duration of the user acceptance testing activity, which is 20 person days, from the LF of node 10, which is 155 person days. Therefore, the LF of node 8 is 135 person days. Similarly, the LF for node 5 is calculated subtracting the duration of the user training activity from the LF time of node 8. The LF time for node 5 is 130 person days. The LF time for node 6, which has a dependent relationship with node 8, is the same as the LF time of node 8. In a similar manner you can calculate the LF time for the rest of the activities in the network schedule.

Figure 8.12 shows the network schedule with the LF time calculated for all activities.

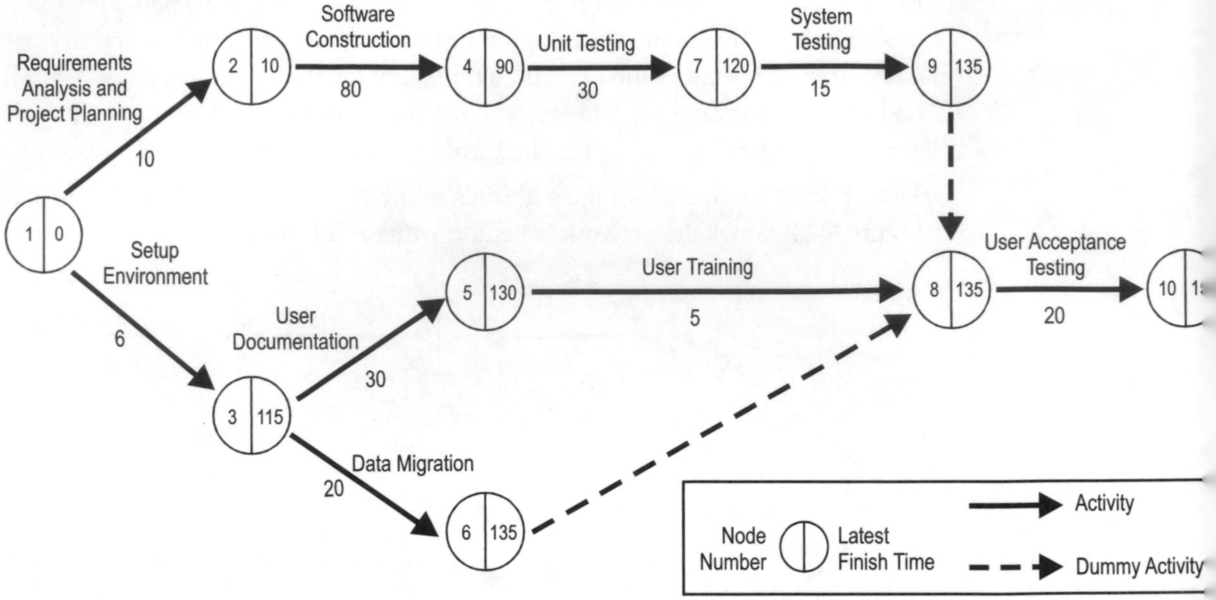

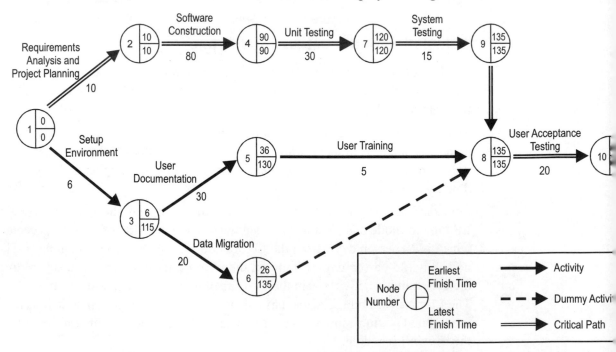

Figure 8.12: Network Schedule with LF Times Calculated

Deriving Critical Path

To determine the critical path of a network, you identify the nodes where the EF time and the LF time are equal. Then, compare the EF time and the LF time calculated for the network schedule. For example, combining figures 8.11 and 8.12 determines the critical path for the network schedule with the activities defined in Table 8.2. This is displayed in Figure 8.13.

Figure 8.13: Network Schedule with Critical Path Determined

COMPARISON OF PROJECT MANAGEMENT TOOLS

The three project management tools discussed in this chapter are used for a variety of software-related and nonsoftware-related projects. However, each tool is suited to a particular application. In addition, each tool has its advantages and disadvantages that permit or limit you from using the tool in specific conditions. This section provides you with a comparative analysis of Gantt, PERT, and CPM for the purpose of creating and monitoring software project schedule.

Gantt Chart

You use Gantt charts in simple software projects where the software development life cycle is linear. For example, the structure of a software product for the banking industry is well defined because of the numerous banking applications that already exist.

However, Gantt charts have a few disadvantages. The three primary disadvantages of a Gantt chart are related to:

- Interdependence of activities
- Tracking the project progress
- Representing uncertainties

Interdependence of Activities

A Gantt chart cannot represent the interdependence of activities in a software project properly. The bar graph format is unsuited if you want to display a large number of activities that are concurrent. For example, in a software project, there are various activities that happen either simultaneously or overlap. Using a Gantt chart, you cannot distinguish between the activities that occur simultaneously from those that share some dependency.

Tracking Project Progress

You also cannot use a Gantt chart as a control device to track a software project. The bar graph format of the Gantt chart does not provide you with any method of tracking the progress of a software project. You can only check the different activities within the software project, their start dates, and their end dates.

Representing Uncertainties

A Gantt chart cannot reflect the uncertainties within a complex software project. You can only use it for simple software projects where all the activities are known and for which the start and end dates can be easily determined. However, uncertainties are the norm in modern software projects, and project schedules often require rescheduling to adjust for uncertainties. If a project is large and complex, such as creating automated error-checking software for a communications satellite, the different activities and sub-activities cannot be determined at the time the project commences. There is an uncertainty about the activities in the later stages of the project until that stage is reached. In addition, Gantt charts cannot reflect the tolerance levels during various activities.

PERT and CPM

PERT and CPM are useful techniques that allow you to manage the complexity of interdependencies within a software project. In addition, both techniques allow you to schedule and track a software project more efficiently than Gantt charts.

Advantages of PERT/CPM

Both PERT and CPM use network schedules to represent a project schedule. Although PERT and CPM were developed separately, both techniques were combined over time and began to be referred to as PERT/CPM.

The advantages of PERT/CPM relate to:

- Precedence relationships
- Interdependencies
- Large projects
- Simple structure
- Preplanning
- Project tracking

Precedence Relationships

PERT/CPM allows you to organize the activities in a project according to a sequence. In a network schedule, each activity must have a preceding activity and a succeeding activity. This rule is applicable to all activities except the first and last activities. Therefore, PERT/CPM allows you an advantage over Gantt charts that arranges the activities in terms of their duration.

Interdependencies

Unlike the Gantt chart, which is unable to depict interdependencies between various activities, PERT/CPM allows you to show the interdependencies. For example, you can use the network schedule to specify that an activity will begin only after specific preceding activities are complete. Similarly, you can also show that two activities need to be executed simultaneously for the succeeding activity to start.

Large Projects

PERT/CPM is suited for one-time, large, and complex projects that have a lot of uncertainties. In a complex software project, it is very difficult to identify each activity in the software project in advance. Most activities are identified and defined in terms of their start and end dates only during the relevant stage of the project. PERT/CPM allow you to create a project schedule while taking project uncertainties into consideration.

Simple Structure

PERT/CPM is based on simple mathematical concepts. The technique uses network schedules to describe a project schedule. The graphical nature of the network schedule is easy to understand. Even a layperson can understand the scope of the entire software project by looking at a summary network schedule. The PERT/CPM schedule can also be used as a medium of communication between groups within and across projects to convey the project status and progress.

Preplanning

PERT/CPM forces you to plan the software project in advance and achieve better coordination of work. As the network schedule demands that each activity must have a preceding and succeeding activity, you are forced to identify as many activities as possible and sequence them. The identification of as many activities as possible reduces the chance of important activities being omitted from consideration. The identification and sequencing exercise helps identify potential problems and bottlenecks in project execution. This allows you to resolve the problems on paper before they materialize.

Project Tracking

The network schedule focuses your attention on the critical path and critical activities. This enables you to complete the project within the shortest time and least cost. You can track the progress of the project because the start and end dates are known for each critical activity. PERT/CPM also allows you to monitor costs and check if the project is within the allocated budget.

Disadvantages of PERT/CPM

Although PERT/CPM provides many benefits in creating a project schedule, the technique is not foolproof. The disadvantages of PERT/CPM relate to:

- Activity definition
- Precedence relationships
- Time estimates

Activity Definition

PERT/CPM requires that each activity in a software project must be clearly defined. In addition, no activity can overlap with another activity in terms of the task being achieved. However, in a large and complex software project, it is not always possible for you to identify all the activities and sub-activities. If you attempt to create a network schedule with an incomplete list of activities, important activities may be left out.

Precedence Relationships

As a software project manager, you may not always be able to identify all the activities and sub-activities in a software project. When a software project commences, you have clearly defined activities only for a few phases of the project. The rest of the activities are defined when the project reaches to the relevant stage. Lack of clarity on all activities in the project prevents you from defining the precedence relationships between all activities. This hampers the creation of a network schedule.

Time Estimates

In PERT, you estimate the time required to complete an activity. Therefore, the PERT network schedule represents only a probabilistic estimation of time. A project schedule created on the basis of probabilistic time estimates can give you only a rough idea of the project timelines. On the other hand, the deterministic approach of CPM treats the time required to complete an activity as a known value. This approach is based on the assumption that the activities in the project are clearly defined and the project manager knows the time required to complete each activity. In reality, neither the probabilistic nor the deterministic approaches are a foolproof method to design a software project schedule.

SUMMARY

✓ Software projects get delayed because of a variety of reasons. A few of these reasons are:

- The initial estimate of the effort and the resources required to complete the software project was incorrect.

- Changes in client requirements were not accounted for in the project schedule.

- The initial deadline set for the project was unrealistic.

- The project management team failed to recognize the problem and take corrective action.

✓ A software project manager needs to balance limited time and resources to meet deadlines.

✓ A software project schedule allows the software project manager to:

- Determine the duration of the project and the phases within the project.

- Distribute the estimated effort over the defined critical activities.

✓ The basic principles of software project scheduling are:

- Classification of all similar activities into groups

- Interdependence of activities

- Time and effort allocation for activities

- Validation criteria for time and effort allocation

- Defined responsibilities and outputs for team members

✓ Three primary aids to create and monitor a project schedule are Gantt charts, PERT, and CPM.

✓ Gantt charts are used to create schedules. In a Gantt chart, you plot time on the horizontal axis and activities on the vertical axis. You represent an activity by a horizontal bar on the Gantt chart.

✓ In a Gantt chart, the position of a horizontal bar shows the start and end time of an activity while the length of the bar shows the duration of activity.

✓ Network scheduling techniques, such as PERT and CPM, use network schedules to trace the completion of predetermined activities.

✓ The components of a network schedule include:

- Activities

- Nodes

- Network

- Critical path

- ✓ Rules for creating a network schedule include:
  - Each activity has a preceding and succeeding node.
  - Each node has a distinct number.
  - The network schedule has no loops.
  - A dummy activity represents the dependency between activities in a network schedule and does not have a description or duration.
- ✓ PERT is a probabilistic technique that uses three time estimates to calculate the duration for an activity.
- ✓ The three time estimates used in PERT are: the optimistic time, the pessimistic time, and the most likely time to complete an activity.
- ✓ CPM is a deterministic technique that assumes that the time duration estimates for an activity are a known value.
- ✓ CPM is used to derive the critical path of a network schedule.
- ✓ CPM uses the time estimates as derived by PERT.
- ✓ To derive the critical path, the earliest finish and latest finish times are calculated for each node in the project schedule.
- ✓ On a comparative basis:
  - The Gantt chart is suitable for small and simple software projects, where the software life cycle is defined.
  - PERT/CPM is suitable for large and complex software projects, with various interdependencies and uncertainties.

HOMEWORK EXERCISES

The following table lists the activities for a software project. The table also provides information about the precedence relationships of the activities and their time durations. Create a network schedule for the project, calculate the EF and LF times, and derive the critical path.

Activity ID	Activity Name	Precedence Relationship	Duration (person days)
1	Scope Definition	-	4
2	Requirement Analysis	1	5
3	High Level Design	2	10
4	Low Level Design	3	20
5	Construction	4	110
6	Unit Testing	5	25
7	Integration Testing	6	10
8	System Testing	7	15
9	User Acceptance	8	10
10	Prepare Function Specifications	4	15
11	Prepare User Manual	5	10
12	Prepare System Manual	5	10
13	Prepare Implementation Plan	12	3
14	Implementation	9	5

LAB EXERCISES

1. Why are software projects delayed? How can you resolve the delay in a software project?

2. What are the five basic principles that guide software project scheduling? Why is it necessary to classify similar groups and activities within a software project? Identify the tool used to break up a project in terms of the different activities and classify similar activities together.

3. Create a Gantt chart using the following details. A project consists of activities A, B, C, D, and E. Time allocated to these activities is 10, 20, 30, 35, and 40 person days, respectively. Activities A, B, and C are carried out sequentially. Activities A, D and E can be carried out in parallel, and activity D follows activity C.

4. The following table lists different activities and their respective durations.

Activity	Duration (person days)
A	3
B	6
C	4
D	8
E	13
F	7
G	6
H	5

The activities are arranged as follows:
a. Activities A and H are the first and last activities, respectively.
b. Activities C, D, and F start concurrently after activity B is complete.
c. Activity E starts concurrently with activity H.
d. Activity G starts after activity E is complete.
e. Activity H starts after activity F completes.
Draw the network schedule for the activities listed above and derive the critical path.

5. What are the disadvantages of PERT/CPM for a large software project? How do they impact the project?

Chapter 9

Using a Project Management Tool: Microsoft Project 2000

Objectives:

- ☐ Define types of tasks that can be performed by using the Project menu.
- ☐ Add deadlines, constraints, and relationships between tasks by using the Tools menu.
- ☐ Add resources and resource costs to a project plan by using the Project menu.
- ☐ Update the status of a task by using the View menu.
- ☐ Reschedule incomplete tasks by using the Tools menu.
- ☐ Modify a project life cycle plan by using the Tools menu.
- ☐ Create, modify, and print reports by using the View menu.

MANAGING TASKS IN MICROSOFT PROJECT 2000

Project management is a highly specialized and professional task. The chances that a project can go haywire are very high because project management includes numerous activities, such as planning, resource allocation, risk management, and estimation. You can automate all these activities using a tool, *Microsoft Project 2000*. Activities such as project planning, resource and cost allocation, and project tracking can be done easily using the various user-friendly features of Microsoft Project 2000.

Microsoft Project 2000 is a popular project management tool that also enables you to schedule and track your project plan. In Microsoft Project, every unit of work, which consumes effort, time, and money, is called a *task*. You use Microsoft Project to specify tasks and the expected duration of each task. Using the task-related information, Microsoft Project prepares a project schedule. The schedule displays a plan consisting of the start and end dates of each task. In addition, it plots a pictorial Gantt chart. The Gantt chart view depicts the extension of tasks across days along with the corresponding resources.

This chapter helps you create and modify a project plan in the Gantt chart view. You will learn how to define different types of tasks. You will also learn to add resources, constraints, and deadlines to tasks. This chapter will also enable you to monitor a project plan by comparing the actual performance of a project with the baseline. Finally, you will learn to create and modify reports for resources.

In this chapter, you will learn to use Microsoft Project with the help of an example of an organization named XYZ Inc.

Creating Tasks

To manage a project efficiently, it is important to treat the project as a decomposable entity that can be analyzed and resolved. A problem first needs to be broken into units and then analyzed for solutions because it is always easier to focus on micro level units. Microsoft Project enables you to perform these tasks. It assumes that you have performed the WBS exercise for the project. The WBS exercise helps you to come up with indivisible units called *tasks*. Therefore, a task is an activity that has a defined start and end dates.

For example, XYZ Inc. has to develop an ERP project. They plan to complete the project in five phases: analysis, design, development, testing, and implementation. During the analysis phase, the WBS exercise is performed and a list of tasks is defined for each of the subsequent phases. Using Microsoft Project, you can create tasks for each phase, specify their duration, and assign resources to them. You can also set relationships between tasks to identify the successor and predecessor tasks.

Microsoft Project enables you to create three types of tasks.

- General
- Milestone
- Recurring

General Tasks

General tasks are the usual tasks that are independent and have no special characteristics related to their duration or time. For example, Analysis is a general task that XYZ Inc. plans to conduct. To create the Analysis task, you can use the Project menu on the Microsoft Project worksheet. The steps to create the Analysis task are as follows.

1. Click the **Project** menu.

   This displays the Project menu that contains all the task-related commands. Figure 9.1 displays the Project menu.

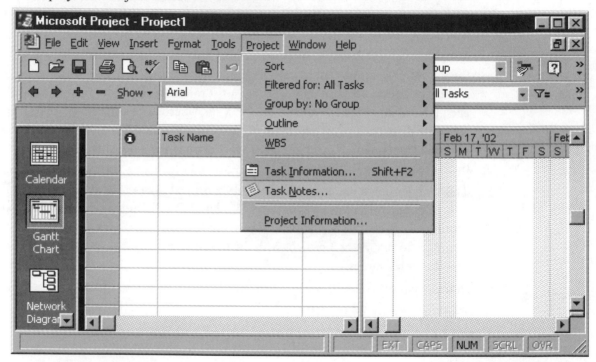

Figure 9.1: Project Menu

2. Click the **Task Information** command on the Project menu.

   This displays the Task Information dialog box where you specify the details of the task being created.

As shown in Figure 9.2, the Task Information dialog box contains five tabs: General, Predecessors, Resources, Advanced, and Notes. You use the General tab of the Task Information dialog box because you need to create a general task. The other tabs have specific purposes for each task. For example, you can specify the details for a task by using the Advanced tab. For the same task, you can use the Notes tab to add notes.

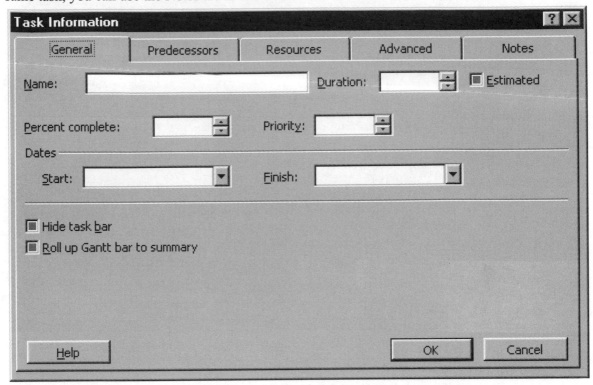

Figure 9.2: Different Tabs in the Task Information Dialog Box

Tip

In addition to the access key *I*, you can display the Task Information dialog box by using the *Shift and F2* shortcut key combination.

3. Type **Analysis** in the **Name** text box.

4. Specify the duration of the Analysis task as **5d** in the **Duration** text box.
   The duration of a task signifies the period for which the task lasts in a project schedule. The start date is preset as the current date unless you enter a specific date. The finish date for the task is displayed as five days after the current date in the Gantt chart view. Duration can be specified in minutes, hours, days, weeks, months, or years.

If you are not sure of a confirmed duration, you can specify an estimated duration of a task. Figure 9.3 displays the Task Information dialog box where task details are specified.

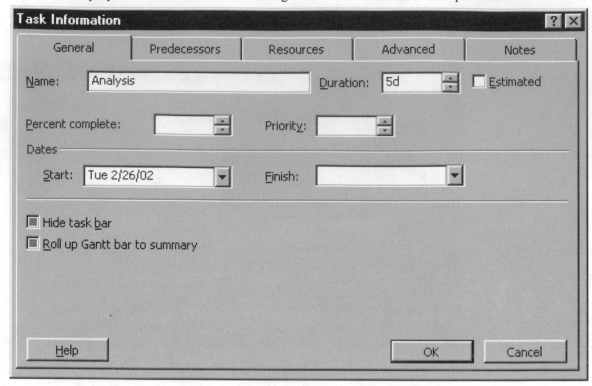

Figure 9.3: Task Information Dialog Box

Tip

To specify an estimated duration for a particular task, you can precede or succeed the duration with a question mark. Alternatively, you can select the Estimated check box next to the Duration text box.

5. Click **OK** to confirm the details provided by you.

After a task is created, you can specify the subtasks below it. For example, Project scope determination is a subtask of the Analysis task. To specify the subtask, you first create the Project scope determination subtask by using the Task Information dialog box. Next, you specify a summary designation for the Analysis task. A summary designation indicates that the task represents a parent task for a group of related tasks below it. The start date of a summary task is the start date of the first subtask. Similarly, the finish date of the summary task is the finish date of the last subtask under the summary task.

To designate Analysis as the summary task, perform the following steps.

1. Create a task named **Project scope determination** using the **Project** menu.
    You need to create this task below the Analysis task.

2. Select the **Project scope determination** task.

3. Click the **Indent** icon on the Formatting toolbar.
   The Indent icon is the green arrow pointing towards right.

Clicking this icon indents the selected task to the right. Notice in Figure 9.4 that Microsoft Project formats the summary task in bold. Alternatively, you can use the left indent icon to make the Analysis task as a summary task.

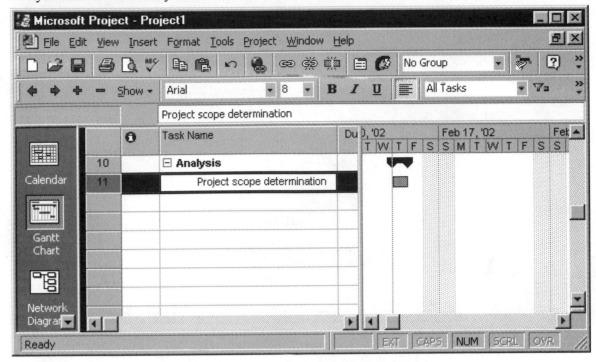

Figure 9.4: Creating Summary Tasks

Similarly, you create the rest of the tasks listed in the project plan of XYZ Inc. and specify subtasks below them. You store the list of tasks and their details in a file with an extension .mpp in Microsoft Project.

Milestone Tasks

Milestone tasks are the second type of tasks that you can create using Microsoft Project. These tasks have no duration. They serve as markers or reference nodes for significant accomplishments in a project. Examples of a milestone task are project startup, project end, pilot implemented, and SRS document sign off. Creating a milestone task is similar to creating any other task. The only difference is that after the task is created, you select an additional option named *Mark task as milestone* in the Task Information dialog box.

For example, in the analysis phase, XYZ Inc. has a milestone task named Analysis Complete. To indicate that Analysis Complete is a milestone task, perform the following steps.

1. Click the **Advanced** tab in the **Task Information** dialog box.
   This tabbed page contains specialized options that enable you to create milestone tasks. It also contains options to specify constraints and deadlines.

2. Type **Analysis Complete** in the **Name** text box.

3. Select the **Mark task as milestone** check box.
   You do this to specify a task as a milestone task.

4. Click **OK** to close the **Task Information** dialog box.

Figure 9.5 displays the Mark task as milestone check box selected.

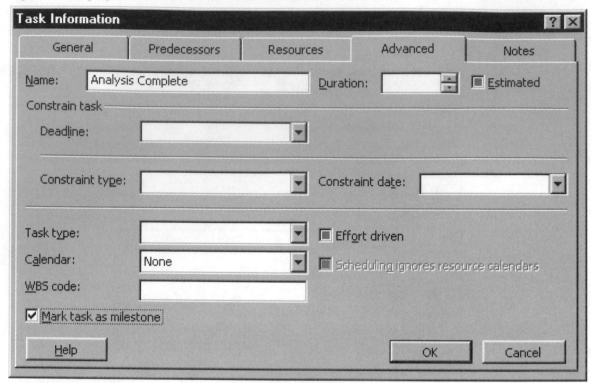

Figure 9.5: Creating Milestone Tasks

A milestone task is displayed as a task with no duration next to it in the Gantt chart view. Similarly, you create other milestone tasks in the Project file.

Recurring Tasks

Recurring tasks, as the name suggests, occur repeatedly at regular intervals. For example, a weekly project meeting with all the team members is a recurring task. You can schedule a recurring task in a project plan cycle as daily, weekly monthly, or yearly. You make this selection after deciding the seriousness of the nature of the task. The seriousness of the nature of the task determines how often the task needs to recur.

For example, if it is a simple meeting to take stock of the situation, you can select the weekly option. Similarly, you can annually schedule a high-level meeting of the board of directors. However, if an ongoing project is faltering due to frequent slippages, you need to closely monitor the activities of the project. To monitor the project activities effectively, you can convene a meeting every day.

You can also schedule the start and end dates of a recurring task. For example, for XYZ Ltd. you need to create the recurring task Project Meeting under the Analysis task. The Project Meeting task recurs every Friday until March 14, which is the project end date. You can create this task by using the Insert menu, and then specify the details in the Recurring Task Information dialog box. To create the recurring task, you perform the following steps.

1. Select the task row where you want the task to appear.

2. Click the **Insert** menu.

3. Click the **Recurring Task** command to display the **Recurring Task Information** dialog box.

4. Type **Project meeting** in the **Name** text box.

5. Select the **Friday** check box in the **Recurrence pattern** group box.
    This step specifies that the task should recur every Friday. Note that the Weekly option button is selected by default.

6. Click the **End by** option button.
    This ensures that the weekly task should continue only until February 14. Figure 9.6 displays this step.

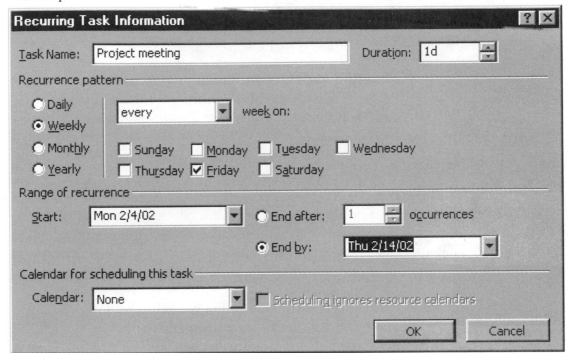

Figure 9.6: Creating Recurring Tasks

7. Select **February 14** from the calendar.

8. Click **OK** to close the **Recurring Task Information** dialog box.

A recurring task appears with a special circular arrow symbol in the indicator field. In the Gantt chart view, it appears at intervals on all the days it is scheduled until the last date specified.

Adding Constraints to Tasks

Constraints are defined as limitations that negatively affect the schedule and quality of a project. Some of the typical project constraints are mentioned below.

- Duration of a project

- Resources of a project

- Performance goals of a project

A constraint also affects other constraints. For example, you may need more resources if you reduce the project duration. You may also have to forgo some of the goals and features of the project if you decide to reduce the project duration. Therefore, it is important that you decide the tradeoff judiciously.

In Microsoft Project, you can specify constraints as limitations that are enforced on a task. For example, you can specify that a task must start on a particular date or not finish later than a particular date. Therefore, schedule-related constraints are available in Microsoft Project.

You can define eight types of schedule-related constraints in a project.

- As soon as possible (ASAP)
- As late as possible (ALAP)
- Start no later than (SNLT)
- Finish no later than (FNLT)
- Start no earlier than (SNET)
- Finish no earlier than (FNET)
- Must start on (MSO)
- Must finish on (MFO)

ASAP

When you use this constraint, Microsoft Project schedules a specific task as early as possible. For this reason you do not mention a specific date for such a task. Microsoft Project automatically assigns this constraint when you schedule a new task from the start date of a project. To change this constraint to a specific constraint, you can assign a specific start date to it.

ALAP

When you use this constraint, Microsoft Project schedules a specific task as late as possible. This is the reason why no specific date is mentioned for such a task. Microsoft Project automatically assigns this constraint when you schedule a new task from the finish date of a project. To change this constraint to a specific constraint, you can assign a specific finish date to it.

SNLT

You select this constraint to specify the latest possible start date of a task. For example, you want to conduct a training program on quality standards for the development team. You want to conduct the training program before the development phase begins so that you have enough time on hand. Therefore, you select the SNLT constraint and specify the start date that is before the start of the development phase. This means the training begins on or before the specified date. You also keep in mind the duration of the training. Suppose it is a two-day training program and the project development start date is February 15. Therefore, after selecting the SNLT constraint, you will enter the start date of the training as February 13.

FNLT

You select this constraint to specify the latest possible date by which a task can be completed. For example, you want the project proposal task to be completed on or before the analysis phase, which is scheduled to start from February 20. Consequently, by enforcing this constraint on the project proposal task, you ensure that the finish date for this task is the same as the start date for the analysis phase.

SNET

This constraint enables you to schedule the start date of a task as early as possible. This is different from the ASAP constraint because the ASAP is a vague constraint with no specific start dates for a task. However, by choosing the SNET constraint, you can specify an early start date for a task. For example, the task to create test cases is dependent upon the construction and the unit testing phases. Therefore, the task to create test cases cannot begin unless the earlier two tasks are over. In this case, you would enforce the SNET constraint on the creation of test cases and specify a start date. This start date cannot be before the end date of the preceding tasks. Consequently, you can create test cases any time on or after this start date but not before.

FNET

You select this constraint when you do not want a task to be complete before a scheduled finish date. For example, during the unit-testing task you discover there were many bugs that were addressed by the developers. This makes you skeptical about the quality of the product. Therefore, you want to extend the finish date of unit testing and enforce the constraint FNET on it. Consequently, you will not be able to finish the unit-testing task before the specified date.

MSO

This constraint indicates that you must begin a task only on the specified start date and not later or before that. This is an inflexible constraint. It is usually enforced during a short cycle duration project when you are unsure whether each task may or may not start on time. This may disturb the planned schedule of the entire project. You can enforce the MSO constraint for critical projects depending upon client requirements.

MFO

If you use the MSO constraint, it is most likely that you would use the MFO constraint also. Using the MFO constraint enables you to focus on completing a particular task. It is useless if you enforce a strict start date with no strict finish date for completing a task. You can again enforce this constraint for critical projects depending upon client requirements.

You enforce or use a constraint on a task by specifying the details in the Advanced page of the Task Information dialog box. In that dialog box, you can also specify the start and the end dates of a constraint depending upon the type of constraint that you choose.

For example, for XYZ Inc. you need to add a constraint to the Develop test plans task. This task is a subtask of the Testing task. After creating both the tasks, you specify the duration of the Develop test plans task. You want that the task should not carry on for more than two days. You also need to impose a constraint that the task should not finish later than August 10. However, the management would appreciate if the task finishes before that.

To add the constraint to the Develop test plans task, you use the constraints feature in the Task Information dialog box. To access the constraints feature, you perform the following steps.

1. Click the **Advanced** tab in the **Task Information** dialog box.

2. Type **Develop test plans** in the **Name** text box of the **Advanced** tabbed page.

3. Type **2** in the **Duration** text box.
   This specifies the maximum time allotted to complete the task.

4. Click the **Constraint type** box.

5. Select the **Finish No Later Than** option in the displayed list.

6. Click the **Constraint date** list.

7. Select **August 10** as the finish date from the calendar that is displayed. Figure 9.7 displays this step.

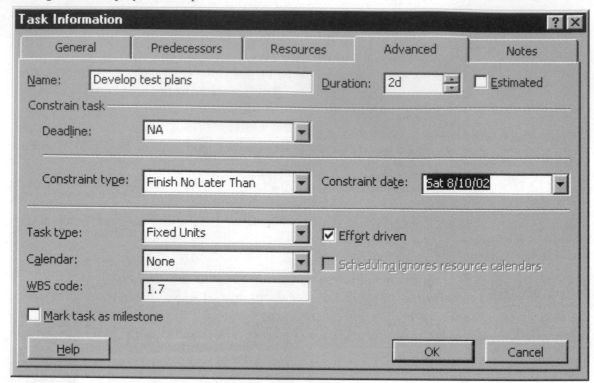

Figure 9.7: Adding Constraints

8. Click **OK** to close the **Task Information** dialog box.

The Develop test plans task is displayed with an icon for Finish No Later Than constraint in the Task sheet of the Gantt chart view.

Tip

After specifying a constraint type and its date, it is a good idea to specify the details of choosing a particular constraint type and its date. Subsequently, you may want to share this information with your colleagues in meetings. This can be done by clicking the *Notes* tab in the Task Information dialog box and entering your comments.

Adding Deadlines to Tasks

Deadlines are strict finish dates for a particular task. Microsoft Project considers a deadline to be a target date to complete a task. You add a deadline to a specific task if you track the progress of that task. Setting realistic deadlines to tasks also enables you to schedule the subsequent tasks.

Deadlines are important because they depict the finish date of a task. Therefore, you can track whether a task has exceeded the planned time or is completed before time. If the task is taking longer than expected, you can take remedial measures such as adding resources. Adding deadlines does not affect project schedule nor does it enforce a date constraint. However, it marks a task that has crossed its deadline with an indication mark next to it.

In the .mpp file that you are creating for XYZ Inc., you need to set July 15 as the deadline for the task Assign development staff, which is a subtask of the Development task. To set the deadline, you perform the following steps.

1. Create the task **Assign development staff** by using the **Project** menu.

2. Select the **Assign development staff** task.
   This is the task for which you need to set a deadline.

3. Click the **Advanced** tab in the **Task Information** dialog box.

4. Click the **Deadline** list box in the Advanced page.
   This is done to specify the deadline for the Assign development staff task.

5. Select **July 15** in the calendar to specify the deadline date.

6. Click **OK** to close the **Task Information** dialog box.

Similarly, you can add deadlines for the other tasks for the XYZ Inc. project.

Setting Dependencies Between Tasks

There is dependency between tasks when a particular task cannot begin until its preceding task is completed. For example, the creation of the high-level design of a project cannot start until the client signs off the SRS document. The SRS document serves as a prerequisite for the immediate subsequent phase.

In Microsoft Project, you can specify four types of dependencies.

- Finish-to-Start (FS)
- Start-to-Start (SS)
- Finish-to-Finish (FF)
- Start-to-Finish (SF)

FS

In dependency relationships of tasks, the name of the relationship consists of the start or finish dates of the predecessor task and the start or finish date of the successor task. For example, the relationship between the task to finish the SRS document and the task to begin the high-level design is FS. This is because you link the finish status of the predecessor task to the start status of the successor task. FS is the default relationship when you link any two tasks.

SS

In addition to FS, you can also begin two tasks at the same time. For example, you can begin the task to do functional testing and integration testing of the testing phase simultaneously. The dependency in a SS relationship occurs when both the predecessor and the successor tasks start at the same time. This is because these tasks do not share any common component nor are they dependent on each other. Therefore, the link between them is SS.

FF

You can also begin two tasks that finish simultaneously. In such a case, the dependency relationship between the two tasks is called an FF relationship. For example, the task to prepare a checklist for implementing a software product cannot end unless implementation testing for that software product is complete.

SF

Finally, you can have a SF relationship between tasks. This relationship indicates that a task cannot end until its preceding task starts. This relationship usually takes place when a project is scheduled from the project finish date. This relationship helps to minimize the risk of delay of a predecessor task if the successor task is dependent on the start of the predecessor task. For example, the testing phase can only start after the coding phase is complete.

Lag and Lead Time Between Tasks

While adding dependencies to tasks, you can also specify lag and lead times for any two interdependent tasks. Lag time is defined as the excess time that is allowed to lapse between predecessor and the successor tasks. This results in a delay in the start of the successor task. For example, you may use this option if you feel that the tasks of the analysis phase are taking more than the planned time to complete. Consequently, you might not want to start the high-level design task as planned but postpone it. In this case, you would calculate the maximum lag time for the high-level design to start.

You specify the lag time for a task as a positive value in the Lag field cell of the Predecessors page. This page exists in the Task Information dialog box.

Lead time is defined as the overlap that exists between two dependent tasks. For example, you could decide to start testing units when developers have partially completed creating the applications for a project. Therefore, you move ahead of the schedule of a successor task before time.

You specify the lead time for a task as a negative value in the same Lag field cell of the Predecessors page. This page exists in the Task Information dialog box.

Consider an example to link two tasks, procuring resources and drafting a project plan. According to the plan, securing resources is a predecessor task while drafting a project plan is a successor task. You need to link the two tasks using the start-to-finish relationship because it is anticipated that the task to draft a plan cannot start before the resources are procured and incorporated in the project plan. During the course of the project, you feel that the successor task cannot begin as planned because procuring resources is too time-consuming. You analyze and deduce that the project plan can only be drafted four days after resources are procured.

You link the two tasks by using the Edit menu. After linking the two tasks, you set the type of relationship as start-to finish. Assume that for the XYZ Inc. project, you need to link the Develop code and Developer primary testing tasks. You have created the Development summary task before. Now, you create these two tasks under the Development summary task. Then, you set a relationship between the tasks. Finally, you set a four-day lag time between the two tasks. To link tasks and set the lag time between them, perform the following steps.

1. Create a task named **Develop code** by using the **Project** menu.
2. Create another task named **Developer primary testing** below the **Develop code** task by using the **Project** menu.
3. Select **Develop code**.
4. Select **Developer primary testing** with the **Ctrl** key pressed.
5. Click the **Edit** menu.
6. Click the **Link Tasks** command.
   The two tasks are displayed as linked to each other in the Gantt chart view as you see in Figure 9.8.

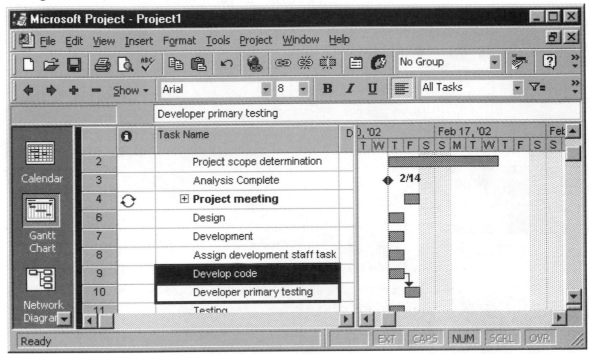

Figure 9.8: Linking Tasks

7. To establish the start-to-finish relationship between the two tasks, select the **Developer primary testing** task and click the **Project** menu.
8. Click the **Task Information** command.
   This action displays the Task Information dialog box wherein you can establish a defined relationship between the two tasks by using the Predecessors tab.
9. Click the **Predecessors** tab in the Task Information dialog box.
10. Select the **Start-to-Finish (SF)** relationship in the **Type** field cell.
    This defines a start-to-finish relationship for the tasks.

11. Type **4d** in the **Lag** field cell to specify four days lag time between the two tasks. This step is displayed in Figure 9.9.

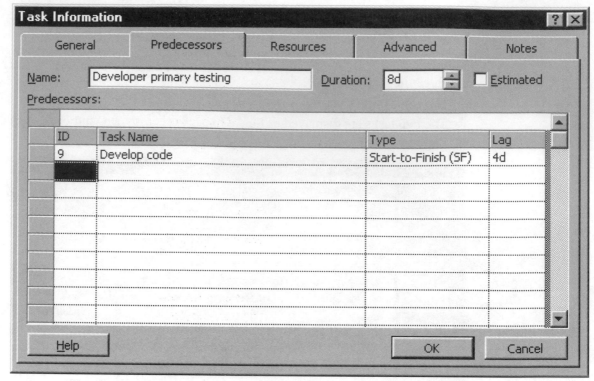

Figure 9.9: Specifying Value for the Lag Field

12. Click **OK** to close the dialog box.

The tasks Develop code and Developer primary testing appear linked to each other with the symbol of Start-to-Finish relationship in the Gantt chart view.

Splitting Tasks

A split in a task is defined as an abrupt and sudden interruption in the planned schedule. The need to split tasks arises because practically no task can be completed without a break. Due to resource crunch, a planned task are normally halted for some time.

For example, at XYZ Inc., both the tasks to train developers and to test a software module require a Windows 2000 Server. However, depending upon the criticality of the tasks, you can split one of the noncritical tasks. In this case, you decide to stop testing the software module and continue training the developers. To specify the task using Microsoft Project, you first create a Testing task as the summary task. After creating the Testing task, you create the Unit testing task under the Testing task. Next, you split the Unit testing task.

To split the Unit testing task, you perform the following steps:

1. Create a task named **Unit testing** below the Testing summary task.

2. Select the **Unit testing** task.

3. Click the **Edit** menu.
   The Edit menu contains the command that enables you to split a task.

4. Click the **Split Task** command on the Edit menu.

Upon clicking the Split Task command, the shape of the cursor changes. In addition, a small yellow box with a tool tip suggesting how to split a task hovers on the task view of the Microsoft Project window.

5. Drag the changed mouse cursor over the task in the Gantt chart view.

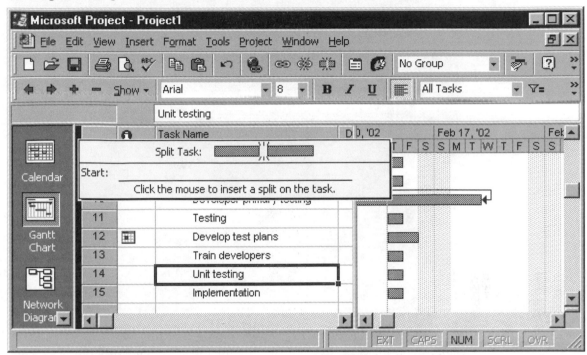

Figure 9.10: Splitting Tasks

In Figure 9.10, you can see the task being split into the required number of days. To split a task for a specified number of days, you drag the mouse pointer to a particular date. For example, a task is scheduled to start from May 5. You want a part of the task to start again from May 15. Therefore, there is a gap between May 5 and May 15. To start the task again from May15, you drag the last end of the task and release the mouse pointer on May 15 in the Gant Chart view.

Assigning Resources and Resource Costs to Tasks

Resources are means that help convert input to a task into output for the task. Resources are assigned to tasks for the following reasons:

■ To track the costs of each resource

■ To track the work completed and the material resources used in a project

There are two types of resources, work and material. Work resources refer to the people and equipment. At the end of a project, these resources are not consumed. Unlike work resources, material resources are used completely by the end of the project. For example, to complete the task of writing the code for a module, you need human and material resources. You also need material resources such as hardware, software, and electricity

Assigning resources to a task is a two-step process. First, you add the available resources to a project. You can do this by adding resources by using the View menu and then clicking the Resource Sheet command on the View menu. When you click the Resource Sheet command,

Microsoft Project changes the default Gantt chart view to the Resource Sheet view. Figure 9.11 displays the Resource Sheet view.

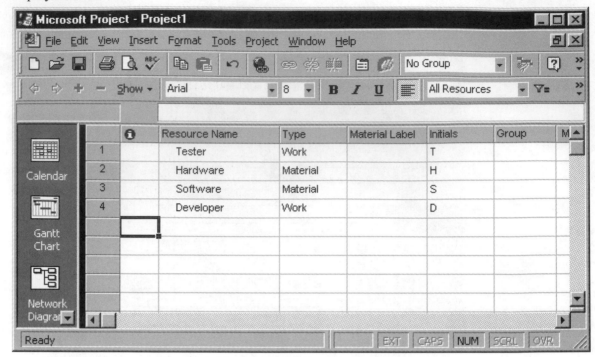

Figure 9.11: Resource Sheet View

Suppose for the XYZ Inc. project, you want to add a hardware resource in the Develop prototype task. The steps to add the resource are as follows:

1. Create a task named Develop prototype below the Analysis summary task.

2. Select the Develop prototype task.

3. Click the Tools menu.
    The Tools menu contains the command to add a resource.

4. Point to the Resources command.
    When you point to the Resources command, the Assign Resources command of the Resources submenu is displayed.

5.   Click the Assign Resources command. Figure 9.12 displays the Assign Resources dialog box.

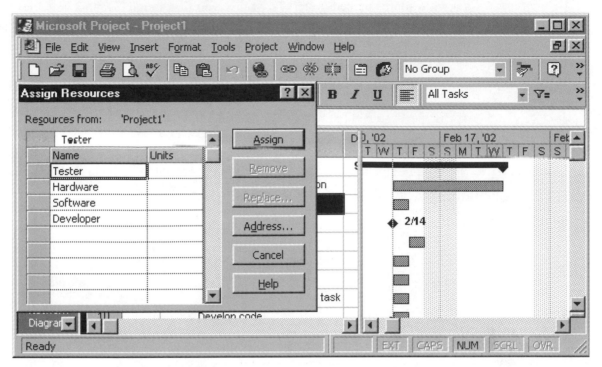

Figure 9.12: Assigning Resources to Tasks

The Assign Resources dialog box contains two fields, Name and Units. The Name field indicates the name of the available resources in the resource pool of a project. The Units field indicates the number of resources that can be used for a particular resource.

You can use the Assign Resources dialog box to assign units for both work and material resources. The unit for work resources is specified in terms of percentage. However, the unit for material is specified as a numeric value.

For example, you may select three computers or five workstations for the development team of a project. These values are not more than the predetermined value set for a resource in the Max.Units field of every resource in the Resource Sheet view.

Select the hardware resource for the Develop prototype task. You close the Assign Resources dialog box by clicking the Close button.

The hardware resource is added next to the Develop prototype task.

Assigning Costs to Tasks

Cost is an important aspect of project scheduling. Controlling costs ensures the optimal use of resources. For example, to complete a specific task in a project plan, you can assign more resources to that task. Alternatively, you can increase the duration of that task depending on the cost of the resources that are used by that task.

You can assign two rates for any type of a resource. The rates for work resources are calculated on an hourly basis. However, the rate at which the material resources are calculated can be:

■   Standard rate: The normal rate at which a resource is procured

■   Overtime rate: The rate that you pay if you overuse a work resource

For example, for the XYZ Inc. project, you need to specify the standard and the overtime rates for a work resource named Tester. To do this, you first assign the work resource Tester to the Unit Testing task that you created earlier. After assigning the resource to the Unit Testing task, perform the following steps to assign rates to the resource:

1. Click the **Resource Sheet** view of Microsoft Project.
    The Resource Sheet view is used to display all resources and their respective costs.

2. Type **Tester** in the first cell of the **Resource Name** column.

3. Select **Tester.**
    You do this because that is the work resource for which you need to specify the standard and overtime rates.

4. Click the **Project** menu to display the **Resource Information** command.

5. Click the **Resource Information** command on the **Project** menu.

6. Click the **Costs** tab in the dialog box.
    The Costs tab provides information about the standard and overtime rates and the cost per unit of a particular resource.

7. Type **$30.00/h** in the first cell of the **Standard Rate** column as shown in Figure 9.13.

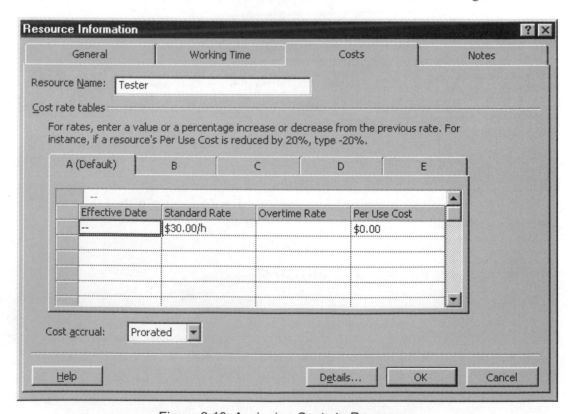

Figure 9.13: Assigning Costs to Resources

8. Type **$10.00/h** in the first cell of the **Overtime Rate** column.
    The rates can also be entered as negative values to denote the decrease in rate as compared to

previous rates or as positive values to denote a comparative increase in rate, such as +20% or −20%.

9. Click **OK** to close the **Resource Information** dialog box.

While calculating costs for work resources, Microsoft Project calculates the resource cost by the hourly rates that you specify and the time required for completing a task. However, when you assign a material resource to a task, Microsoft Project automatically calculates the total cost of the resource by using the material resource rate specified by you and the quantity of material required for completing the task.

TRACKING A PROJECT PLAN

Project management is a multiple-phase undertaking. The first phase is the project initiation or the project planning phase. This phase is followed by the project-tracking phase. Finally, you wrap up a project with the project-end phase. Project tracking is an extremely important activity in an organization. Unless a project is tracked effectively, it might never come close to termination. Project tracking also ensures strict adherence to project plans, requirements, and schedules.

Progress Lines

To track a project plan, you first view the progress of a project. You can view the progress of a project by applying progress lines to the tasks in the project. You can display progress lines in three ways.

You can choose to display progress lines always at the current status of a project. To do this, you need to select the Always display current progress lines check box in the Progress Lines dialog box. Selecting this option displays progress lines every time based on the current status of a project.

The second way to display project lines is to display them on selected dates of a project plan. For example, you use this option when you need to know the progress status of a project on the day development is completed. In this case, you select the Display selected progress lines check box to display progress lines on that day. Similarly, you can use this option to display progress lines on the day when testing is completed or the project-end date.

Finally, you can display progress lines at regular intervals such as daily, weekly, or monthly. If you choose daily, you can further define its preciseness by choosing everyday, every second, or every third day, and so on. Alternatively, if you choose monthly, you can refine your choice by selecting the month and day when a progress line is displayed. To display progress lines for all the tasks listed in the Sample-Project.mpp file every third day, you perform the following steps.

1. Click the **Tools** menu.

2. Point to the **Tracking** command to view different options for creating progress lines.

3. On the Tracking submenu, click the **Progress Lines** command.

4. The Progress Lines dialog box is displayed. In the dialog box, select the **Display progress lines at recurring intervals** check box.

5. After selecting the **Display progress lines at recurring intervals** check box, select the **Daily** option button.

6. To specify that the progress lines must be displayed every third day, click the every box and select the **every 3rd** option in the list.

7. You can further choose to display the progress lines every third day of a week on a workday. This is shown in Figure 9.14.

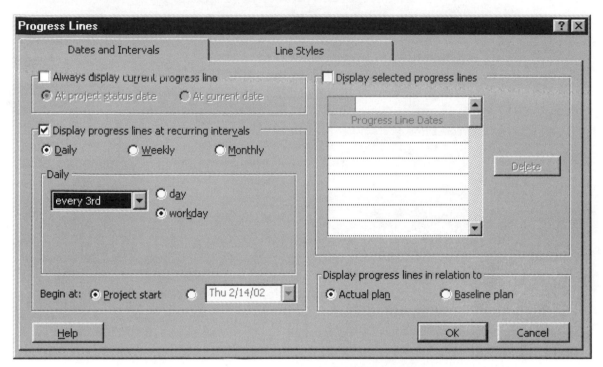

Figure 9.14: Setting Options for Progress Lines

8. To confirm the specifications and close the **Progress Lines** dialog box, click **OK**.

Figure 9.15 displays the progress lines of the tasks in the Gantt chart view.

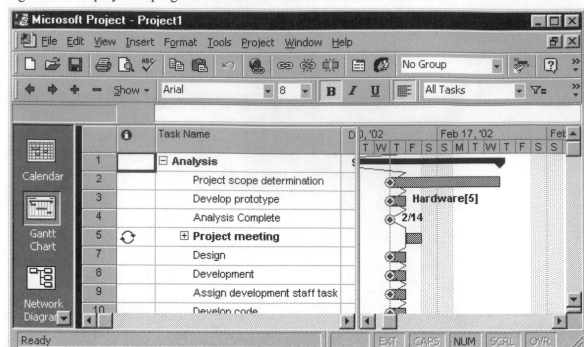

Figure 9.15: Progress Lines in the Gantt Chart View

Project Baselines

Project baselines are another way of depicting the progress of a project. Baselines are indicators that help you compare the actual start date with the planned start date of a project. They also help compare the actual cost incurred with the planned cost for a project. After preparing a project plan for tasks, you can save the plan as a baseline. This serves as an ideal plan for you to compare the actual performance of the project with the baseline that you save.

To save a project plan as a baseline, perform the following steps:

1. Click the **Tools** menu, and point to the **Tracking** command.

2. Select the **Save Baseline** command on the Tracking submenu.

3. In the **Save Baseline** dialog box, select the **Save baseline** and **Entire project** option buttons to save a baseline of the entire project.

4. Click **OK** to close the **Save Baseline** dialog box.

You can also save a part of the project plan by saving a few tasks as baselines by clicking the Selected tasks option button.

To view the deviation from a baseline performance to the actual performance of a project, perform the following step:

5. In the **Project Information** dialog box, click the **Statistics** button to view the project statistics for the Sample-Project.mpp dialog box. This dialog box is displayed in Figure 9.16.

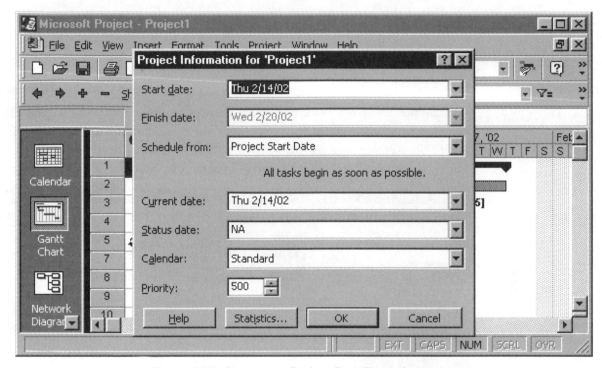

Figure 9.16: Displaying Project Baseline Information

The dialog box displays critical and summarized information about the variance values of the start and finish dates of a project, work completed in hours, cost, and duration in days. Higher the variance of a column, higher is the degree to which a project does not conform to the baseline plan. The actual values are displayed in the dialog box.

You can compare the baseline values for all these factors with the actual values of a task to conduct project plan analysis.

Recording and Updating Tasks

One way of tracking a project schedule is by determining the actual work done by a resource. After doing that, you compare it against the total work to be done initially. Using these factors, you can calculate the remaining work that needs to be done in the rest of the project cycle.

For example, you need to check the status of the Test component modules task in the XYZ Inc. project. This task exists under the Testing summary task. You use the Task Sheet view to record the actual work done by a resource and calculate the work that remains to be done. To do that, perform the following steps.

1. Select the task **Unit testing** for which you want to view the task completion status. This task exists under the Testing summary task.

2. Click the **View** menu.

---

3.   Click the **Table:Entry** command.

4.   Click the **Work** command on the Table::Entry submenu.

After doing this, four fields appear: Work, Baseline, Actual, and Remaining.

You update the Actual field value with the current amount of work done. Microsoft Project automatically updates the Remaining value after comparing the Actual value with the value in the Work field. Alternatively, you can update the value of the remaining field to a number that you feel is correct. Consequently, Microsoft Project updates the Total figure in the Work field. It also displays the difference in the previous Work and the current Work values in the Variance field.

For example, the Work field in Figure 9.17 displays the value 20. You update the Actual field with the value 13. Consequently, the remaining field would automatically show 7. However, you can modify the Remaining field to display the value 10 if seven days are not adequate. Notice that the Work field displays the value 27, and the value in the Variance field is 3.

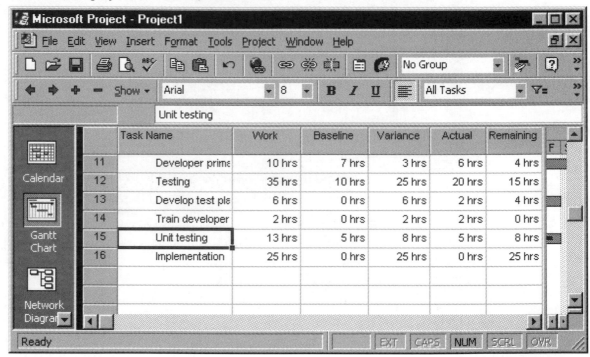

Figure 9.17: Updating the Status of Tasks

Note

You can also update the percentage of work completed by specifying the value in the Percent complete spin box. The Percent complete spin box is present in the General tab of the Task Information dialog box. Consequently, Microsoft Project updates the actual and remaining work in the Work sheet of tasks.

Rescheduling Tasks

Using Microsoft Project, you can reschedule the tasks of a project. Rescheduling involves modifying the start or finish dates of a task. For example, you need to reschedule the start date of the Create user manuals task. This task exists below the Development summary task. To reschedule an incomplete task, perform the following steps:

1. Create a task named **Create user manuals** under the Development task.

2. Make the **Development task** a summary task by using the left indent icon.

3. Select the **Create user manuals** task.

4. Click the **Tracking** command on the Tools menu.

5. Click the **Update Project** command on the Tracking submenu to display the Update Project dialog box. Figure 9.18 displays this dialog box.

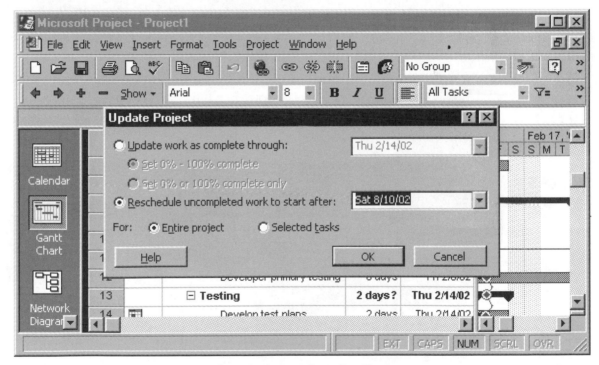

Figure 9.18: Rescheduling Tasks

6. In the Update Project dialog box, select the **Reschedule uncompleted work to start after** option. This option is used to reschedule an incomplete task.

7. Specify a new start date for the Create user manuals task.

8. Select the **Selected tasks** option to reschedule a task. If you need to reschedule an entire project, choose the **Entire project** option.

9. Click **OK**.

Modifying the Duration of a Project Plan

During the course of a project, schedule, cost, and effort slippages are quite common. Therefore, you sometimes need to modify the project start and end dates. Normally the start date is modified for short cycle projects that need an early head start. Finish date is modified when you are unable to meet the project end date due to slippages. Assume that a project starts on February 15 and you change its finish date from June 10 to June 15. To do this, perform the following steps:

1. Click the **Project** menu.

2. On the Project menu, click the **Project Information** command. This displays th Project Information dialog box.

3. In the Project Information dialog box, click the **Schedule from** list box.

4. Select the **Project Finish Date** option from the Schedule from list.

5. Click the **Finish date** box, and select June 15 from the calendar of the month June. This step is shown in Figure 9.19.

6. Click **OK**.

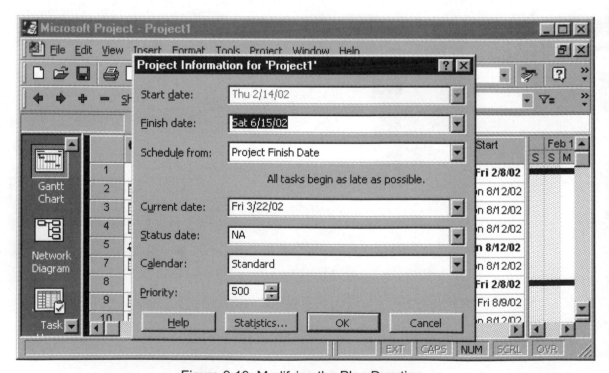

Figure 9.19: Modifying the Plan Duration

You have modified the project finish date from June 10 to June 15. You can view the change in the Gantt chart view of the project.

DISPLAYING PROJECT INFORMATION USING REPORTS

You create reports to display project-related information in a tabular format, which is easily comprehensible. Project reports provide a picture of the status of a project. The status of a project helps measure the progress of it. Reports can be prepared for a specific phase or for all the phases at one time.

Creating Standard Reports

Using Microsoft Project 2000, you can create two types of standard reports:

■ Standard resource report

You create standard resource reports to display resource allocation and the costs incurred on them.

■ Standard task report

You create standard task reports to display information regarding tasks and the duration to complete each task in a project.

To create a report on the resources listed in the Sample-Project.mpp file, perform the following steps:

1. Display the **Resource Sheet** view of Microsoft Project.

2. Click the **View** menu.

3. Click the **Reports** command.
   This command displays the Reports dialog box. This contains the various report formats.

4. Select the **Custom** icon to create a new resource report.

Figure 9.20 displays the Custom icon.

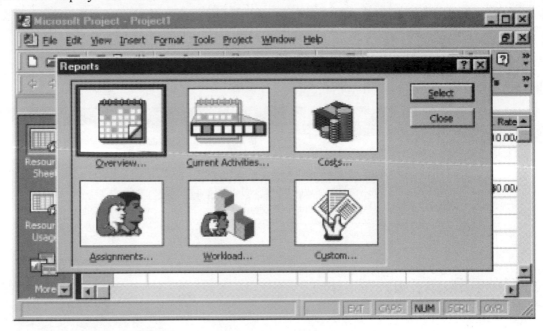

Figure 9.20: Displaying the Custom Icon in the Reports Dialog Box

5. Click the **Select** button.

    This displays the **Custom Reports** dialog box.

6. Click the **New** button.

    This way, you create a new type of a resource report that is not part of the list of reports displayed. The Define New Report dialog box is displayed as shown in Figure 9.21.

Figure 9.21: Defining New Reports

7. In the Report type box, select the **Resource** option.
   You do this to create a report displaying the various resources used in a project.

8. Click **OK** to confirm your selection.
   The Resource Report dialog box is displayed as shown in Figure 9.22. In this dialog box, you specify the name of the report. In the same dialog box, you can sort the information to be displayed in the report.

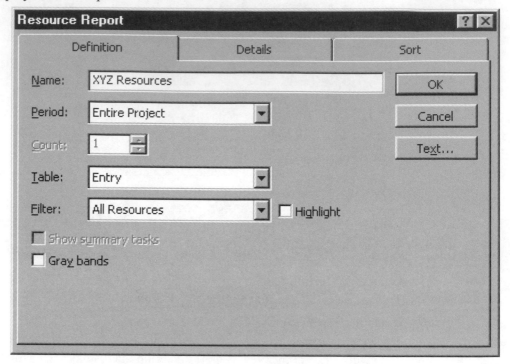

Figure 9.22: Resource Report Dialog Box

9. Click **OK** to confirm your specifications.

After the Resource Report dialog box is closed, the Custom Reports dialog box is displayed.

10. Click the **Preview** button to view the report.

The report is shown in Figure 9.23. To be able to view the report, you configure a printer to the computer that has Microsoft Project.

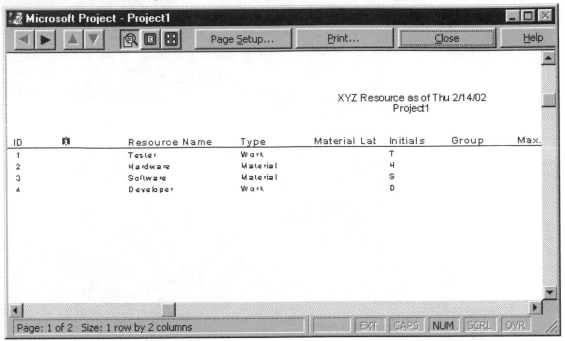

Figure 9.23: Report on the Resources Listed in the Project1.mpp File

Similarly, you can also view a report on tasks. To view the report on tasks, repeat the procedure for creating a report on resources in the Gantt chart view of Microsoft Project.

Modifying and Printing a Standard Report

You might need to modify a report to display more information or to display the existing information in a different format. To modify the ways in which a task is displayed, you use the Task report dialog box.

You can modify an existing standard task or a resource report by clicking the Edit button on the Custom Reports dialog box. This displays the relevant reports dialog box.

For example, to modify an existing report to display only summary tasks and add gridlines to each task for the XYZ Inc. project, perform the following steps:

1. Click the **Definition** tab in the Task Report dialog box.

The Task Report dialog box is displayed in Figure 9.24.

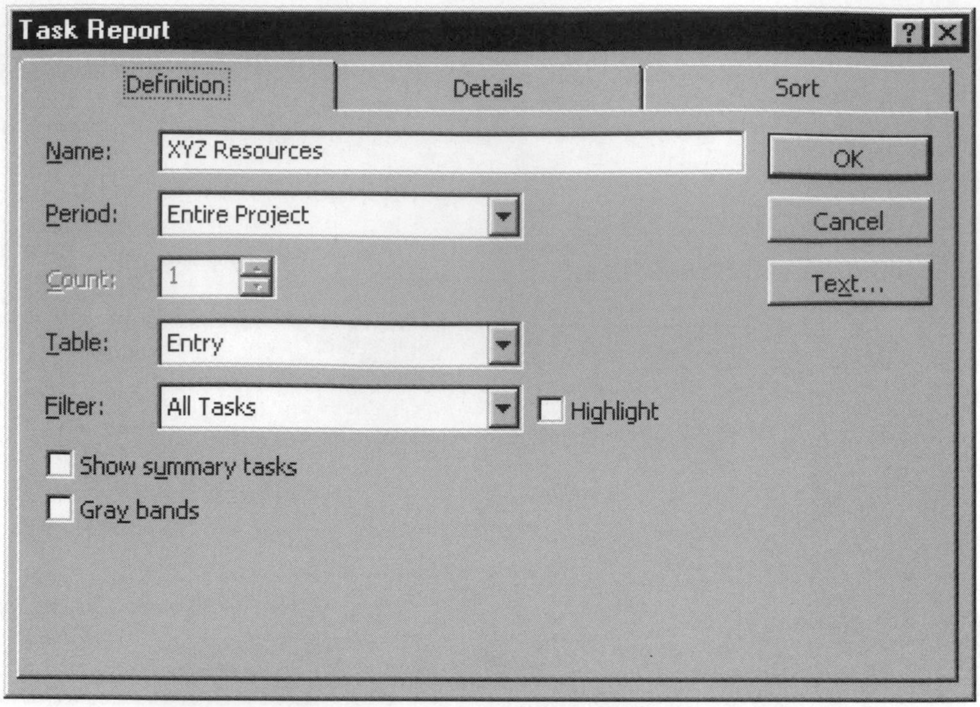

Figure 9.24: Modifying Reports

2. Click the **Show summary tasks** check box.

   This check box is used to display only the summary tasks in a project. For example, in the current project file, selecting this check box would display only the broad-level tasks, Analysis, Design, Development, Testing, and Implementation and not the subtasks below each one of them.

3. Click the **Details** tab.

4. On the **Details** page, select the **Gridlines between details** check box.

The Gridlines between details check box is shown selected in Figure 9.25.

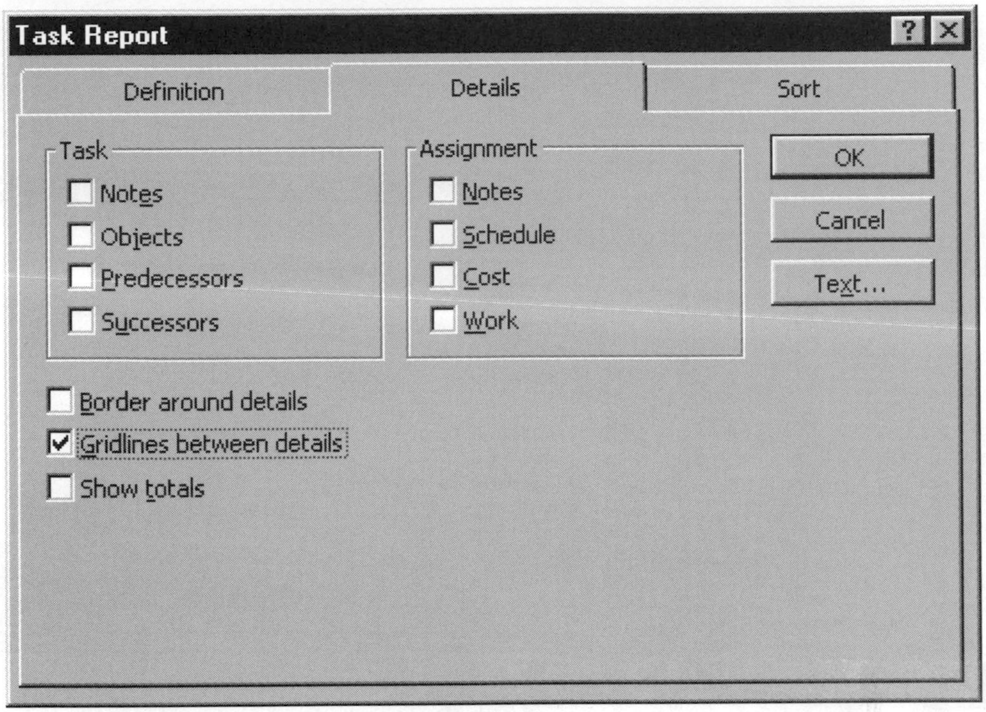

Task Report dialog box with **Definition**, **Details**, and **Sort** tabs. The **Details** tab is active, showing:

- **Task** group: Notes, Objects, Predecessors, Successors (all unchecked)
- **Assignment** group: Notes, Schedule, Cost, Work (all unchecked)
- Border around details (unchecked)
- ☑ Gridlines between details (checked)
- Show totals (unchecked)
- Buttons: OK, Cancel, Text...

Figure 9.25: Selecting Gridlines between details Check Box

5. Click **OK** to close the Task Report dialog box.

In Task Report dialog box, you can display specific fields in the Definition tab. In addition, you can also use the Details tab to display a summary of tasks in gridlines and resources.

You can also sort a report on different fields displayed on a report.

Printing a Standard Report

Printing a standard report is really simple. In the Define New Report dialog box, you click the Print button to print a report.

Figure 9.26 displays the Define New Report dialog box. Clicking the Print button in the Custom Reports dialog box, displays the Print dialog box.

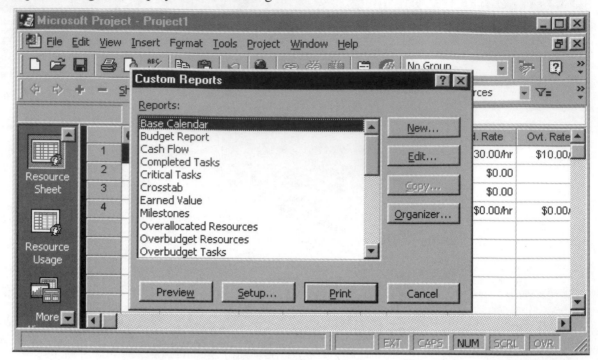

Figure 9.26: Printing a Report

Finally, you can see the Sample-Project.mpp file that you are creating for XYZ Inc. complete with all the components that you have added.

Conclusion

Microsoft Project is a useful software application that helps you create and monitor your project plans and schedules. It helps you create tasks, assign resources to tasks, and calculate the cost that would be incurred on completing each task. Apart from this, it provides features to modify the project plan and reschedule the start and end dates of the project. In addition, you can create and print reports to present the status of your project in meetings.

SUMMARY

✓ You can create general, milestone, and recurring types of tasks by using the Project menu.

✓ Microsoft project enables you to add deadlines, constraints, and relationships between tasks by using the Tools menu.

✓ Constraints are limitations that are set on tasks. When you set constraints on a task, Microsoft Project restricts the use of resources and duration specified for that task. Setting constraints on tasks is important because constraints affect the allocation of resources and the start and finish dates of subsequent tasks.

✓ You can set the following constraints on a task in the Task Information dialog box.
- ASAP
- ALAP
- SNLT
- FNLT
- SNET
- FNET
- MSO
- MFO

✓ Setting relationships between tasks is necessary because it helps adjust the start and end dates of dependent and nondependent tasks.

✓ You can also split tasks that need to be interrupted for some time due to lack of or diversion of resources to comparatively more critical tasks.

✓ You can also add costs to resources in a project. In addition, you can also assign costs to the tasks in the resource pool that you have created in the Resource Sheet view.

✓ You can track a project by using one of the following:
- Using baselines
- Using progress lines

✓ You can update the actual work done or even modify the remaining work to be done based on decisions made by the management. To update the status of a task, you can use the View menu.

✓ You can use the Tools menu to reschedule an incomplete task.

✓ As part of project tracking, you can also modify the start and end dates of a project. You can do this by using the Tools menu.

✓ Microsoft Project also enables you to present information related to a project in the form of custom reports.

✓ You can create two types of reports, reports of tasks and resources.

✓ The View menu allows you to create, modify, and print reports by specifying precise details about a report.

LAB EXERCISES

1. The list below depicts various tasks in the testing phase of an SDLC. Create these tasks in the sequence they are presented using the Project menu.

    a. Conduct testing orientation training for developers and testers.

    b. Create a test plan.

    c. Conduct meetings with developers and testers.

    d. Validate test cases.

    e. Perform functional testing.

    f. Perform integration testing.

    g. Testing complete.

2. After creating the tasks, enter the start and finish dates of the following tasks as in the table.

Task Name	Start Date	Finish Date
Conduct testing orientation training for developers and testers.	March 8	March 9
Create a test plan.	March 10	March 11
Conduct meetings with developers and testers.	March 15	March 15
Validate test cases.	March 16	March 19
Perform functional testing.	March 20	April 10
Perform integration testing.	April 11	April 21
Testing complete	April 22	April 22

3. Mark the Testing complete task as a milestone task.

4. Mark Conduct meetings with developers and testers as a recurring task. The recurring task should occur every Friday of a month until June 15. Set the duration of the recurring task as one day.

5. Perform functional testing can only begin after Validate test cases task is complete. Establish an appropriate relationship between the two tasks.

6. Add the following resources in the Resource Sheet view.

    a. Laptop

    b. Jim Lewis

    c. Susan Ward

7. In the Gantt chart view, assign the following resources to the tasks.

Task Name	Work/Material Resources
Conduct testing orientation training for developers and testers.	Laptop
Perform functional testing.	Jim Lewis
Perform integration testing.	Susan Ward

8. The percentage of work complete on the *Conduct testing orientation training for developers and testers* task is 70 percent. However, only 35 percent of work is completed on the *Create a test plan* task. Update the status of the work completed on the two tasks in the Task Information dialog box.

9. Subsequently, view the progress of the project by using progress lines. You need to enable progress lines for the project on every fifth working day.

10. The task *Perform integration testing* needs to be halted in between due to lack of resources. Reschedule to complete this task on April 15.

11. Accordingly update the finish date of the *Perform integration testing* task because the total duration of this task is of 10 days.

12. Create a project report named *Project Resources* displaying the resources that have been used during the course of the project.

Chapter 10

Software Project Management Metrics

Objectives:

- ☐ Define the need for metrics in software project management.

- ☐ Identify the characteristics of a metric.

- ☐ Sequence the steps to create a metric.

- ☐ List the commonly used types of software metrics.

- ☐ Use design metrics to measure the complexity of a software project.

- ☐ Use various project metrics to execute a project.

- ☐ Use product metrics to measure the quality of deliverables in different phases.

- ☐ Use maintenance metrics to measure maintenance projects.

SOFTWARE METRICS

Tom DeMarco has said in the book, Controlling Software Projects: Management, Measurement, and Estimates, "*You can't control what you can't measure.*" The same thought can be applied to project management. To control a project effectively, it is imperative to measure the activities and processes that comprise the project. By measuring processes, you can easily evaluate and improve them and produce quality work products.

Continuous improvement in processes is an important goal of project management. Continuous improvement is required to evolve best practices that accelerate the speed of development while keeping a strong focus on meeting project schedules and quality targets. To understand processes, you need to quantify and measure the entities that comprise a process. Software entities such as delays, effort, personnel skills, and quality are abstract entities. However, they still need to be defined and quantified to ensure better project management.

In this chapter, you will learn about metrics that can be used to measure the efficiency of the processes that are followed in software projects. This chapter details the metrics of design, project, product, and maintenance so that you can use them effectively in the various phases of the SDLC. Using these metrics, you can implement measures to keep the project on track. Finally, this chapter will also help you to identify the qualities of ideal metrics and create them for an organization.

What is a Metric

A metric enables you to measure the quality of a factor. For example, to measure the quality of a product deliverable, such as a prototype, the metric could be the number of defects reported for the prototype.

You can measure and quantify a factor only if the factor has numeric values. The numeric value assigned to a qualitative factor can be analyzed and compared to similar values for other factors. The analysis of metrics enables you to make important decisions related to project management. For example, while measuring the quality of a prototype, the data for defects recorded for the prototype enables you to identify the causes of the defects. After categorizing the defects into different types, you can devise solutions to deliver a quality prototype in the future.

After the defects are identified, you can assign a severity level to each defect. Severity of defects are classified as follows:

- Severe
- Major
- Minor

Severe defects critically affect the functionality of a product. For example, when a user clicks the Display button in a report dialog box, the client computer is disconnected from the server. Major defects logically affect the functionality of a product. For example, there is no provision for a user to quit an application by using a button on the main menu screen. A minor defect is a slight defect that may act as an irritant for users but does not disturb the functionality of the application. An example of a minor defect is a spelling mistake on a user interface.

Prototype1	Categorization of Defects			
	Severe	Major	Minor	Total
Planned less than equal to	0	5	20	25
Actual	3	9	25	37

Table 10.1: An Example of a Metric

Table 10.1 displays a table of defects in a prototype. The number of defects that were estimated and those that were actually reported by the client are listed in the table. The estimated number of defects is derived from the past experience of the organization. After categorizing the defects, it is evident that the actual number of defects reported for all categories was much more than the permissible number. For example, no severe category of defects per KLOC was permissible for the product. However, Prototype1 had three defects categorized as severe.

The increase in the number of defects is a cause of concern for the management. The management needs to take appropriate remedial actions to ensure that in future projects, the actual number of defects does not exceed the permissible number.

Therefore, from the preceding example, the explanation of a metric can be elucidated. A metric quantifies a qualitative factor. In the example, the qualitative factor is the quality of the prototype. As a result, a metric that measures the quality of a product is named a quality or defects metric. The quantification of a qualitative factor defines the need for a metric. The need for a metric is to record, measure, and monitor the changes in a qualitative factor. Referring to the same example, the quality of the prototype is measured in terms of the number of defects that are captured and analyzed for it. After you analyze the changes in a metric, you can decide whether that particular factor requires improvement or not. Improvement in that factor would also impact the overall management of the project. After referring to the example, you can decide that the quality metric certainly requires improvement. Improvement can be by reducing the number of all types of defects. In addition, the organization that created the prototype needs to strengthen its defects prevention mechanism and monitor it regularly.

Characteristics of a Metric

A metric must have certain characteristics so that it is effective. These include:

- Goal-oriented approach
- Measurable
- Analyzable
- Programming language-independent
- Timely

Goal-oriented approach

A metric should be goal-oriented. For example, the goal of a metric can be to reduce the expenses incurred in different phases of a software project or to reduce the time spent on it. The goal of the metric is used to define a baseline value. A baseline value is a specification that is formally reviewed and agreed upon. It serves as the basis for further development. Baseline can be changed only through formal change control procedures. During the development cycle of a project, the actual data of a particular metric is compared with the baseline data to compute deviations. The magnitude of deviation enables the management to track and control costs, effort in terms of the time spent, productivity, or improve the quality of the product.

Measurable

Apart from being goal-oriented, a metric should be measurable. Measurability denotes that a metric can be used to measure a software entity to a high degree of accuracy, if not completely accurately. Measurability of a metric ensures consistent results for all processes in a project. For example, it might be a good idea to measure the productivity of employees in a project, but the same may not be applicable when measuring the reusability of a piece of code. Measurement of code reusability is not a good metric because each programmer has an individual style to approach and solve a problem. Therefore, the metric to measure code reusability is not advisable because it does not yield objective results consistently.

Analyzable

Another important characteristic of a metric is that it should be suitable for analysis. If a metric is not suitable for analysis, it is futile to monitor it for improvement in a project. For example, an organization uses a metric to measure client satisfaction. Over the years, the organization has experienced changes in client preferences and technological advancement in hardware and software. As a result of these changes, it is necessary that the organization test and analyze the metric again. The metric can be modified based on the result of the analysis.

Programming-language independent

A metric should also be independent of the programming language used for software development. Metrics that change with a change in the programming language cannot provide reliable results. For example, a software project is divided into three main modules. The interface module is coded in Visual Basic (VB) 6.0. The event functions and procedures are written in PowerBuilder, and the programming for the database is done in Oracle. In such a case where many languages are being used, the metrics that can measure the size, complexity, or the effort spent in coding in all three languages differ. Due to the discrepancy, the organization will be unable to obtain accurate results to track a project or plan it further. In addition, the use of such metrics may cause confusion to project managers and developing teams.

Timely

Finally, a good metric is timely. This means that the data to produce results using the metric should always be available when it is needed.

Steps to Create a Metric

A process group engineer, a system analyst, or a project manager is primarily responsible for designing metrics. Broadly, there are four steps to create a metric.

- Define the goal of the metric
- Identify the requirements of the metric
- Identify the organizational baseline value for the metric
- Review the metric for its usability

The first step in creating a metric is to define its goal. The definition of a goal is important because it allows the metric to be designed based on the goal. The goal should be as clear, measurable, and as explicit as possible. For example, a metric can have a goal to measure the number of defects reported by clients. The Figure 10.1 depicts the first step to create a metric.

Define the goal of a metric.

Figure 10.1: First Step to Create a Metric

After defining the goal of the metric, the next step is to identify its requirements. The requirements include human resource, data collection techniques, and methodologies used to process the data. For example, the requirements of a metric that measures the number of defects reported by clients include the availability of quality assurance professionals and past data to specify severity criteria.

Figure 10.2 represents the first two steps in creating a metric.

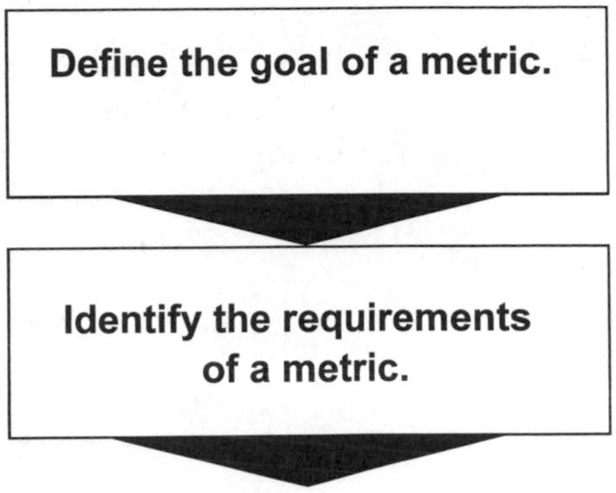

Define the goal of a metric.

Identify the requirements of a metric.

Figure 10.2: First and Second Steps to Create a Metric

The third step in metric creation is the identification of an organizational baseline value for the proposed metric. A baseline value is an average value that an organization may have identified based on prior experience. A metric is designed so as to achieve the baseline value. For example, an organization decides not to have more than 20 severe defects in the acceptance-testing phase. However, a client detects 42 defects during the acceptance-testing phase. In this example, the value 20 is called the baseline value. To measure the worth of a software project, the baseline value is compared with the actual value. If the actual value is greater than the baseline value, the management needs to discuss ways to reduce the number of defects for similar projects in the future. In contrast, if the number of defects is less than 20, the management can explore the reasons for defects fewer than the baseline value. The first three steps are depicted in Figure 10.3.

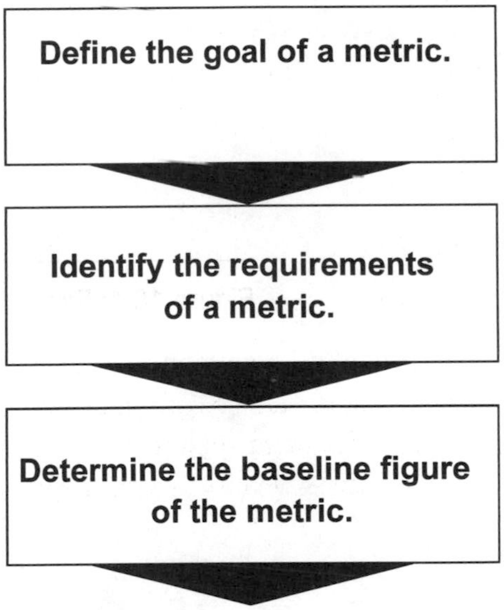

Define the goal of a metric.

Identify the requirements of a metric.

Determine the baseline figure of the metric.

Figure 10.3: First, Second, and Third Steps to Create a Metric

Finally, review the metric for its usability. Process experts can be asked to test and provide feedback on the metric. The feedback can be used to enhance the functionality and the user-friendliness of the metric.

The final step to create a metric is depicted along with the previous steps in Figure 10.4.

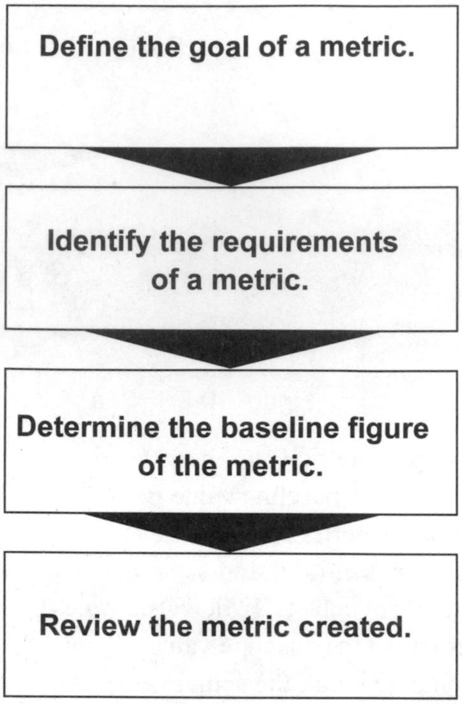

Define the goal of a metric.

Identify the requirements of a metric.

Determine the baseline figure of the metric.

Review the metric created.

Figure 10.4: Complete Steps to Create a Metric

TYPES OF SOFTWARE METRICS

Four types of metrics are usually used in an organization. All these metrics operate with a single objective to improve the quality of processes and products in an organization. The types of metrics commonly used by organizations include:

■ Design metrics. These are used to record design issues, which correspond to the requirements document. Design metrics enable you to decide how much you have deviated from the requirements of the project. Lesser the deviation, fewer the number of defects. Design issues need to be addressed as soon as they are recorded so that the same are not repeated in the later phases of the SDLC.

■ Project metrics. Project metrics is a set of metrics related to all SDLC phases. Project metrics measure the effectiveness of the processes followed in each phase.

■ Product metrics. These metrics are used to measure the quality of deliverables produced in a software project life cycle.

■ Maintenance metrics. These measure the progress of a maintenance project.

Design Metrics

During the design phase it is possible to measure the characteristics of a software program. Complexity is a characteristic measured during this phase. Complexity can be measured for the structure, data components, and the interface design of a software program. Complexity can affect the size, testability, and effort spent on developing and testing the modules of a project. The measure of the complexity of a software design is called a design metric. Design metrics are seldom used in organizations because organizations find it time-consuming to analyze their results. Moreover, design metrics are difficult to implement.

There can be many varieties of design metrics. One variety is architecture design metrics.

Architecture Design Metrics

An architecture design metric measures the complexities of a software program by referring to the design of the program. All software projects are developed from a blue print. The blue print or the architecture design of the software is crucial for predicting the features and functionality of the final product.

An architecture design metric addresses three types of complexities of a software program. As a result, there are three types of architecture design metrics. These are listed below:

- Structural complexity

- Data complexity

- System complexity

The number of fan-out modules in a software program defines the structural complexity metric. A fan-out module refers to a module invoked by a module parent to it. For example, a module, Chk-name, invokes a module to check for a user name that exists on a database. Chk-name also invokes another module that checks for a string of not more than 12 characters. In addition, a module checks for invalid numeric and alphanumeric strings. Therefore, the module Chk-name invokes three modules as represented in Figure 10.5. This indicates that the fan-out value is three. Multiple fan-out modules increase the complexity and the speed of execution of a software program. This can affect the testability requirements of the modules as well.

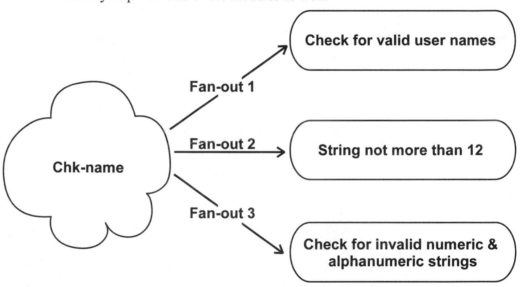

Figure 10.5: Fan-out of a Module

The data complexity metric measures the complexity of the internal interface of a software program. An internal interface is defined by its input and output variables. For example, a module, chk-dt validates a date entered by a user in the mm/dd/yy format. For this, an input variable accepts a date value. An incorrect date value is replaced by a corrected date value in an output variable. Existence of such variables increases the complexity of a software program.

You obtain the system complexity metric by combining the values of structural complexity and data complexity. As you have seen, system complexity provides a complete view of the complexity in a software program. After determining the complexity of a program by manually counting the fan-out and data variables in the module of a software program, you can plan the effort required to develop and test the software. For example, there are three main modules in a project. Module 1 invokes modules 2 and 3. Module 3 contains maximum number of variables. In such a situation, you can plan for more resources and time to test and develop module 1 first. Subsequently, module 3 can be developed and tested. Module 2 that neither invokes any other module nor is relatively complex can be planned for later development and testing.

Project Metrics

Project metrics are specific to the actual execution of a project. They enable you to execute a project with a systematic and technical approach. Project metrics can help you avoid project delays. You can also use them to avoid and mitigate project risks. Project metrics are also used to assess the quality of a finished product on a periodic basis. Examples of project metrics are the metrics that measure the size, complexity, or the time and effort spent on a project.

Five important project metrics are commonly used in an organization. The following metrics are applied in the different phases of the SDLC.

- Effort
- Productivity in FP
- Cost
- Size
- Defects
- Testing

Effort Metric

The effort metric enables you to determine the amount of effort required to complete a project. Effort is generally estimated close to accuracy in all the phases of the SDLC. To define an effort metric, you create a metric like the one shown in Table 10.2. The table depicts effort in man-months. A man-month is the amount of effort required to complete work in a month.

Metric(s)		Analysis	Design	Construction	Testing	Total
Effort	Planned effort (man-months)	5	12	25	10	52
	Actual effort (man-months)	8	14	35	8	65
	Percentage of increase in effort	60	16.5	40	-20	20

Table 10.2: An Effort Metric

The planned value for effort is known as the baseline value because it serves as the nodal point for comparing the planned and the achieved values. You can calculate the actual effort in man-months by using the actual effort data from the daily effort-tracking database. For example, in Table 10.2, the planned effort to complete the analysis phase is 5 man-months. However, the actual effort spent on analysis is 8 man-months. On the other hand, the planned effort to complete the testing phase is 10 man-months whereas actually it takes 8 man-months to complete testing. The difference between planned and actual effort is expressed in percentage. This difference is termed as the increase in effort. For example, the difference between planned and actual effort during the analysis phase is 60 percent. This increase in effort is a cause of concern for the management. The management should strive to gradually reduce it. On the contrary, the testing phase displays negative percentage increase in effort. The management needs to investigate what was done differently in the testing phase so that the effort was curtailed.

Many international organizations also calculate the effort for onsite and offshore development activities to calculate the total effort on development.

Productivity Metric

Another project metric is the productivity metric. In a software project, you measure human effort according to the number of hours spent on an FP of work. The effort in performing an FP of work in an hour is called *productivity*. To calculate productivity, you first determine the total amount of FP for the software project. Then, distribute the total FP among the phases in the SDLC.

To calculate accurate productivity for a particular phase, you need two types of data:

■ Actual effort expressed in person hours

■ Actual size of the project in FP

Just like you did for the effort metric, you can retrieve the actual effort data from the daily effort-tracking database to calculate productivity. On the other hand, the actual size of a project in FP is retrieved from the project plan. The project plan contains the estimated size of the project, which is finalized during the analysis phase.

To understand how a productivity metric is calculated, consider Table 10.3. The table displays the planned effort versus actual effort for a software project. The effort data is expressed in terms of hours per FP. Assume the actual software size is 100 FP. To complete 100 FP of work in the project, the estimated productivity required is 8 hours per FP. Note, that this value is a total of the productivity required for all the phases. However, the actual productivity reflected in the table is 7.9 hours per FP. This indicates that the productivity is lower than planned. The productivity metric in Table 10.3 makes it clear that productivity was lower in the initial phases of development as compared to the later ones. In this situation, the management needs to figure out the cause of low productivity in the initial phases. They may even want to find out what was done differently in the later phases to improve productivity.

Metric	Analysis	Design	Construction	Testing	Total
Productivity in hours/FP					
Planned	1.2	1.6	2.8	2.4	8.0
Actual	1.0	1.4	3.0	2.5	7.9
Difference (+/-)	0.2	0.2	-0.2	-0.1	0.1

Table 10.3: A Productivity Metric

Cost Metric

Cost is yet another project metric that enables you to manage a project efficiently. A cost metric measures the planned versus actual expense incurred on a project. An important component of the cost metric is the cost of resources. This includes the human resource and material resources required for a project. Incidentally, cost is the most difficult metric to control. This metric usually runs out of control during a project. Cost overrun can be attributed to a rise in the price of the required resources, change, or shift in project objectives, or increase in the requirement of resources.

Table 10.4 displays a sample cost metric. In the table, the cost metric includes the cost of travel and communication for project-related purposes. You can calculate the expenses incurred during every phase and record them as shown in Table 10.4. This enables you to control and reduce costs in different phases.

Metric		Analysis	Design	Construction	Testing	Total
Cost in US dollars ($)						
Resources	Planned	40,000	100,000	200,000	100,000	440,000
	Actual	55,000	130,000	300,000	250,000	735,000
Communication	Planned	10000	7000	1000	1000	19000
	Actual	20000	4500	700	500	25,700
	Total planned	50,000	107,000	201,000	101,000	459,000
	Total actual	105,000	134,500	300,700	250,500	790,700
	Total Deviation in percentage (actual-planned/planned*100))	110	25	50	148	72

Table 10.4: A Cost Metric

You can also use the cost metric to measure the deviation in the total planned expenditure when compared with the actual expenses incurred during a project. For example, the data in the table reveals that there is an increase in communication costs over the plan in the analysis phase. During the subsequent phases, the cost deviations related to communication with the client reduce.

The deviation in costs enables you to calculate the amount of additional investment that needs to be provided for the project. Determining the estimated cost at project initiation helps map the budget with the resource allocation required for a project.

Size Metric

Another important project metric is the size metric, which is calculated for an entire project and not for any particular phase of a project. The size of a project may vary with respect to the changes required by the client. You may record data related to the size of a project in a table format as displayed in Table 10.5.

The size metric directly affects the effort, testing, and productivity metrics of a project.

Metric		Total
Size in FP		
	Size Planned	100
	Size Actual	120
	Change in size	+20
	Growth of size in %	16

Table 10.5: A Size Metric

There are two main components of the size metric.

- Change in the required effort due to change in project size

- Percentage growth in project size

A change in the effort simply measures the effort in terms of FP for every change requested by the client and accepted by the development team. The same data can also be presented as percentage. The growth of size in percentage metric reflects the change in the size of a project compared to its original or planned size. This is an important metric because frequent changes in the size of a project may involve additional effort and resources, which have to be deployed by the management. Frequent changes in the size of a project also mean that the design specifications are not clearly defined at the start of the project. By using the size metric, you can avoid the design pitfalls observed in one project in future projects.

Defects Metric

Defects are errors that occur in a work product. The number of defects defines the quality of a project. If the number of defects is large, the quality of the product is inferior. In contrast, if the number of defects is small, the quality of the product is superior.

Defects can occur during any phase of the SDLC. There can be defects related to the analysis of project requirements, design, or coding of software. Defects not detected in a particular phase continue to be present during the subsequent phases in the SDLC. To facilitate calculation and categorization of defects, many organizations use automated tools and techniques. These tools and techniques also help you in defining the severity of defects.

You can use the displayed Table 10.6 to record and track the number of defects reported per KLOC in every phase.

Metric		Analysis	Design	Construction	Testing	Total
Defects per KLOC						
Severe	Planned (less than equal to)	0	0	0	0	0
	Actual	5	3	15	8	31
Major	Planned (less than equal to)	5	2	5	10	22
	Actual	3	6	12	18	39
Minor	Planned (less than equal to)	20	15	15	20	70
	Actual	12	10	12	25	59

Table 10.6: A Defects Metric

Table 10.6 depicts the defects in various categories in every phase of the SDLC. It is evident from the table that the management had expected no defects in the severe category in all phases. However, there is a considerable increase in severe defects in all phases.

Similarly, less than equal to 10 major defects per KLOC were estimated during the testing phase but 18 major defects were reported in this phase. In the same phase, 25 minor defects per KLOC were also reported as compared to the expected value of 20 minor defects. The management needs to study the causes for an increase in the number of defects in all phases.

Testing Metric

The testing metric is used to measure the number of test cases required to test software. Test case is a specification that needs to be executed to test a particular module in a software program. There are separate test cases for integration testing and unit testing. Integration testing refers to the overall black box testing of the entire software project. In contrast, unit testing refers to testing individual modules of a software project.

You can use the format displayed in Table 10.7 to record the number of test cases required for every phase.

Metric(s)		Construction
Testing	Test cases per FP	
	Planned	5
	Actual	4

Table 10.7: A Testing Metric

The size of a phase determines the number of test cases. Test cases enable rigorous testing of every module of the entire software. From Table 10.7, it can be observed that during the construction phase, the number of test cases per FP were less than planned. This is a cause of concern for the management. The management and the QA department should find out the reasons for such discrepancy. If the number of test cases is less than planned, it implies that software is not tested rigorously. It may also imply that software is not tested according to the software specifications developed in the analysis phase. If a software product is expected to be complex and extensive, it is advisable to develop more test cases per FP.

Product Metrics

Analysis done using the product metrics can provide you an insight into the quality of work done by the development teams. Product metrics trace and measure the quality of a deliverable in different phases. For example, a source code is the output deliverable of the construction phase. A set of metrics measures the quality and timeliness of the deliverable. To measure the metric of source code, you can use the format displayed in Table 10.8.

Deliverable name		Effectiveness (%)	Conformance to requirements (%)
Source code	Planned	100	100
	Actual	72	90

Table 10.8: Format of a Product Metric

In Table 10.8, two factors that are measured:

■ Effectiveness

■ Conformance to requirements

Effectiveness of a deliverable is measured in terms of the quantity of the deliverable completed and the number of quality goals achieved. You can use the following formula to calculate effectiveness of a deliverable:

```
Effectiveness = Quantity in % * Quality in % / 100
```

For example, 80 percent of source code is completed and 90 percent of the quality goals are achieved in developing that source code. Therefore, after substituting the values in the effectiveness formula, you can calculate effectiveness as follows:

Effectiveness = 80 * 90 / 100

Effectiveness = 72

It is also clear from the table that the source code conformed to most of the requirements mentioned in the requirements document. To calculate the conformance to requirements, you count the number of requirement in the requirements document sent by the client. Next, you count the number of requirements that are actually completed. Finally, the difference between the two values is calculated and expressed in terms of percentage. The value indicates the extent of deviation between the planned and actual conformance to requirements.

Maintenance Metrics

Maintenance metrics are used for maintenance projects. Maintenance projects require enhancements based on client feedback or changes in the market, technology, and user preferences. The client fills up a change request form in which the changes and the types of changes required are mentioned. Table 10.9 displays a sample change request form.

Project Name:	
Name:	Date:
Functional description of the change desired	
Type of Change (Tick the appropriate one)	Change Trigger Component (Tick the appropriate one (s))
Correction	Requirements specification
Enhancement	Design
Adaptation	Code
Re-engineering	Other
Total effort required to perform change	
Responsibility of performing change	

Table 10.9: A Sample Change Request Form

There are two types of measurements performed for maintenance projects. These are:

▓ Extent of change required

▓ Type of maintenance requested by the client

The first type of measurement is to gauge the extent of change required. To do this, you count the total number of modules in the software application launched. You also keep track of all the modifications done in any module of the application. In addition, the modules added and deleted from the previous version of the application are also tracked. You can use the format displayed in Table 10.10 to track these details.

No. of modules remaining unmodified	No. of modules added to a released software program	No. of modules modified in a released software program	No. of modules deleted from a released software program
6	3	10	2
Total=21			

Table 10.10: A Module Track Metric

The second type of measurement performed for maintenance projects is in terms of the type of maintenance requested by the client. There are two metrics used to measure maintenance activities in an organization.

■ Corrective

■ Upgrades

Corrective maintenance addresses the software-related defects reported by the client. The defects can be either related to the functionality of software or violation of requirements specifications. An organization should strive to keep this maintenance under control because it clearly indicates basic design defects in the design structure of software.

The other type of metric used for maintenance in an organization is upgrades. These include enhancements on software to incorporate additional functionality. In addition, upgrades include adapting software to the changing technology and making preventive changes to the software to eliminate anticipated problems.

Type of Maintenance	Planned in %	Actual in %
Corrective	17	70
Upgrades	83	30

Table 10.11: A Maintenance Metric

Table 10.11 displays the corrective and upgrades maintenance metrics in an organization. Note that the percentage of corrective defects that the organization initially planned is much lower than what it actually addressed. In contrast, upgrades that were actually addressed formed a much lower percentage of what was actually planned. This indicates that the organization is spending effort in addressing basic design defects as compared to enhancements. This may also imply that unit and functional testing of software was ineffective.

You can use the data collected for a maintenance metric to calculate the software maturity index (SMI). This indicates the stability and reliability of a software product. If the value of SMI is less than 1, the software product is not very stable and needs transformations for improvement. When the SMI value reaches 1, the software product is said to be stable. A stable software product is unlikely to change frequently in response to user and market preferences. However, the software can always be open to technological breakthroughs and enhancements.

SUMMARY

✓ Metrics assign values to quantitative factors.

✓ Metrics facilitate project planning, scheduling, and improving the SDLC process and product quality. There are four main types of metrics used widely during the SDLC of a project. These are:

- Design metrics
- Project metrics
- Product metrics
- Maintenance metrics

✓ Design metrics help in measuring the design and architecture of a software project.

✓ Project metrics is a set of the following metrics:

- Effort
- Productivity
- Cost
- Defects
- Size

✓ Project metrics measure the effectiveness of the important factors for a project. They are implemented in every phase of the SDLC.

✓ Product metrics measure the quality and conformance to the requirements of the deliverables of a phase. They also measure the timeliness in the delivery of project deliverables.

✓ Maintenance metrics are a set of metrics similar to the metrics for a development project. They are used to measure the cost, effort, productivity, and defects associated with a maintenance project.

✓ You use maintenance metrics to track the number of required changes implemented in a maintenance project.

HOMEWORK EXERCISES

1. Create a metric table of corrective measures and enhancements in a software project. The percentage of corrective measures is planned to be 20 and the percentage of enhancements is 80. However, the organization actually recorded 12 percent of corrective measures and 88 percent of enhancements. Based on the preceding values, analyze the table you create and comment on the following.

    a. The design structure of the project
    b. The testing activity performed for the software
    c. The technical capability of the development team

LAB EXERCISES

1. An organization needs to develop five test cases per FP. The size of the project is estimated to be 200 FP. However, 300 test cases were developed for the entire project. Suggest action points that you would undertake to address any concern that you foresee.

2. You need to design a metric that tracks system-related problems recorded in a year. The organization has estimated for less than or equal to 15 system-related problems in a year. After creating the metric table, what mechanism you would use to collect data on system-related problems?

3. The number of system-related problems recorded is 27. Comparing this information with the preceding information, answer the following questions.

   a. What do you infer from the system-related metric?

   b. Discuss the reasons that could have caused an imbalance between the planned and actual system-related problems reported?

   c. Discuss some corrective measures that you would take to prevent such system-related problems?

Chapter 11

Managing a Project: Quality Assurance and Configuration Management

---

Objectives:

- ☐ State the need for software quality assurance.

- ☐ Select the factors that determine the quality of a software product.

- ☐ Identify the role of standards and procedures in maintaining software quality.

- ☐ List the various software quality assurance activities.

- ☐ Describe the software review techniques.

- ☐ Describe the software testing techniques.

- ☐ Create a software quality assurance plan.

- ☐ State the need for software configuration.

- ☐ List the software configuration management activities.

- ☐ Distinguish between baseline and interim versions.

SOFTWARE QUALITY ASSURANCE

Suppose you are flying, and there is an announcement: "We are trying out our new aircraft control systems, hope you enjoy your flight." How would you react? Your heartbeat would definitely increase at the thought of being a guinea pig for this new system. You would wish the system was tested and tried before being run. In such a situation, the successful functioning of the system becomes critical. Similarly, with the growing application of information technology in major industries, the successful functioning of software products has become critical. The success of a software product depends on its ability to satisfy client needs consistently. In the current scenario of competition, it is the quality of the product that distinguishes a good product from a great one.

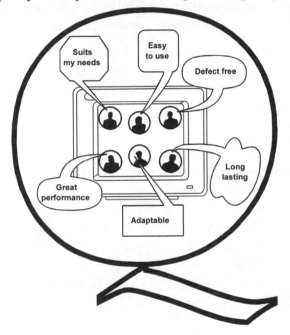

Figure 11.1: Quality

In this chapter, you will learn about the following:

- Software quality concepts

- Quality standards and procedures

- Software quality assurance (SQA) activities

- Software configuration management (SCM)

In short, this chapter will help you answer the all-important question "How to manage quality?"

Software Quality Concepts

According to American Heritage Dictionary, quality is defined as "an inherent or distinguishing characteristic or a property". The distinguishing characteristics of a software product are the *cyclomatic complexity*, *cohesion*, function points, and lines of code. These characteristics of a software product define the quality of the product. Product quality depends on its conformance to software requirements, development standards, and implicit requirements.

During software development, the quality of a product depends on the quality of the design. The quality of product design, in turn, depends on how effectively the product designer captures the client requirements and specifications. At times, the client has some implicit requirements that are not captured in the requirements document. There are three things that guide requirements: want, desire, and wish. Usually, wants are captured explicitly in the requirements documents. However, if you manage to capture desires and wishes, the product becomes a great success. The product designer needs to state these implicit requirements clearly during analysis. The adherence to these implicit requirements is the key attribute that sets one product apart from another.

The product quality also depends on how strictly and to what degree the developer adheres to design specifications. This is what the concept 'quality is meeting or exceeding our client's needs and requirements' means. The product quality is said to be high if the product is manufactured according to design specifications.

Quality Cost

The cost of quality is nonconformance to product requirements. In other words, quality translates to cost. Quality needs to be measured so that the management is aware of the cost incurred in maintaining quality. By measuring quality, the project manager can prioritize the problems and decide the corrective action to be taken. Quality measurement also indicates the efforts required in maintaining quality. More importantly, by measuring quality you can calculate the cost incurred due to nonconformance. This is called PONC. If you recall the tragic crash of space shuttle Challenger in 1986, you realize the importance of conformance to quality standards. A small mechanical snag during take-off resulted in a crash. Here, the loss of life and the failure of mission were the PONC incurred by the project. In short, PONC is the cost of waste. When you improve quality, you reduce PONC and increase your overall earnings.

Quality Control

Quality control is a series of review activities, such as inspections, reviews, and tests, used throughout the SDLC of the software product. The objective of quality control is to find problems as early as possible and fix them. Quality control ensures that the software product meets the requirements defined at every stage in its development. There is provision for feedback mechanism during quality control. Any slippage in meeting the requirements during the development process is communicated to the development team immediately. Feedback ensures that errors or misses found during quality control are rectified as soon as they are detected. During software development, quality control plays a valuable role by evaluating products against standards and specifications. Quality control activities can be fully automated, manual, or a combination of these.

Quality Factors

There are a number of factors that determine the quality of a software product. These factors can be measured either directly or indirectly. McCall (MCC77) and his colleagues proposed some software quality factors based on three most important aspects of a software product: product operation, product revision, and product transition.

Product Operation Factors

The product operation factors determine the quality of software when a program is executed. Good quality software is not only correct and reliable but also delivers correct performance in all circumstances. Some of the factors of product operation are correctness, reliability, efficiency, integrity, and usability. You can look at the factor description in Table 11.1.

Correctness	Accuracy of the program and the extent to which it fulfills design specifications
Reliability	Extent to which the program is secure and its ability to recover quickly from failure
Efficiency	Performance of the program and its ability to perform tasks within a time frame
Integrity	Ability of the program to take care of security and the extent to which it can prevent unauthorized access
Usability	Ease with which a user can learn, operate, and use the program

Table 11.1: Product Operation Factors

Product Revision Factors

Product revision factors focus on the ease of maintenance of the software product. Maintenance tasks could be either correcting faults in the original design or making improvements to adapt the functionality to changing environments. Product revision covers the following factors: maintainability, flexibility, and testability. These factors are described in Table 11.2.

Maintainability	Ease with which a program is debugged
Flexibility	Ease with which a program is modified
Testability	Ease with which a program is tested

Table 11.2: Product Revision Factors

Product Transition Factors

The product transition factors determine the quality of programs that are designed for open systems. Here the focus is more on the portability and reusability of a software product. To help a system run on different platforms, certain parts of a system may be reused. The product transition factors are portability, reusability, interoperability, configurability, and expandability.

These factors are described in Table 11.3.

Portability	Efficiency with which a program runs on different platforms or operating systems
Reusability	Extent to which a program can be used in more than one program or system
Interoperability	Effort needed to transfer a program to another system
Configurability	Ability of the program to be installed at more than one location with different features at each location
Expandability	Ability of the program to support an increase in data and users

Table 11.3: Product Transition Factors

Quality Standards and Procedures

As discussed earlier, SQA is a systematic approach toward the evaluation of software product quality. The quality of software is said to be high if it meets the standards and procedures defined for the product. Standards are criteria to which the products are compared. For example, there may be standards that govern the quality review process. Documentation standard, design standard, and code standard are the three types of standards that software projects usually follow. Documentation standard specifies the form and content for planning, control, and product documentation. Design standards provide rules and methods for translating the software requirements into software design. The design standards are specified in the form and content of the product design. Unlike documentation standard, code standard defines the language in which code should be written. The standard clearly mentions the structures, style conventions, and rules for data structures and interfaces that will be implemented in the project.

Procedures are criteria to which the development and control processes are compared. Procedures are explicit steps followed in a process. Procedures need to be properly documented because they are needed for configuration management, nonconformance reporting, corrective action, testing, and formal inspections. Proper documentation of procedures is necessary because SQA activities rely on them for project compliance. Organizations normally enforce quality standards with the help of checklists, common error lists, and standards and guidelines.

SOFTWARE QUALITY ASSURANCE ACTIVITIES

SQA is the process of evaluating the quality of a product and enforcing adherence to software product standards and procedures. It is an umbrella activity that ensures conformance to standards and procedures throughout the SDLC of a software product. There are a large number of tasks involved in SQA activities. These include:

- Formulating a quality management plan
- Applying software engineering techniques
- Conducting formal technical reviews
- Applying a multitiered testing strategy
- Enforcing process adherence
- Controlling change
- Measuring impact of change
- Performing SQA audits
- Keeping records and reporting

Formulating a Quality Management Plan

One of the tasks of SQA is the formulation of a quality management plan. The quality management plan identifies the quality aspects of the software product to be developed. It helps in planning checkpoints for work products and the development process. It also tracks changes made to the development process based on the results of the checks. The quality management plan is tracked as a live plan throughout the SDLC.

Applying Software Engineering Techniques

Application of software engineering techniques helps the software designer to achieve high quality specifications. The designer gathers information using techniques such as interviews and FAST. Using the information gathered, the designer prepares project estimation with the help of techniques such as WBS, SLOC estimation, or FP estimation.

Conducting Formal Technical Reviews

Formal technical review (FTR) is conducted to assess the quality and design of the prototype. It is a meeting with the technical staff to discuss the quality requirements of a software product and its design quality. FTRs help in detecting errors at an early phase of development. This prevents errors from percolating down to the latter phases and resulting in rework.

Applying a Multitiered Testing Strategy

Software testing is a critical task of SQA activity, which aims at error detection. Unit testing is the first level of testing. The subsequent levels of testing are integration testing and system level testing. There are various testing strategies followed by organizations. At times, developers perform unit testing and integration testing with independent testing support. There are also occasions where testers perform functional testing and system level testing with developer support. Sometimes beta testing with selected clients is also conducted to test the product before it is finally released.

Enforcing Process Adherence

This task of SQA emphasizes the need for process adherence during product development. In addition, the development process should also adhere to procedures defined for product development. Therefore, this is a combination of two tasks, product evaluation and process monitoring.

Product Evaluation

Product evaluation ensures that the standards laid down for a project are followed. During product evaluation, the compliance of the software product to the existing standards is verified. Initially, SQA activities are conducted to monitor the standards and procedures of the project. Product evaluation ensures that the software product reflects the requirements identified in the project management plan.

Process Monitoring

Process monitoring ensures that appropriate steps to follow the product development procedures are carried out. SQA monitors processes by comparing the actual steps carried out with the steps in the documented procedures.

Product evaluation and process monitoring ensure that the development and control processes described in the project management plan are correctly carried out. These tasks ensure that the project-related procedures and standards are followed. They also ensure that products and processes conform to standards and procedures. Audits ensure that product evaluation and process monitoring are performed.

Controlling Change

This task combines human procedures and automated tools to provide a mechanism for change control. The change control mechanism ensures software quality by formalizing requests for change, evaluating the nature of change, and controlling the impact of change. Change control mechanism is implemented during the development and maintenance stages.

Measuring Impact of Change

Change is inevitable in the SDLC. However, the change needs to be measured and monitored. Changes in the product or process are measured using software quality metrics. Software quality metrics helps in estimating the cost and resource requirements of a project. To control software quality, it is essential to measure quality and then compare it with established standards. Software quality metrics are used to evaluate the effectiveness of techniques and tools, the productivity of development activities, and the quality of products. Metrics enables mangers and developers to monitor the activities and proposed changes throughout the SDLC and initiate corrective actions.

Performing SQA Audits

SQA audits scrutinize the software development process by comparing it to established processes. This ensures that proper control is maintained over the documents required during SDLC. Audits also ensure that the status of an activity performed by the developer is reflected in the status report of the developer.

Keeping Records and Reporting

Keeping records and reporting ensure the collection and circulation of information relevant to SQA. The results of reviews, audits, change control, testing, and other SQA activities are reported and compiled for future reference.

Software Review

Software review is an effective way of filtering errors in a software product. Typically, an error found after the product release costs 50 times as much to correct as one detected during the design phase. This means the cost of fixing a defect rises dramatically if it is found late in the development life cycle of the product. Therefore, you need to filter errors as early as possible. Software review is used as a filter at various points of software development. Reviews conducted at each of these phases, analysis, design, coding, and testing reveal areas of improvement in the product. Reviews also indicate those areas that do not need any improvement. You can use software reviews to achieve consistency and uniformity across products. Reviews also make the task of product creation more manageable. Some of the most common software review techniques practiced across software organizations include:

- Inspections
- Walkthroughs
- Formal technical reviews

Inspections

Inspections improve the reliability, availability, and maintainability of a software product. Anything readable that is produced during software development can be inspected. The readable material can be requirements specifications, design documents and models, test plans, system documentation, and user aids. Group inspections enable team members to exchange knowledge and ideas during an inspection session.

Inspections can be combined with structured, systematic testing to provide a powerful tool for creating defect-free programs. The inspection activity follows a specified process and the participants play well-defined roles. An inspection team consists of three to eight members who play the roles of moderator, author, reader, recorder, and inspector.

Moderator leads the inspection, schedules meetings, controls meetings, reports inspection results, and follows up on rework issues. Author creates or maintains the work product being inspected. Reader describes the sections of the work product to the team as they proceed through inspection. Recorder classifies and records defects and issues raised during the inspection. The moderator might perform this role in a small inspection team. Inspector finds errors in the product. All participants play the role of inspectors. However, good inspectors are those who have created the specification for the work product being inspected. For example, the designer can act as an inspector during code inspection while a quality assurance representative can act as standards enforcer. It also helps to have a client representative participate in requirements specification inspections.

Walkthroughs

The term walkthrough refers to a group activity in which the developer of the product guides the progress of the review. Walkthroughs are less rigorous than either formal inspections or peer reviews in which the developer plays a more passive role. Normally walkthroughs turn into a presentation by the author. The focus of finding errors is diluted. Such misadventures make walkthroughs usually less successful at detecting bugs than the more formal review methods.

Two useful walkthrough approaches adopted worldwide are group reviews with individual preparation and individual peer desk-checks. Group reviews are not very rigorous like inspections. The group reviews involve many of the same activities and roles, such as individual preparation and the use of a moderator and a recorder. Usually the overview meeting and the follow-up steps are skipped and checklists are used sparingly. At the end, the readers paraphrase their interpretation of what a program is doing.

Individual peer desk-checks are quite cost-effective. Only one person besides the author examines the material. This approach can be more effective if there are individuals who are extremely good at finding defects on their own.

 Tip

If someone consistently finds most of the group-identified defects during the individual preparation step, such a person is fit to perform individual peer desk-checks.

Formal Technical Reviews

One of the most common, yet important, software quality assurance activity performed is FTR. This activity is performed to check errors in logic, function, or implementation for any representation of the software. Using FTR, you can verify whether or not the software product adheres to the defined standards. FTR is also conducted to check for consistency in the software product and audit the manageability of the software product. It includes activities such as walkthrough and inspection. FTR focuses on specific parts of the software product, such as the requirements components, detailed design module, and the source code listing for a module. FTR also concentrates on the entire product. The participants in FTR are the developer, the project leader, and all the reviewers. At the end of the review meeting, the issues recorded are formalized into review issues list. The minutes of the meeting are summarized into a review summary report as displayed in Figure 11.2.

Technical Review Report		
Review Identification		
Project Name	Current Phase	Review Number
Product Identification		
Item Reviewed	Version No.	Developer
Brief Description		
Documents Referred (along with versions, if any)		
Start Time	End Time	
Review Material Attached: Yes/No		
Participants	**Role**	**Preparation Time**
Total Review Time (No. of Participants * Actual duration of meeting)		
Total Review Person Hours		
Product Appraisal		
Accepted as is ( )	With Minor Modifications ( )	
Not Accepted Major Revision ( )	Minor Revisions ( )	
Review Not Completed (Explanation as follows)		
Supplementary Material Attached		
Issues Lists:	Others	
Revise and Reschedule (if required)	Target Date for Next Review	
Verification of Defect Closure		
Responsibility of:	Planned Date of Verification	
Recommended for Release	Signature:	Date:

Figure 11.2: Technical Review Report

Tip

To prepare realistic schedules, you can collect data from past projects. Speak to related project managers regarding time estimation for reviews, the review capacity of the reviewer, and estimate the review effort accordingly.

Software Testing

Software testing is a quality control activity performed to detect errors in a program. Testing is performed to find the difference between the expected and observed behavior of the program. The flip side of testing is that testing can only prove the presence of bugs not their absence. However, testing is the ultimate review of specification, design, and coding. Testing indicates the reliability and quality of the product. Testing needs to be planned soon after the design phase. All tests need to be planned and designed before any code is generated. Testing is most effective when conducted by a third party.

The testing process begins with the preparation of the test plan. A good test plan has all details of the testing process. The test plan lists the types of tests to be conducted, mentions the milestones of the testing process, and specifies the tester details. A good test plan should include:

- Details of tool and strategies used for SQA activities

- Precedence of the tests

- Reviews and inspections details

- Details of staff performing testing

- Test products details

- Plans to identify and reduce risks

- Product release criteria

- Entry and exit criteria for each phase

As a project manger, you need to design test cases that have the maximum chances of finding errors by using minimum effort and time. The test cases are designed during the design phase. The more the number of test cases, the more rigorous is the testing. The test cases should test all aspects of software before it is released.

Kinds of Testing

The kind of testing that is done depends on the approach that you follow for testing a software product. There are two approaches usually followed in software testing, black box testing and white box testing. Black box testing is not based on any knowledge of internal design or code. Tests are based entirely on requirements and functionality. White box testing is based on the knowledge of internal logic of an application code. These tests are based on the coverage of code statements, branches, paths, and conditions.

Apart from categorizing testing on the basis of the approach followed, you can categorize testing on the basis of the level at which the testing is conducted. Testing can be conducted at various levels. These include:

- Unit testing
- Integration testing
- Validation testing
- Security testing
- Stress testing
- Performance testing
- Volume testing
- Beta testing

Unit Testing

Unit testing focuses on the smallest unit of software. The smallest unit can be either a module or code. In unit testing, usually the developer and not the tester tests the functions or code modules. Unit testing follows the white box approach. This type of testing requires detailed knowledge of the internal program design or code, which a developer knows better than a tester. Unit testing is normally done during software construction.

Integration Testing

During integration testing, the combined parts of an application are tested to determine if they function together correctly. The parts can be code modules, individual applications, client and server applications on a network, etc. All modules could work independently but when combined, the modules might generate errors. Integration testing detects the errors associated with interfacing. This type of testing is especially relevant to client/server and distributed systems.

Validation Testing

Validation testing is performed after the integration testing of software. At the end of integration testing, software is assembled, interfacing errors are corrected, and software is subjected to a final series of validation tests. Validation testing is performed to test whether or not software conforms to requirements. *Configuration review*, also called audit, is an element of validation testing. Configuration review ensures that all elements of software configuration are properly developed and catalogued.

Security Testing

Security testing is done to detect the presence of protection mechanisms in the system. In security testing, you verify whether the security of the system is strong enough to protect the system against unauthorized internal or external access. The ultimate objective of a good security testing is to test whether it is easy to penetrate the security mechanism of the system by unauthorized means. Some organizations also use professional hackers to check whether the security of the system is foolproof.

Stress Testing

Stress testing is used to describe tests such as system functional testing under unusually heavy loads or heavy repetition of certain actions or inputs. Stress testing is performed to find out the maximum stress that a program can take. For example, a system that has a capacity to support 20 users is tested under a load of 20 to 30 users. Stress testing verifies the behavior of a system when subjected to heavy load. The load can be input of large numerical values, large complex queries to a database system, or high memory requirements.

Performance Testing

Performance testing is used to test the run-time performance of a system. Performance testing occurs at all steps in the testing process starting from the unit level testing. However, the actual performance of the system is determined after the system is fully integrated. Ideally, performance criteria are defined in the requirements documentation, the QA plan, or the test plan.

Volume Testing

In volume testing, you subject a system to a series of tests where the volume of data processed is the subject of the test. The systems subjected to volume testing can be transactions processing systems capturing real time sales, database updates, or data retrieval. Volume testing verifies the physical and logical limits of a system.

Beta Testing

Beta testing is done after development is completed and you need to detect bugs before the final release. Beta testing is done by end-users and not by programmers or testers. The product is made available to the select group of users who execute the system and provide necessary feedback before it is released.

Testing Tools

To automate the testing process, you can use various tools available in the market. The categories of tools available in the market are unit testing tools, functional or regression testing tools, and performance testing tools. Functional testing verifies the functional requirements of an application. Regression testing is re-testing after fixes or modifications of the software or its environment. Functional or Regression Testing Tools are automated testing tools especially used for this type of testing. Performance testing is used to test an application under heavy loads.

Some of the testing tools and their features are mentioned in Table 11.4.

Testing Tools	Features
Unit testing tools	Provide a simple framework for building and executing unit tests
	Build a test-suite incrementally during development
	Help in automatic construction of composite tests
	Provide multithreaded test cases
Functional or regression testing tools	Provide simple test creation process
	Insert checkpoints to compare actual and expected results
	Verify database values to ensure transaction accuracy
	Record test cases and enhance or reuse them based on changes in business requirements
	Provide interactive reporting tools to analyze the results obtained
	Ensure easier verification of transactions
	Provide sophisticated introspection capabilities
Performance testing tools	Simulate real Web traffic, and measure the end-user experience of the site
	Capture business process to create virtual user scripts, record behavior of real-time users, and allow parameterization of the same
	Create realistic load scenarios.
	Support environments to provide for more accurate online monitoring of performance
	Identify and isolate performance problems
	Provide a large number of performance monitoring graphs

Table 11.4: Testing Tools and Features

Tip

To be most effective, testing should cover 30 to 40 percent of the entire development phase.

SQA Plan

The SQA plan serves as the template for SQA activities planned for each software project. The SQA group and the project team develop the SQA plan. A sample of an SQA plan is displayed in Table 11.5. The initial two sections of the plan describe the purpose and references of the SQA plan. The next section records details of the roles and responsibilities for maintaining software product quality.

The Documentation section of the SQA plan describes each of the work products produced during the software process. This section defines the minimum set of work products that are acceptable to achieve high quality. The Documentation section consists of:

- Project documents such as project plan, requirements documents, test cases, test reports, user manual, and administrative manuals

- Models such as ERDs, class hierarchies

- Technical documents such as specifications, test plans

- User documents such as help files

All applicable standards to be used in the project are listed in the Standards and Guidelines section of the SQA plan. The standards and practices applied are the document standards, coding standards, and review guidelines.

Table 11.5 displays an SQA plan.

Software Quality Assurance Plan

1) Purpose

2) References

3) Responsibilities

Task	Responsibility	Date

4) Documentation

Document Name	Author	Date	Details

5) Standards and Guidelines

Document	Details	Phase

6) Audit Schedule

Serial No.	Planned Date	Actual Date	No. of Nonconformances

7) Testing Strategy and Plan
Objective
Schedule

Activity	Planned Start Date	Planned End Date	Actual Start Date	Actual End Date

8) Defect Reporting and Corrective Action
Defect Report

Defect Location	Comments	Severity Level	Developer Comments	Status (After Verification)

9) Tools, Techniques, and Methodologies
Testing Tools
Analysis and Design Tools
Configuration Management Tools

10) SCM

Baseline	CI	Phase	Acceptance Criteria	Approval Authority	Planned date	Actual date

11) Training Needs

Name	Skills Required	Skills Required Date	Training Required	Training Mode	Planned date	Actual date

12) Risk Management

Risk Description	Probability of Occurrence	Impact on Project	Risk Factor	Mitigation Steps	End date

Table 11.5: Software Quality Assurance Plan

The audit dates and nonconformance, if any, are noted in the Audit Schedule section of the document. Similarly, the Testing Strategy and Plan section has details of the testing objective, schedule, and test plan.

The details of the defect report, which is generated after the testing process, are entered in the Defect Reporting and Corrective Action section. The section defines procedures for reporting, tracking, and resolving errors and defects, and identifies the organizational responsibilities for these activities.

The Tools, Techniques, and Methodologies section has details of the software test plan and procedure. It also has information on the testing tools, the analysis and design tools, and configuration management tools to be used.

The remaining sections in the plan define the software configuration management procedures, the training needs of the SQA members, and risk management steps to be undertaken.

Phase-specific Software Quality Assurance

In addition to the general SQA activities discussed above, there are some phase-specific SQA activities undertaken during the software acquisition life cycle. The SQA activities undertaken at the end of each phase help the project manager decide about the next course of SQA activities to be initiated in the following phase. Some of the SQA activities undertaken in each DLC phase are described below.

SQA Activities During the Analysis Phase

SQA should be involved in both writing and reviewing the Management Plan to assure that the processes, procedures, and standards identified in the plan are appropriate, clear, specific, and auditable. During this phase, SQA also provides the quality assurance section of the Management Plan. While the product requirements are finalized, SQA assures that software requirements are complete, testable, and properly interpreted as functional requirements, performance requirements, and interface requirements.

SQA Activities During the Design Phase

SQA activities during the preliminary design phase ensure adherence to approved design standards mentioned in the Management Plan. In this phase, SQA activities are undertaken to ensure that all software requirements are allocated to software components. SQA activities check whether a testing verification matrix exists and is kept up-to-date. SQA activities also ensure that the Interface Control Documents agree with the standard in form and content. SQA also reviews the Physical Design Review documentation and ensures that all action items are resolved. Placing the approved design under configuration management is also an SQA activity of this phase.

In the detailed design phase, SQA activities ensure that approved design standards are followed. SQA activities supervise the inclusion of allocated modules in the detailed design. They also verify whether or not the results of design inspections are included in the design. SQA also reviews the Conceptual Design Review documentation and ensures that all action items are resolved.

SQA Activities During the Coding and Testing Phase

In the coding and testing phase, SQA activities check the readiness of the deliverable items for testing. SQA checks ensure that all tests are run according to test plans and procedures. Nonconformances to the test plans, if any, are reported and resolved. SQA checks at this phase ensure that test reports are complete and correct, testing is complete, and software and documentation are ready for delivery.

SQA Activities During the Software Implementation and Evaluation Phase

SQA activities during the implementation and evaluation phase include the audit of results of coding and design activities. SQA activities include reviewing the schedule contained in the software development plan and checking the status of all deliverable items. SQA checks also monitor the configuration management activities, audit the software development library, report nonconformance, and verify corrective actions.

SOFTWARE CONFIGURATION MANAGEMENT

SCM is an integral part of SQA. SCM involves assessing the impact of the changes made during SQA activities and making decisions based on cost and benefit analysis. SCM can be defined as the art of identifying, organizing, and controlling changes in a software project with the objective of minimizing mistakes. SCM is different from software maintenance. Software maintenance is required after the software is delivered to the client and is put into operation. As opposed to this, SCM is a set of tracking and controlling activities that begins when a software project begins and ends only when the software is taken out of operation.

Software Configuration Management Activities

SCM is used to establish and maintain integrity of software items and ensure that they can be traced easily. Using SCM, you can define a library structure for storage and retrieval of software items. SCM needs to be performed at all phases in the SDLC of a software project. The various SCM activities are:

1. Identifying Objects

2. Controlling Versions

3. Controlling Changes

4. Auditing

5. Communicating changes

Identifying Objects

The first activity in SCM involves identifying software configurable items (SCIs). SCI is an aggregation of software that is designated for configuration management. It is treated as a single entity in the configuration management process. For example, design documents, program code, test case, and custom requirement document are configurable items.

You can use the Item Traceability Matrix to identify SCIs at the end of each phase. A sample of Item Traceability Matrix is displayed in Table 11.6. In the table, you can see the different SCIs in different phases of the development process.

Deliverable Name	Phase			
	Requirement Analysis	Design	Construction	Testing
Requirement Analysis Document	Requirement Analysis Document			
Design Document		Functional Specification Document and Program Specification Document		
Code			Code A Code B Code C	
Test Document				Unit Test Cases System Test Cases
Database Design Document		Database Design Specification		

Table 11.6: Item Traceability Matrix

To identify SCIs, you need to first breakdown the project deliverable to the SCI level. Each phase in the project has its own deliverables. To trace the deliverables, you need to map the SCIs to the phases in which they are delivered.

Controlling Versions

Version control combines procedures and tools to manage different versions of configuration objects that are created during software product development. To control versions, you can use Version Control Register. In Version Control Register, you enter the details of components, such as component identification numbers, their versions, and dates of validity. It is advisable to release a baseline after a version is released. Baseline is a specification or a product that is formally reviewed and agreed upon. This serves as the basis for further development. Baseline can be changed only through formal change control procedures. A baseline consists of a set of SCIs that are logically related to each other. Baselines are established when subsequent changes to the SCIs need to be controlled. Version control is essential so that everybody uses only the latest version. Any kind of version mismatch might result in rework.

Controlling Changes

Uncontrolled change can lead to chaos. Change control combines human procedures and automated tools to provide a mechanism for controlling change. The purpose of change control is to monitor and control changes in order to baseline SCIs. There are various reasons that trigger changes. A problem report might call for a change. Similarly, suggestions or ideas from brainstorming sessions and feedback from clients can result in change. Modifications or addition to functionality and changes in environment can also cause changes. The Figure 11.3 explains the formal change control process using a flow chart.

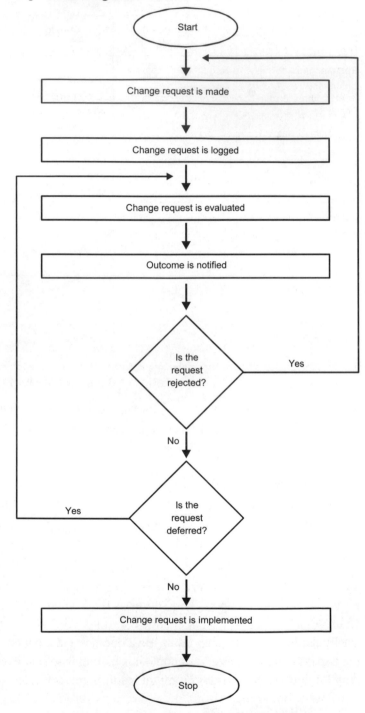

Figure 11.3: Formal Change Control Process

A request for change triggers the change control procedure. Then request is logged in the change request register. Next, the change request number is recorded in the change request evaluation plan. The request is evaluated and analyzed to check if the change is valid. Change request is also evaluated in terms of the number of items affected and the effort involved in effecting the change. Finally, the possible outcome of the change request is communicated. The request for change is rejected, deferred, or approved. If the request for change is rejected, the requestor needs to log a fresh request. A deferred change request is evaluated at a later date while the change request that is approved is implemented.

There are tools that provide facilities to check in and check out so that the same version of the object is not updated more than once. The check-in and checkout facilities provide synchronization control. Synchronization control helps to ensure that parallel changes performed by two different people do not overwrite one another.

Auditing

Configuration audit is conducted formally by the SQA group in projects where SCM is a formal activity. The identification, version control, and change control tasks help the developer maintain order and decorum in an environment of change. However, the control mechanisms track a change only until an item is generated. FTRs and software configuration audits (SCA) are conducted to ensure that change is properly implemented. FTR verifies the technical correctness of the SCI that is subjected to change. SCA assesses those characteristics of an SCI that are not considered during FTRs. Audit verifies whether the changes specified in the request for change are made and additional modifications, if any, are also noted. Audits ensure that FTRs are conducted to check for technical correctness. Audits verify that changes made are highlighted in the SCI. The change date and change author are specified and the attributes of SCI reflect the change. The SCM procedures for noting, recording, and reporting change are also followed. Audits also ensure that related SCIs are updated.

Communicating Changes

Another task of SCM is communicating changes. This task ensures communication between different members in the project. It notes the activities performed, the time when they are performed, those involved in the activities, and those affected by the activities. In short, the task is all about status reporting. In a large project, there is a possibility of miscommunication among various people involved in the project. This is usually done using configuration status report shown in Table 11.7. The table contains the name of the SCI, the latest released version, the date of release, brief description of changes performed, and associated change request. Further details of the changes can be obtained from the associated change request.

There can be instances where two developers may be trying to modify the same software configurable item with different and conflicting intentions. Absence of status reporting could result in incorrect decisions being taken or important decisions not being communicated. At times, those who should be pointing out the serious side effects caused by a change are not aware of the implementation of the change. There are also instances of version mismatch when teams are unaware of the latest version to be followed. To avoid such hazards due to lack of communication among the project team, changes are communicated among team members. Therefore, status reporting provides information about each change to those who need to know. Software configuration management takes care of changes in a software process. SCM identifies, controls, audits, and reports modifications that occur during software development. SCM helps maintain the integrity of configurable items produced during software development.

Project:			Version:	
Configurable Item Name	Version	Date Released	Changes Done	Related Change Request ID/Problem Report ID

Table 11.7: Configuration Status Report

Baselines vs. Interim Versions

SCM differentiates between baselines and interim versions. A baseline is a tested and certified version of a system. Baselines can be assigned version numbers such as 1.0, 2.0, 3.0, and so on. A baseline usually undergoes intensive testing. Interim versions, on the other hand, have version numbers, such as 1.1 or 1.2. The interim version is a temporary version. Interim versions have a short life and survive only during bug fixing, testing, or debugging. However, interim versions also have a unique version number or name. Baselines are more visible with the marketing team and the vendors than the interim versions. However, as part of SCM, all versions of changes are saved, clearly labeled, and archived. Archiving is the process of maintaining controlled copies of prior versions. Archiving helps in re-creating earlier versions in the event of data loss or data corruption.

SUMMARY

✓ Software quality is defined as conformance to explicitly stated functional and performance requirements, documents, and standards.

✓ The factors that affect software quality are a complex mix of conditions that can be measured based on certain data such as auditability, completeness, consistency, error tolerance, expandability, hardware independence, software system independence, modularity, security, and simplicity.

✓ Software quality assurance is a planned and systematic approach necessary to ensure the quality of a software product.

✓ Software reviews filter the product of all errors. Software reviews can be conducted at all stages in the DLC of a software product such as analysis, design, and coding.

✓ Testing is an important element of SQA activity. There are various testing tools to automate the testing process.

✓ The SQA plan is used as the template for all SQA activities planned for a software project and includes details of the SQA activities to be performed during project execution.

✓ SCM is used to establish and maintain integrity of software items and ensure that they can be traced easily.

✓ SCM helps define a library structure for storage and retrieval of software items.

✓ SCM helps assess the impact of a recommended change and make decisions depending on the costs and benefits.

✓ SCM needs to be performed at all phases in the DLC of a software project. The various SCM activities are identifying changes, controlling changes, controlling versions, implementing changes, and communicating changes.

✓ SCM activities are independent of the supervision of the project or the product manager. This is to ensure objectivity in SCM.

✓ The scope of SCM is not limited by code. The scope includes requirements, design, database structures, test plans, and documentation. SCM procedures vary from project to project.

HOMEWORK EXERCISES

1. List the software quality management activities explaining each activity in at least two sentences.

2. Explain the steps in the change request procedure by using a diagram.

LAB EXERCISES

Suppose you have created an application for your organization that helps employees log requests for cabs on a cab request database. Employees working beyond office hours are provided transport to their respective homes. To avail this opportunity, an employee can submit a request for a cab in this application and await sanction from the supervisor. The application has a front-end component and a back-end component.

The front-end component is a screen where employees can submit information about their current office location, destination, departure time, and the name of the supervisor.

The back-end component is a batch process that sends a message using e-mail to the supervisor for approval. The message has a link that the supervisor clicks to gain access to the form. The supervisor either approves or disapproves the request. The status mail is sent to the requesting employee, and the corresponding record is updated.

Employees can log requests up to a specified time. After this, the actual processing of the requests takes place.

1. Discuss the different types of testing that can be performed on the application.

2. Suppose you have to incorporate a change in the system after implementation. The change is incorporated to ensure that the employee cannot request for a cab for a date other than the current date. This change will be incorporated on an item "A" that is a program to validate the date of request. Discuss the various change management activities that you will perform.

Chapter 12

Software Implementation and Maintenance

Objectives:

- ☐ Describe the prerequisites for software implementation.
- ☐ List the software implementation activities.
- ☐ Define the need for project maintenance.
- ☐ Identify the types of project maintenance.
- ☐ Identify the phases in maintenance process.
- ☐ Describe the process of software reengineering.
- ☐ List the best practices of maintenance process.

SOFTWARE IMPLEMENTATION

After the software product is developed, the challenge lies in seeing the system work successfully at the user-end. Product implementation is the crucial activity of actually handing over the product to the users. The product moves from the theoretical environment of the development team to the practical environment of the user. Implementation begins with the preparatory activities of planning, training the user staff, and testing the system. After the preparatory activities are complete, the new system is installed and configured at the user end. Implementation marks the end of product development. After this, the product is handed over to the maintenance team.

In this chapter, you will look at both software implementation and maintenance. In the first section, you will look at the process of implementing the software product in the user environment. You will look at the prerequisites to facilitate a successful product implementation. You will also learn about the implementation activities that facilitate system installation and configuration. The second section covers software maintenance. In this section, you will learn about the maintenance activities performed during the maintenance process.

Implementation Prerequisites

The purpose of implementation is to organize and implement the new or updated system. Most of the time, implementation is a contract-based activity. The contract provides details of the implementation activity. Implementation procedure includes details such as the scope, method, and duration of implementation. There are some prerequisites of implementation. They are finalizing the number of licenses, procedures for error logging, scheduling system changeover, and procedure for maintaining data backups. However, the primary task is to organize a team to monitor implementation.

An implementation coordination committee is set up to monitor implementation. The line manager whose department is the most affected by implementation chairs the committee. Other committee members include line managers of other departments and members of the development team.

The committee performs various activities. It identifies various requirements of implementation process, such as arranging for software licenses, project software, and other standby facilities. The committee looks into the implications of the system environment, staff allocation for implementation tasks, and internal communication. The committee also devises alternative methods of facilitating system changeover.

The various activities performed during implementation are preparing an implementation plan, a training plan, an acceptance plan, and a system support plan.

Implementation Plan

The first task of implementation is the creation of the implementation plan. The implementation plan contains details of the methods of system transfer and the timescale for implementation.

Details of hardware and software needed for implementation are also mentioned in the plan. The plan contains details of date, location, and timescale for implementation. The plan also mentions the prerequisites of implementation, such as the existing network environment and the availability of related software. You can look at an implementation plan in Table 12.1.

Implementation Plan					
1) Implementation Schedule					
Serial No.	Location	Start Date	End Date	Days	Resources
2) Resource List					
Serial No.	Resource Name	Contact Number	Pager or Mobile No.	E-mail ID	Key Resource (Y/N)
3) Software Components for Installation					
3.1) Server					
Serial No.	Software Name	Version	Space Required	Location	
3.2) Client					
Serial No.	Software Name	Version	Space Required	Location	
4) Data Migration					
Serial No.	Data to be Migrated	Location of Server	Data Migration	Mode of Migration	Batch or Script

Table 12.1: Implementation Plan

In the implementation plan, Implementation Schedule section records details such as location and duration of implementation. The Resource List section has a list of the resources and their contact numbers. The plan has details of the server and clients in the Components of Installation section. Finally, the plan also contains data migration details.

Training Plan

Preparing a training plan is one of the tasks of implementation. The training plan contains details of the participants to be trained. It also mentions the focus area and the audience for the training session. Training schedule containing the training venue, training name, start date and end date is a part of the training plan. The plan conveys budgetary details and the roles and responsibilities of participants as well as the faculty. A training plan is displayed in Table 12.2. The plan has details of the focus areas of training, courses identified for training, and training schedules. Roles and responsibilities of trainer are also included in the training plan.

Training Plan						
1) Focus Areas for Training						
Serial No.			Focus Area			
2) Training Courses						
Serial No.	Course Title	Duration	Category	Faculty	Details	Number of participants
3) Training Schedule						
Serial No.	Course Title	Code	Start Date	End Date	Venue	
4) Roles and Responsibilities						
Member	Role		Back-Up Member	Responsibilities		

Table 12.2: Training Plan

Acceptance Plan

The purpose of an acceptance plan is to determine the details of acceptance testing. The plan contains details such as the order of testing of functions, location, date, and duration of testing. Details of participating members, coordinators, and users are also mentioned in the plan. The acceptance plan lists the procedure for bug fixing, version control, and verification and validation details. Procedure for the creation of acceptance test cases and setting up software and hardware environment is also mentioned in the plan.

The acceptance plan in Table 12.3 contains details of the acceptance schedule, acceptance criteria, list of resources, and a bug report form.

Acceptance Plan						
1) Schedule						
Serial No.	Module	From Date	To Date	Days	Resource Name	Documentation
2) Acceptance Criteria						
Serial No.	Item Name			Acceptance Criterion		
3) Resource List						
Serial No.	Resource Name		E-mail	Telephone/Pager		Key Resource (Y/N)
4) Bug Reporting Procedure						
Serial No.	Module	Bug	Reported By	Report Date	Closure Date	Assigned To	Fixed On

Table 12.3: Acceptance Plan

System Support Plan

The implementation team prepares the system support plan either during or before product installation. The system support plan contains details of how the system will be supported after it is implemented. Typically, the support plan has a warranty clause. The warranty clause usually lasts for a year. The warranty covers details of people in the support activities, details of agreement, the response time, and support details.

Implementation Activities

After the prerequisites are in place, implementation activities begin in right earnest. Now, all the plans created for implementation are put into practice. Implementation activities include acceptance testing, user and operator training, data migration, installation and configuration, product sign-off, product wind-up, post mortem, and product delivery.

User Acceptance Testing

You must have heard the proverb, "the proof of the pudding lies in the eating!" This applies for the software product also. The success of the software product depends on how the user responds to the product. One of the important implementation activities is user acceptance testing. This aims at ensuring that the system is working according to the user requirements. UAT is done to ensure that the desired product design matches the actual product design.

UAT is the final testing performed by the end user after using the product over a limited period of time. As part of the implementation process, the project manager prepares the User Acceptance Test plan. The UAT plan is the last stage of the testing process where the user tests the product. The user tests the product and identifies whether it is acceptable or not.

Ideally, UAT is conducted in the same environment as the one in which the product is designed. The UAT plan consists of the activities to be conducted, functions to be tested, and the time, date, and environment in which software will be tested. Often test cases are attached with the UAT plan. The user validates the software based on the test cases. The executable product is installed in the test environment and configured for use. Then the user executes the test supplied. After the user tests the software product, the implementation team takes care of the bugs or problems identified by the user. The bug fixing and closing of issues continue iteratively until all the problems are solved. The software product is then ready for use. The user representative gives a signoff on the prescribed format to indicate satisfaction with the product. This marks the end of the development activity. The final bug-free version is delivered to the user.

Training

To familiarize the users with the new system, you need to train them. Apart from the users, there are the operators who also need to be trained to handle the system. Training for both the users and operators has separate goals. Training sessions aim at providing the participants with the specific skills required in handling the new system. Training aids used are documents, icons and online helps, and demonstrations or classroom sessions. The user training focuses on major system functions and the users' need to gain access to them. Some of the activities that a user might need to perform are simulating activities, analyzing data, drawing graphs, and searching for information. The user is trained on navigation skills, information searching skills, and security functions. The users are trained on the differences between the old and new activities to familiarize them with the differences.

The operator training focuses on the support functions of the system. The support functions include granting user access, granting file access, recovering damaged files, installing new devices and software, and making backups. Therefore, the operators' training focuses on two function areas. First, the operators learn to run the system, and second they learn to support the users.

Another important approach to training is documentation. Documentation can be in the form of user manuals and guides. The use of documentation in training will depend on the target audience. Therefore, you need to ensure that your development team does not neglect training and documentation. This should be planned and tracked from the project start as soon as the requirements analysis is complete. You also need to ensure that training and documentation for users and operators is updated periodically.

Data Migration

At times, the user might want to transfer data from the old system to the new system during implementation. The implementation team migrates data from the old system to the new system. This task can be automated by using scripts and tools. Data migration is an important activity. As a project manager, you need to ensure that all data is successfully migrated. At times, data migration involves a large amount of data from heterogeneous sources. This entails lot of work, which might be beyond the handling capacity of the implementation team. Typically, in such situations, data migration activity is subcontracted to an external agency. If the data is in the form of documents, data entry operators could also be hired. Although the activity is subcontracted, as a project manager, you need to plan and monitor its progress continuously.

Installation and Configuration

To make the system available to end users, the implementation team needs to install and configure the system. This involves making the system run and prepare it for actual work. The implementation team does this by deploying the system on user machines. During installation, the files, components, and executables are copied to the user machine.

Configuration is the act of making necessary changes in the system parameters that are specific for target users. This activity is performed along with installation. Installation and configuration activity can be automated by using many tools. You can perform installation and configuration at multiple locations by using tools. These tools create installable disks that can be used to install and configure. This enhances the productivity of the implementation team to a great extent.

At times, the project manager might need to outsource the installation activity. Then great care needs to be taken to ensure that correct versions are installed. At times, Web-based automatic installation facilities are used to simplify the process further. At times, the implementation team might need to install the system at multiple locations simultaneously. The team prepares separate plans for each location. The implementation team also configures the installed system.

Product Sign-Off

At the end of acceptance testing, the user-representative gives the sign-off in the form of an acceptance letter. This marks the formal end of the implementation phase. This means that all issues raised during the acceptance testing are solved and closed. As a project manager, you need to ensure that the contractual obligations with the user are fulfilled. You need to verify that the client accepts all documents and deliverables as mentioned in the contract. You also ensure that the sign-off is according to defined guidelines and is in the form of an acceptance letter.

Project Wind-Up

Project wind-up marks the formal closure of the development phase. This activity begins after obtaining a sign-off from the user. The key activities performed during project wind-up are analyzing what went wrong and what could have been better. Major learning from the project is summarized at the end of the project. Certain completion criteria are finalized at the project start. These criteria prevent the project from dragging on endlessly. Certain activities are performed to ensure that the project ends on time.

- Monitoring deliverables that are not yet complete
- Monitoring progress

- Controlling change requests
- Monitoring work yet to be done

Usually a senior project manager supervises the project-wind up activities. During project wind-up, you need to gather feedback both internally as well as from the client. The various wind-up activities performed during project end include obtaining client feedback of the project. You also need to update and close the project plan. Another activity is updating project-related statistics at the end for resource estimation. You can determine the level of success of the project based on the quality of the delivered system and the level of satisfaction of all concerned.

During project wind up, the project manager also plans for the allocation of the project staff. The deliverables list is checked to ensure that all requirements are met. The project manager also verifies the financial completion of the project. A contract is also drawn to deal with the problems later for a defined period under a warranty. The project is evaluated for adherence to schedule, budget, technical goals, and client and project team satisfaction.

Another important project-end activity is data collection. Data accumulated during the project is collected and organized after completion. This data helps in resource estimation and quality assurance of future projects. The data collected regarding the actual cost per task, cost overrun and under-run per task, unplanned tasks, and planned task that were not required are estimated. Data about software change requests and bug statistics is also noted.

The performance of the project team is also evaluated at the end of the project. The team members are evaluated in terms of their ability to accomplish project tasks. The time taken, the quality achieved, and the adherence to cost and schedule is also noted. The team members are also evaluated based on their innovative approach to accomplishing a task. The ability of the team member to work as a team, communicate, and support each other is also judged. The team members are also asked to evaluate themselves in terms of their strengths and weaknesses.

Post Mortem

The post mortem activities involve collecting valuable information at the end of the project. The knowledge gained from the project is documented for use by other projects. Similarly, the recommendations for enhancements are also documented. You also need to submit project-related items, hard copies, and files to the project library. Usually, post mortem activities are conducted among the team members. The team members exchange feedback about each other regarding interpersonal communication and work processes within the team.

Finally, the project manager prepares a project closedown report. This report contains suggestions on what should be done to improve software quality in the next project. This report contains details of what the team has failed to deliver and the lessons learned from the project. This report will help detect and eliminate long-term problems. The project closedown report contains the following details:

- Description of the project
- Success assessment
- Schedule, budget, and technical details
- Problems while implementing solutions
- Data updates regarding cost estimation

Product Delivery

Product delivery marks the last leg of implementation. In this phase, the packaged software, documentation, and other items mentioned in the contract are passed on to the maintenance team. As a project manager, you need to ensure the smooth transfer of knowledge from the development team to the maintenance team. The maintenance activities are discussed in detail in the next section.

SOFTWARE MAINTENANCE

According to surveys, changeability is one of the most important attributes of complex, multifunction software systems. This calls for continuous adjustments of the software to suit the changing environment. While changes are inevitable, it is not always possible to create products foreseeing the changes. Therefore, the product needs to be changed according to the changing scenario. You might need to upgrade the software product based on new system requirements or remove redundant functionality. The need for a change brings software maintenance into the picture. Maintenance activities can either be in-house or outsourced. In the case of in-house maintenance, the development team performs the maintenance activities. On the other hand, an independent maintenance team performs outsourced maintenance activities.

Software maintenance deals with the sustenance of a piece of software after it is released. Maintenance activity is needed when errors are detected after the software product is released. Changing requirements of the software product also require maintenance activity to cater to the changes.

Maintenance activity assumes greater importance for a project manager. This is because managing software maintenance is more challenging than managing software development. Consider an example. You are maintaining a banking operation. A small program change is introduced as part of the maintenance activity. Suppose this change results in an incorrect interest calculation. You can well imagine the kind of confusion this error will create, not to mention the loss of client faith and goodwill in the bank. Therefore, as a project manager, you need to be extra cautious while managing a maintenance project.

Types of Maintenance Activities

Maintenance is an important phase in SDLC. The need for maintenance activities has increased with the increase in software packages. Maintenance activities include correction and prevention of defects, enhancements to incorporate changing needs, and porting of applications and adaptability. The changing hardware and software scenarios have increased the demand for software maintenance. Today, in the entire SDLC of a software application, the maintenance effort is about 80 percent and the development effort is only 20 percent.

There are four types of maintenance activities:

- Corrective
- Adaptive
- Perfective
- Preventive

Corrective maintenance is about fixing bugs. This takes approximately 17 percent of the maintenance time. During corrective maintenance, the existing code is used to correct the fault that causes the code to deviate from its documented requirements. Here, the focus is on fixing defects.

During adaptive maintenance, the existing code is changed to adapt the new features and functionality. These new features are usually part of a new release of a code. This change normally takes 18 percent of the maintenance time.

Perfective maintenance improves the maintainability of the code. During this activity, the code is restructured to make it easily understood and to remove ambiguities. The enhancement of code occupies 60 percent of the maintenance time.

Preventive maintenance is undertaken to protect the code against failure. Here, the focus is on adhering to coding standards and reduce the chances of code failure. Preventive maintenance activity takes around 5 percent of the maintenance time.

In the above list of maintenance activities, you can see that out of total maintenance effort, only 20 percent is spent on corrective maintenance and 80 percent on the rest. This refutes the popular belief that maintenance activities is all about fixing mistakes.

Maintenance Activities

To perform maintenance activities, the maintenance team needs to acquire the business and technical knowledge of the client systems. The maintenance process is usually divided into three phases.

- Initiation Phase
- Preparation Phase
- Execution Phase

Initiation Phase

The initiation phase starts with the commencement of maintenance activities. It is primarily a knowledge acquisition phase. During this phase, the maintenance team takes over the system from the development team. The maintenance team familiarizes itself with the ways and functioning of the system. This is essentially a phase of knowledge transfer from the development team to the maintenance team. The major activities of the initiation phase are baseline assessment and operating procedures. During baseline assessment, the interfacing and communication methods between the development and maintenance teams are defined. The user-coordinator from the user side and the information technology help from the maintenance team are identified. During this phase, the plan for acquiring the systems knowledge is also finalized.

During the operating procedures activities, the maintenance team understands the application and the functionality involved in the maintenance task. The maintenance team reviews the current operating procedures of the system. The team also obtains details about the environment set up, deployment of software, the resource allocation process, and priority settings. Other activities such as root cause analysis, work assignment to the development teams, and updating of documentation procedures is also done. The maintenance team refers to the problem management procedures, on-call or escalation procedures, and operational process for handling faults. It also makes decisions based on the severity of the faults, application criticality, and infrastructure issues.

The maintenance team finalizes procedures for transferring support work from the development team. The maintenance team members are initiated to hands-on exposure of the systems. The maintenance team finalizes the quality systems and standards and guidelines to be followed.

Preparation Phase

The preparation phase begins after the initiation phase. During this phase, the maintenance team sets up the administrative and support procedures needed for maintenance activities. In this phase, the environment is set up and hardware, software, and network is made ready for operation. All the procedures decided and finalized during the initiation phase are put into practice in this phase. According to the documentation procedures finalized in the initiation phase, the latest documentation is kept in the library. During this phase, bug reporting, problem solving, and other support methodologies are established. The security measures are also put in place and practiced during this phase.

Execution Phase

The execution phase follows the preparation phase. In this phase, the maintenance team starts executing the maintenance activities after the preparation in the earlier phase. During this phase, the maintenance team is in close touch with the development team for a small period of time. Such communication is recommended to ensure better coordination.

Maintenance Curve

Maintenance activity begins after product implementation. The effort spent on maintenance varies over a period of time. Normally, maintenance effort is very high immediately after implementation. The system faces numerous changes during this time. The changes could be in the form of bugs, changes in network environment, or problems caused by user mishandling. During this time, the effort spent on maintenance activities is very high. With time, the system stabilizes and maintenance activities also slowdown. During this period, the users are more or less satisfied with the system. The system also runs smoothly without requiring any major changes. Therefore, maintenance activity is at its lowest during this phase.

However, over a period of time, business processes change and the system also depreciates. During this period, major changes start coming in. The changes are in the form of enhancements and additions of new systems or modules.

These changes take place continuously to keep the system up-to-date with the changing needs and requirements. Maintenance activities are also at a maximum during this phase.

However, soon the system becomes obsolete and is phased out. Along with the system phase-out, maintenance activities also come to an end.

Figure 12.1 shows the variation of maintenance activity with time. In the curve, maintenance effort is very high during the initial phase. Then the maintenance effort stabilizes during the maturity phase. Finally, the maintenance effort increases sharply just before system phase out. The system is phased out to pave the way for new systems. The old systems are also reengineered to make new systems. You will learn about reengineering later in this chapter.

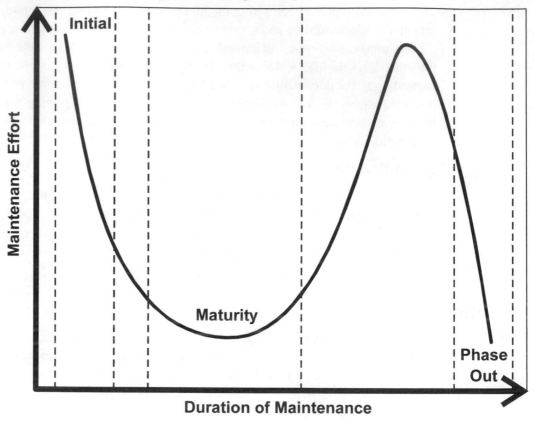

Figure 12.1: Maintenance Curve

Maintenance Process

There are certain prerequisites that you need to follow before beginning with the maintenance process. All documentation needs to be complete and up-to-date. All existing items need to be configured, and the latest copy of the code should be available. The hardware, software, and network environment for testing and maintenance should be made available. Before beginning with the maintenance process, the maintenance team is identified. The user representative from the user side is identified and the maintenance team is constituted. The maintenance team consists of the head of IT, the project coordinator, and team members. The maintenance project manager is the single point contact between the user representative and the maintenance team. The project manager categorizes the type of maintenance activity to be performed based on specifications. The project manager ensures proper communication between all the entities involved in maintenance activity. To ensure that the maintenance process runs smoothly, there is a thorough checking of all deliverables. Maintenance activity is the most critical because the system is running and already in place. Therefore, the project manager needs to ensure that no error arises during the maintenance process.

The common approach followed in the maintenance process is as follows. After the user makes a request for change, the maintenance team performs an impact analysis. Then the team plans for the system release. The system goes through design changes, coding, and testing. Finally, the system is released. The maintenance activities undertaken are corrective maintenance, adaptive maintenance, perfective maintenance, and preventive maintenance.

Corrective Maintenance Process

The corrective maintenance process begins with the user representative reporting bugs to the project coordinator by using the problem report form. The project coordinator analyzes the problem and assigns the problem to one of the team members for corrective action. If the bug fixing leads to any changes in the system, the change is carried out based on the change request process. The team member requests the SCM team to check out the item to be modified. Then the bugs are fixed and tested in the test environment. After this, the user acceptance is carried out for the successful completion of the corrective maintenance process. Finally, the SCM team releases the modified item. All related documents are modified to reflect the changes and the project coordinator closes the problem report.

Adaptive Maintenance Process

In the adaptive maintenance process, changes are made to the system to accommodate changes in its external environment. Adaptive maintenance includes work related to enhancing software functionality. During this process, certain system changes, additions, insertions, deletions, and modifications are included to meet the evolving needs of the user and the environment. At times, the original environment of the software product might change For example, there might be changes in operating system, business rules, and external product characteristics. Adaptive maintenance refers to modifications that adapt to these changes. The project coordinator plans the changes to be made. The detail plan and the quality goals are defined for the changes. The team is formed based on the quantum of work. The change request procedure is followed to carry out the changes. Finally, the changes are deployed based on a deployment strategy.

Perfective Maintenance Process

Perfective maintenance refers to enhancements that make the product better, faster, smaller, better documented, better structured with more functions and reports. It includes all efforts to improve the quality of software. Perfective maintenance extends the software beyond its original functional requirements. During perfective maintenance, the user or the system personnel initiates the changes to the system. The initiator raises the change request to the project coordinator. The changes could be a result of enhancements of new functionality in the existing system. After tracking the changes, an impact analysis is done and a detail plan is made to carry out the changes. Based on the amount of changes, a dedicated member or a team works on the changes. The testing is done in the testing environment and changes are implemented in the system based on the deployment strategy.

Preventive Maintenance Process

Preventive maintenance activities make changes to software programs so that they can be more easily corrected, adapted, and enhanced. During the preventive maintenance process, the project coordinator identifies the potential risks. Recommendations are made to the management for approval of the maintenance actions. The project coordinator prepares the project detail plan for carrying out the changes. The preventive maintenance team is formed based on the quantum of work. The team implements the change based on the request procedure. Finally, deployment happens based on the deployment strategy.

The maintenance process begins when the user initiates a request for a change. The process ends when the system changes are tested and the change is released for operation. In between, there are many activities that are coordinated and planned using change management.

Reengineering

Reengineering is a process of abstraction of a new system from an old system. Reengineering is the modification and evolution of software product to meet the constantly changing business requirements. Failure to reengineer can prevent an organization from remaining competitive and persistent. This is because every system faces the risk of being phased out sooner than they were earlier. Therefore, you need to develop systems that support multiple platforms and are open to modifications and changes. Here, the role of reengineering comes into play. Reengineering comprises reverse engineering and forward engineering.

Reverse Engineering

Reverse engineering is a process of recovering the design of the running system from the source code. Reverse engineering involves analyzing a software system to achieve two objectives. First, reverse engineering helps to identify the system components and their interactions. Second, it helps make representations of the system on a different, higher level of abstraction.

Suppose, you want to retrieve the design of a product whose design document is not available. You can recover the design by working backwards on the product from the source code to the design requirements. At times, you might need to reengineer programs developed many years back. The specifications of such programs are either unclear or was not developed at all. In such a situation, you use reverse engineering to analyze the program at a higher level of abstraction. Therefore, you perform reverse engineering to add a significant functionality to the old program. You can also use it to make the system cost-effective and to adopt new technologies.

Certain prerequisites are necessary for reverse engineering. The existing system should be in a running condition. The latest source code should be available. During reverse engineering, the reverse engineering team gathers information about the source code and the design and specifications documents. They also obtain information about the knowledge and experience of the developer. Then the team studies the existing code and the existing documents. Then they create a draft document from the existing code. The team discusses with the users and modifies the draft document based on the discussions.

To perform requirement reengineering, the team first prepares a prototype. After this, it provides the demo of the prototype to the users. Then the system requirement specification document is modified based on the discussions. The team obtains approval from the users on the requirements.

During design reengineering, the team studies the existing data model and the new requirements. Then they map the requirements with the existing data model and conduct gap analysis. After this, they modify the data model based on the gap analysis. The team studies the behavior of the existing programs and prepares program specifications based on the behavior and the existing code. Then the unwanted functionality is removed from the program specifications. The program is then modified based on the new requirements.

During construction reengineering, the team comments on the unwanted code from the programs. Then they add remarks in the filtered code, and modify the programs based on the new functionality. Finally, the team tests the reengineering process. Testing involves preparing the unit level test cases, the test code, and fixing the defects. Then the code for integration testing is released. The various testing methodologies followed are conducting integration testing, functional testing, independent testing, user acceptance testing, and releasing the code for deployment.

Reverse engineering helps understand the processing of the system, understand data, and eliminate dead code, bad coupling, and no documentation. It also reduces the maintenance efforts. The tools used for reverse engineering arc Rigi and Refine Language Tools, static analyzer, and test editor.

Forward Engineering

Forward engineering is the process of building a new program from the requirements and design specifications of an old program. During forward engineering, old design information is recovered from existing software and is used to reconstitute the existing system. In the process, the quality of the existing system is enhanced and new functions are added. Therefore, forward engineering moves from a high-level abstraction and design to a low-level implementation. Forward engineering is used to improve the overall performance of the system.

Figure12.2 displays the reengineering process.

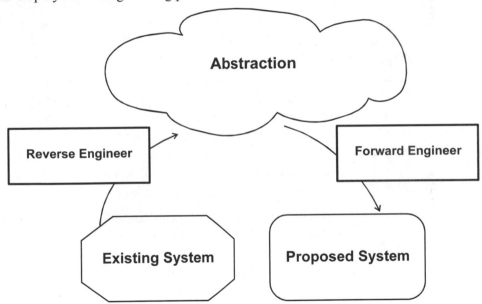

Figure 12.2: Reengineering Process

Maintenance Best Practices

In addition to the maintenance process, there are some maintenance best practices. A maintenance process is successful if the testing and production environment are the same. Version control is strictly implemented using version control tools, such as VSS and PVCS. You need to check that the deployment strategy is clearly defined and tested and the documentation is kept up-to-date.

The members of the maintenance team management should be rotated in different business areas to enhance efficiency. It is very essential to identify backups of the key personnel. There should be a balance between the new development and problem fixing. Ensure proper training, and use the latest technology. Knowledge sharing sessions also help in improving communication within the team. There should be an online help facility for the maintenance team, and helpdesk tools should be available to track the problems. Periodic causal analysis of the nature of problems and corrective action need to be conducted. To ensure successful maintenance process, you need to conduct periodic quality reviews and monitor the quality goals of the team.

SUMMARY

✓ Software implementation marks the closure of software product development.

✓ The prerequisites of implementation are preparing an implementation plan, a training plan, an acceptance plan, and a system support plan.

✓ There are various activities performed during implementation. These activities are:

- Conducting user acceptance tests
- Training users and operators
- Migrating data from the old system to the new system
- Installation and configuration of software at user end
- Obtaining product sign-off from users
- Conducting project wind-up activities
- Performing project post-mortem
- Delivering the packaged software product, documentation, and other deliverables

✓ Software maintenance activities involve correction and prevention of defects after the product is released. They are also performed to incorporate the changes in the product because of changing needs and requirements.

✓ There are four types of maintenance activities: corrective, adaptive, perfective, and preventive.

✓ Maintenance activities are performed in three phases: initiation phase, preparation phase, and execution phase.

✓ Maintenance activities vary over a period of time. The maintenance effort increases immediately after implementation. It then slows down and stabilizes before increasing again when the product is phased out.

✓ Reengineering involves the modification and evolution of software product to meet the changing needs and requirements.

✓ Reverse engineering is the process of recovering the design of the software product from the source code of the product.

✓ Forward engineering is the process of creating a new program from the requirements and design specifications of the old program.

✓ To conduct a successful maintenance activity, ensure that the testing and production environment are the same and versions are strictly controlled.

HOMEWORK EXERCISES

1. Suppose you have to implement a software product at the client end. List the implementation planning steps that you need to perform.

2. Analyze the phases of the maintenance process.

3. Describe how reengineering helps meet changing needs and requirements.

LAB EXERCISES

1. Suppose your team has just completed the user acceptance testing of Interactive Voice Response System. Now, you need to implement the system in Dallas and Atlanta on April 15 and April 25, respectively. You have only one resource to carry out implementation. It will take two days at each place to implement the system. The system requires 600 MB of disk space and one server at each location. There is no client machine installation. The software IVR.exe version 1.0 needs to be run from a CD to the server machine and has to be installed. The data needs to be migrated from a text file by running a batch script transfer.bat.

   a. Describe the implementation planning activities that you would need to undertake for successful implementation.
   b. List the implementation activities to be performed.
   c. Assume that the project was completed well within the schedule and budget allocated. Also assume the possible problems that you could have encountered during implementation. Based on these assumptions, prepare a project closedown report.

2. Suppose AB Corp. has outsourced its maintenance work on its payroll, human resource, and inventory system to your organization. You are supposed to take over the maintenance activities from the existing vendor PPP Maintenance Inc.

   a. Describe the various phases of the maintenance activity that will be performed.
   b. List the maintenance best practices that your team will follow during maintenance.

3. A large organization LMN Inc. has a mission-critical production system running in the organization for several years. The system is running in the old legacy Mainframe environment. LMN Inc. wants to migrate the system to a new client/server-based environment. Some of the design documents were missing, and those that were found were not updated properly. The exact requirement was also unclear because the system had undergone several changes over the years. The people maintaining the system are also not very clear as to how the code works at many places.

   a. What is the approach you will take to migrate the system?
   b. Explain the reasons why you decide on a particular approach.
   c. Discuss the activities you will perform to migrate the system by using a flowchart.

4. What are the different types of maintenance activities? Discuss them briefly. Which type of maintenance activity undertakes bug fixing?

Appendix

ADDITIONAL REFERENCES

Internet Links

- Definitions and concepts of Software Quality Assurance can be obtained from:

  http://satc.gsfc.nasa.gov/assure/agbsec3.txt

- White papers on software configuration management can be obtained from:

  http://www.cmtoday.com/yp/papers.html

- Further information on implementation can be obtained from:

  http://citeseer.nj.nec.com/hankerson00software.html

- To know more about software maintenance, you can refer to the link below:

  http://www.cs.unc.edu/~stotts/COMP145/text/maint.html

- More information on software reengineering can be obtained from:

  http://www.rigi.csc.uvic.ca/UVicRevTut/UVicRevTut.html

- To know more about software process models, you can refer to the links below:

  http://www.cs.qub.ac.uk/~J.Campbell/myweb/misd/node2.html

  http://www.cc.gatech.edu/computing/SW_Eng/people/Faculty/Colin.Potts/Courses/3302/1-08-mgt/

- Additional information on project, size, and productivity metrics can be obtained from:

  http://louisa.levels.unisa.edu.au/1996/se.semester1.96/lectures/t2metric.html

- To know more about the advanced COCOMO technique, you can refer to the link below:

  http://my.raex.com/FC/B1/phess/coco/Modelman.pdf

- For information about different aspects of software project management, you can refer to the links below:

  http:///www.rspa.com

  http://www.comp.glam.ac.uk/pages/staff/dwfarthi/projman.htm

  http://www.clark.net/pub/ajlucero/index.html

  http://www.pmi.org

Recommended Reading

- Pressman, Roger S., *Software Engineering: A Practitioner's Approach*, 5th ed., McGraw-Hill, 2001.

- Schulmeyer, Gordon G. (Editor), McManus, James I., Schulmeyer, Gordo G., *Handbook of Software Quality Assurance*, 3rd ed., Prentice Hall PTR.

- Jalote, Pankaj, *An Integrated Approach to Software Engineering*, 2nd ed., Springer-Verlag, 1997.

- Brooks, Jr., Frederick P., *The Mythical Man-Month: Essays on Software Engineering*, 2nd ed., Addison Wesley Longman, Inc., 1995.

GLOSSARY

B

Behavioral Constraints – The behavioral constraints for a software project include the demographics and attitudes of the users of the final software product.

Brainstorming – Brainstorming is a shared problem solving technique. In a brainstorming session, the attendees attempt to break their existing thought patterns and generate original and creative ideas to solve a problem. The aim of a brainstorming session is to generate creative ideas.

C

Change Control Mechanism - The risks encountered during product development are categorized as development process risks. These comprise developer errors, natural disasters, disgruntled employees, and poor management objectives.

Cohesion – Cohesion is a measure of the relative functional strength of a module.

Component - It is the smallest unit of a system. It is one of the parts that constitute a system.

COnstructive COst Model (COCOMO) - COCOMO is a technique used to calculate effort and duration of a project using cost driver attributes.

Cyclomatic Complexity - It is a software metric that provides a quantitative measure of testing the difficulty and an indication of ultimate reliability of a program.

D

Development Process Risks - The risks encountered during product development are categorized as development process risks. These comprise developer errors, natural disasters, disgruntled employees, and poor management objectives.

Decomposition – Decomposition describes the primary deliverables of a software project in terms of the sub-tasks or sub-elements. It breaks down each deliverable into smaller and more manageable elements for the purposes of planning, execution, and control.

F

Function Points (FP) – FP is a technique of estimating the size of a software project. Function-oriented metrics use function points extensively. Function points are direct indicators of the functionality of a software application from the user's perspective. Function points are also used to express cost, effort, productivity, and defects of a project.

I

Incremental Model – In this model, the development of a software product is in builds. A build is defined as a self-contained unit of the development activity. The entire development cycle is planned for a specific number of logical builds. In each build, a specific set of features is incorporated.

Interview - An interview is an exchange of information between two or more people. Interviews are widely used as a requirements gathering technique. In an interview, the software analyst gathers detailed information about the customer software requirements.

L

Libraries - Software libraries provide the means for identifying and labeling baseline entities and capturing and tracking the status of changes in those entities.

M

Metric - A metric enables you to measure the quality of a factor. For example, to measure the quality of a deliverable product, such as a prototype, the metric could be the number of defects reported for the prototype.

P

Process Model – A process model is a methodology followed for the development of a software project. It defines a structured approach to sequence and identify the requirements for each phase in an SDLC.

Prototyping Model – The Prototyping model is a process model in which a throwaway prototype is created based on the feedback from estimated customer requirements. The prototype need not encompass all the features of the expected final product. It reflects the major features of the final product and how they would be executed.

Product Risks – Product risks are changing requirements during product development. They also include incomplete and unclear requirements and problems in meeting design specifications.

Productivity - Productivity is the effort in performing an FP of work for a project.

Project Wind-Up – Project wind-up marks the formal closure of the development phase. This activity begins after obtaining a sign-off from the user. The key activities performed during project wind-up are analyzing what went wrong and what could have been better.

Post Mortem - The post mortem activities involve collecting valuable information at the end of the project. The knowledge gained from the project is documented for use by other projects.

Program Evaluation and Review Technique (PERT) - PERT is a network-scheduling technique. You can use this technique to perform analysis for a wide variety of projects. It depicts a project as a sequence of activities. This helps you perform an analysis of individual activities or the complete project.

Q

Quality Function Deployment (QFD) - The QFD technique is used to translate the spoken or unspoken customer requirements to technical specifications and deliver a high quality product or service.

Quality control - Quality control is a series of review activities, such as inspections, reviews, and tests, used throughout the SDLC of the software product. The objective of quality control is to find problems as early as possible and fix them.

Questionnaire - A questionnaire is used by a software analyst to ask the customer questions in a structured form. It allows the analyst to ask and receive answers to specific or open-ended questions.

R

Resource Constraints – Resource constraints are caused due to a lack of facilities, equipment, funds, training, or skilled people to execute a project. The availability of these resources is often defined by the budget assigned to a software project.

Risk Mitigation – Risk mitigation is the best possible approach adopted by the project manager to avoid risks from occurring.

Router-to-router VPN Connection – A router-to-router VPN connection connects two private networks. A VPN-enabled router is placed at both networks and connectivity is established between the routers.

Revision - Revision is associated with bug fixing and error correction in logic. Revision does not affect documented functional capabilities because the requirements have not changed.

Release- It is a formal notification and distribution of an approved version.

S

Spiral Model – The Spiral model focuses on identifying and eliminating high-risk problems by careful process design. Its basic goal is to identify and define ways to eliminate risks in the design phase. Consequently, minimum and manageable risks percolate into the development phase.

Source Lines of Code (SLOC) – A screening router firewall examines data packets on the basis of their IP addresses and then performs the function of packet filtering. The screening router can either be a physical piece of equipment or a computer with two or more network interface cards.

Software Requirements Specification (SRS) – An SRS document describes the behavior of a software in detail. The SRS document includes the functional requirements, the nonfunctional requirements, and the design constraints on the software. It provides a complete and comprehensive description of the requirements for the software.

T

Technological Constraints – The technological constraints define how a software project needs to adhere to technological standards. For example, the use of a particular programming technology, platform, or environment is a technological constraint.

V

Version – It is an initial release or re-release of a computer software configuration item. Version also indicates a software configuration item having a defined set of functional capabilities.

W

Waterfall Model – It is the simplest, the oldest, and the most widely used process model or paradigm for software engineering. As the name suggests, the phases in this model flow one after the other just as water flows in a waterfall from a higher to a lower level. A preceding phase is depicted at a higher level than its subsequent phase.